10 0653397 7

Managing Trauma in the Workplace

Managing Trauma in the Workplace looks at the impact of trauma not only from the perspective of the employees but also from that of their organisations. In addition to describing the negative outcomes from traumatic exposure it offers solutions which will not only build a more resilient workforce but also lead to individual and organisational growth and development.

This book has contributions from international experts working in a variety of professions including teaching, the military, social work and human resources. It is split into four parts which explore:

- the nature of organisational trauma
- traumatized organisation and business continuity
- organisational interventions
- building resilience and growth.

Managing Trauma in the Workplace is essential reading for anyone with responsibility to help and support workers involved in distressing and traumatic incidents as a victim, supporter or investigator.

Noreen Tehrani is a chartered occupational, counselling and health psychologist. She is Managing Director of Noreen Tehrani Associates.

Managing Trauma in the Workplace

Supporting workers and organisations

Edited by Noreen Tehrani

BUSINESS LIBRARY

Routledge
Taylor & Francis Group

LONDON AND NEW YORK

10065 33922

First published 2011
by Routledge
27 Church Road, Hove, East Sussex BN3 2FA

Simultaneously published in the USA and Canada
by Routledge
270 Madison Avenue, New York, NY 10016

*Routledge is an imprint of the Taylor & Francis Group,
an Informa business*

© 2011 selection and editorial matter, Noreen Tehrani;
individual chapters, the contributors.

Typeset in Times by RefineCatch Limited, Bungay, Suffolk
Printed and bound in Great Britain by TJ International Ltd, Padstow, Cornwall
Paperback cover design by Sandra Heath

All rights reserved. No part of this book may be reprinted or
reproduced or utilised in any form or by any electronic,
mechanical, or other means, now known or hereafter
invented, including photocopying and recording, or in any
information storage or retrieval system, without
permission in writing from the publishers.

This publication has been produced with paper manufactured to strict
environmental standards and with pulp derived from sustainable
forests.

British Library Cataloguing in Publication Data
A catalogue record for this book is available from the British Library.

Library of Congress Cataloging in Publication Data
Managing trauma in the workplace : supporting workers and
organisations / edited by Noreen Tehrani.
    p. cm.
Includes index.
1. Post-traumatic stress disorder. 2. Psychic trauma.
3. Work environment. 4. Organisation. I. Tehrani, Noreen.
RC552.P67M356 2010
616.85'21—dc22   20100004584

ISBN: 978-0-415-55892-1 (hbk)
ISBN: 978-0-415-55893-8 (pbk)

Contents

Tables

Figures

Contributors

David Alexander MA(Hons), CPsychol, PhD, FBPS, (Hon)FRCPsych is in charge of the Traumatic Stress Clinic, Aberdeen, and is the Director of the Aberdeen Centre for Trauma Research. He has been involved in a number of major incidents, including the Estonia ferry disaster, the Balkans War and the Urals train disaster in Russia. Following the Nairobi terrorist bombing, he was appointed as specialist adviser to the Kenya Medical Association. He has also conducted a review of the Iraq psychiatric services on behalf of the Royal College of Psychiatrists, and a similar role in Sri Lanka following the tsunami disaster. Most recently, he was invited to Pakistan as a clinical adviser following the earthquake. He is a Visiting Lecturer at the Scottish Police College on the management of trauma and hostage negotiation.

Sandra L. Bloom MD is a Board-Certified psychiatrist, Associate Professor of Health Management and Policy and Co-Director of the Center for Nonviolence and Social Justice at the School of Public Health of Drexel University in Philadelphia. Dr Bloom is the founder of the Sanctuary Institute. Distinguished Fellow at the Andrus Children's Center and a Past-President of the International Society for Traumatic Stress Studies. She is author of Creating Sanctuary: Toward the Evolution of Sane Societies. A new book, Destroying Sanctuary: The Crisis in Human Service Delivery, which will be published by Oxford University Press.

Walter Busuttil MB, ChB, MPhil, MRCGP, FRCPsych is Medical Director to Combat Stress, a charity that treats ex-servicemen and combat veterans with mental health difficulties. He served for 16 years in the Royal Air Force and was instrumental in the setting up of mental health rehabilitation services for servicemen returning from the first Gulf War. He was involved in the rehabilitation of the released British Beirut hostages and helped to set up a service at Ticehurst House Hospital in East Sussex for the treatment and rehabilitation of complex post-traumatic stress disorder (PTSD) sufferers. As Medical Director at the Dene Hospital, a female medium-secure hospital in West Sussex, he set up a unique psychological trauma service. He is currently the Chair of the UK Trauma Group and has published and lectured internationally on the treatment and rehabilitation of veterans and chronic and complex PTSD.

Tim Chadwick MBA, MIRM, MBCI, ACII has more than 15 years of financial services experience in insurance, marketing management and risk management. Tim joined Aon in July 2004 from Royal & Sun Alliance, where he held the roles of Group Operational Risk Manager and Global Head of Business Continuity. Tim is currently Aon's Head of Corporate Governance and the Situation Management Team Coordinator, and is the Situation Response Leader for London. He sits on the British Standard Institute (BSI) Risk Management Committee and has played a key role in leading the development of BS31100, the British Standard for Risk Management. Together with his co-author, he won a number of Business Continuity Awards for Royal & Sun Alliance's global BC framework and response to major incidents. Separately, Tim won the Business Continuity Award for Best BC Strategy for Aon.

Eileen Delaney MA is a Health Science Specialist at the National Center for PTSD at VA Boston Healthcare System. She works with Brett Litz PhD, who specializes in PTSD research as well as other mental health problems related to trauma. Eileen is completing her PhD in clinical psychology, with a specialization in behavioural medicine/health psychology, at Bowling Green State University (BGSU). Her dissertation project aims to learn more about how individuals adjust to and cope with being diagnosed and living with HIV/AIDS.

Bernadette Dunne BA, MA has been a Registered General Nurse since March 1983. She graduated in 2001 with a BA in Occupational Health; she also has an MA in Health Care Ethics and Law from Manchester University. She has had a varied career, working with a wide range of organisations as an Occupational Health

Practitioner, with experience in the Engineering, Service and Policing Sectors. She has a strong belief in the unique position of occupational health practitioners in promoting health and wellbeing in society.

John Durkin MSc is carrying out PhD research at the University of Nottingham. He is investigating psychological growth following adversity and the role played by social support in its emergence. His interest in the psychosocial processes that occur in the aftermath of traumatic experience emerged from 17 years working as a firefighter.

Julia Graham FCII, FBCI, MIRM has worked in the world of risk and insurance for over 30 years. She is the Chief Risk Officer for DLA Piper, the largest legal services organisation in the world. Previously Julia was Head of Global Group Risk Management at the insurance company RSA, where she had a background in underwriting, marketing, operational management and risk management, as the company's first Group Risk Manager. Julia is a past Chairman of AIRMIC, the UK association of insurance and risk managers, and Chairman of the Risk Panel of the Managing Partners' Forum, whose membership specifically focuses on professional services organisations. She was Chairman of the British Standards Institution (BSI) committee which published the first British Standard for Risk Management, BS31100, in 2008. Julia is a frequent conference speaker, co-author of *A Risk Management Approach to Business Continuity*, and regular author of articles on risk and insurance.

Sonia Handa MPH is a Health Science Specialist at the National Center for PTSD at VA Boston Healthcare System. Much of her research has focused on the provision of brief interventions, using motivational interviewing techniques among patients in hospital trauma units who have experienced an alcohol-related injury and suffer from alcohol dependency.

Stephen Joseph Phd is Professor of Psychology, Health and Social Care at the University of Nottingham, where he is co-director of the Centre for Trauma, Resilience and Growth and an Honorary Consultant Psychologist in Psychotherapy in Nottinghamshire Health Care NHS Trust. Stephen's research interests are in the study of traumatic stress, resilience and growth following adversity.

Susan Klein MA(Hons), PhD, Cert COSCA is a Reader in Trauma Research at the Aberdeen Centre for Trauma Research (ACTR) and a Principal Member of the Institute for Health and Welfare Research (IHWR) of the Robert Gordon University. She is responsible for managing the wide-based research portfolio for the ACTR and is theme leader for Neurological and Mental Health for the IHWR. She has extensive experience in the design of trauma-related projects, including identifying indicators of the impact of critical incidents on emergency personnel, consultant psychiatrists and NHS staff. She has extensive experience in the development of training materials and is a trainer accredited by the World Health Organization. She is Deputy Chair of the Sudden Trauma Information Service Helpline (STISH) and a member of the UK Psychological Trauma Society and the European Society for Traumatic Stress.

Lillian Krantz BA is a Research Technician at the National Center for PTSD at VA Boston Healthcare System, where she assists with the implementation of trauma studies taking place locally and internationally. She also has previous research experience in health/motivational psychology with Baerbel Knauper at McGill University.

Jörg Leonhardt MSW, MSc in Human Factors and System Safety (University of Lund) is the Head of Human Factors in the Safety Management Division of the German air navigation service provider (ANSP) Deutsche Flugsicherung (DFS). Jörg is a family therapist and Approved Instructor of the International Critical Incident Stress Foundation (ICISF). He developed the DFS CISM programme, conducted peer trainings for several ANSPs throughout Europe, and is first editor of the book *CISM in Aviation*. His current research is on the integration of resilience engineering into high risk industries.

Brett Litz PhD is a Professor of Psychiatry at Boston University School of Medicine and a Professor of Psychology at Boston University's School of Arts and Sciences. He is also a staff clinical psychologist and former Associate Director of the Behavioural Sciences Division (BSD) of the National Center for PTSD at VA Boston Healthcare System (VBHS), as well as the Director of the Mental Health Core of the Massachusetts Veterans Epidemiological Research and Information Center

(MAVERIC). Dr Litz has extensive experience in PTSD and trauma research, which includes examining risk and resiliency factors and developing and implementing early mental health interventions for PTSD and other mental health problems implicated by exposure to trauma.

Tom Lowe BSc, MAppSci, CPsychol, AFBPsS is a Senior Educational Psychologist with North Lanarkshire Council. His work includes being the lead psychologist for his service's critical incident support team and for delivering critical incident training to education staff. In addition, he is a member of the local Choose Life implementation group (the Scottish suicide prevention programme), where he is involved in training, prevention programmes and developing multi-agency intervention guidance (Life Lines).

Stuart McNab PhD, CPsychol, CSci, AFBPsS is Programme Leader of the MSc in Psychological Trauma at the University of Chester and a counselling psychologist in private practice. He has worked as a social worker, probation officer and lecturer in further education before joining the then University College of Chester in 1995. His current research interests include supervising trauma therapists and the use of mindfulness and the natural environment to build resilience and enhance recovery from trauma.

David Murphy BSc, MA, CPsychol is a Chartered Counselling Psychologist who specializes in person-centred psychotherapy and is also an accredited member of the British Association of Counselling and Psychotherapy. He is Lecturer in Trauma Studies at the Centre for Trauma, Resilience and Growth, which is jointly funded by the University of Nottingham and Nottinghamshire Healthcare NHS Trust, where he is Honorary Psychologist in Psychotherapy. Together with Professor Stephen Joseph and Steve Regel, David helped set up and now manages a training placement unit for mental health social workers, based within the trauma centre. The unit is the first of its kind in the UK to specialize in and adopt social and relationship-based approaches to trauma.

Nicky Piper RGN, Diploma in Critical Care, BSc(Hons) is an Occupational Health Specialist Practitioner and the Head of Nursing and Counselling in a large police organisation, where she has been in post for 4 years. Previously she has worked in an occupational health setting in the private and the public sector. She has a special interest in working proactively in the field of traumatic stress.

Christie Rainbird MSc, BSc Health Studies is an Occupational Health and Trauma Practitioner. She led the Post-incident Support Programme for BTP following the bombings in Central London in July 2005. For 5 years she managed the Metropolitan Police Counselling Service and Trauma Support Programme and was closely involved in the World Trade Center disaster, going to New York to support the British Police undertaking family liaison work with bereaved families. Christie currently manages the Occupational Health Service at Oxford Brookes University.

Kate Richardson Dip SW, BA Econ, Postgraduate Diploma in Supervision and Mentorship (Child Care) has worked in children and families social work since 1988 as a social worker and social work manager. Since 1996, Kate has specialized in child protection social work, working as a local authority specialist practitioner and a manager for a number of specialist NSPCC teams. Since 2006, Kate has been the Child Protection Coordinator for the Child Exploitation and Online Protection (CEOP) Centre and manages the social work team seconded from the National Society for the Prevention of Cruelty to Children (NSPCC). Kate has contributed to a number of national and international developments in child protection. She has particular interests in child protection and disabled children and complex child protection joint investigation service development.

Noreen Tehrani PhD is a chartered occupational, health and counselling psychologist with an international reputation for her work in dealing with disasters, crisis and trauma. She works with a number of police forces, fire services and commercial organisations in the development of integrated trauma support programmes. Noreen is the Consultant Psychologist with the Child Exploitation and Online Protection (CEOP) Centre, providing support for the organisation and its workers and involved in undertaking research into the prevention of compassion fatigue, burn-out and secondary trauma.

Sarah Vaughan BA(Hons), DESS (MBA) is a Lecturer in Intercultural Communication and Management with a Business School in France and is currently investigating Corporate Social Responsibility education in France for her DBA at Grenoble Ecole de

Management and the University of Newcastle. Her interest is particularly in the human resource implications of CSR and in the role of French management education in changing a culture of compliance to regulation with regard to workplace violence and conflict towards a culture of well-being at work.

Joachim Vogt PhD is Professor of Work and Engineering Psychology at Technische Universität Darmstadt, Germany. He has worked in the R&D and the Safety Management Division of the German air navigation service provider Deutsche Flugsicherung (DFS) and as Associate Professor for Work and Organisational Psychology at Copenhagen University, Denmark. His research group in Darmstadt focuses on both soft and hard factors in an interdisciplinary approach. Examples are human computer interaction, ergonomics, cost–benefit analysis of human resources programmes, sustainable culture and organisational development.

Preface

Managing Trauma in the Workplace is a book that has been written by practitioners and researchers who are well respected, competent and enthusiastic in working to provide safe working environments for the brave men and women that work to make the world a safer and more compassionate place.

The book was born out of a collaborative vision to create a book that would provide information, research, guidance and tools to help organisations, practitioners and researchers gain insight into the nature, experience and treatment of traumatic stress in the workplace. The collaborative effort has been an extremely rewarding experience for the editor. Together we have created a framework which can be used by others when building new knowledge into this difficult and demanding area of work.

The book is arranged in four interconnected parts, which look at the nature of organisational trauma, how workplace trauma affects organisations, an evaluation of interventions and finally how to create resilient workers and organisations.

Part I brings together practitioners and researchers working in a wide range of organisations. The traditional emergency services are represented in Chapter 2, in which Noreen Tehrani and Nicky Piper interview a number of police officers and staff undertaking high-risk roles, and Chapter 7 examines the impact of working in crime investigation and analysis. The book also recognizes that there are many other workplaces that regularly face the need to deal with traumatic situations or events. Kate Richardson (Chapter 1) provides an insight into the world of the social worker, exploring the difficulties that social workers face when dealing with the needs of vulnerable children and families. Walter Busuttil (Chapter 3), himself a military veteran, brings together years of his research to provide an insight to the difficulties faced by military veterans, a particularly poignant chapter given the increased numbers of war casualties returning from Iraq and Afghanistan. One of the professions that is generally slow to recognize its need to take care of its practitioners is human resources. Chapter 4 looks at the strains and stresses of that role, which can lead these practitioners to begin to experience compassion fatigue and burn-out. The chapter calls for organisations to do more to take more care of this important group and to recognize the level of expertise that is required to undertake this difficult role. Although most people are aware that air traffic control is one of the most stressful jobs in the world, in Chapter 5 Joachim Vogt and Jörg Leonhardt provide an insight into the way that many air traffic control organisations are providing immediate support for their controllers, using the knowledge and skills of trained peers. Chapter 6 is by Tom Lowe, who has a busy role supporting children, teachers and other staff in North Lanarkshire. Tom describes some of the major disasters and traumatic events that can affect the school community as well as the training he provides for the school support teams.

There are four chapters in Part II. The first (Chapter 8), by Susan Klein and David Alexander, provides the reader with a framework to help them understand the issues that all organisations need to consider when trying to put together policies and procedures designed to protect its workers from the impact of traumatic exposure. In the first of her two chapters, Sandra Bloom (Chapter 9) describes how organisations can become traumatized and begin to behave in a way that introduces traumatized behaviours into the way it operates. Sandra provides descriptions of the kinds of behaviours we have all seen, but perhaps have not recognized, as being the result of the organisation absorbing the trauma from its clients. The next chapter, by Sarah Vaughan (Chapter 10), looks at national culture and characteristics and how this can affect the way the organisation deals with bullying and other abusive behaviours. Sarah uses an illustration taken from a French organisation to demonstrate culture in action. Finally, Part II takes a look at the world of risk management and business continuity. Julia Graham and Tim Chadwick are well-known figures in the world of business continuity with a wide experience in dealing with disasters, crisis and trauma at a corporate level. Their chapter (Chapter 11) helps to take the book into the board room, where the organisational cost of dealing with trauma is experienced in terms of the losses incurred when disasters and crisis are not handled appropriately, with the resultant loss of people, reputation and performance.

Part III of the book turns to organisational interventions. There are three chapters in this part of the book, although mention has been made of specific illustrative interventions in earlier chapters. Chapter 12, by Noreen Tehrani, Christie Rainbird and Bernadette Dunne, looks at an evaluation of a post-trauma intervention which took place within British Transport Police, following the 7 July 2005 London bombings on London Transport trains and bus. Chapter 13, written by Sonia Handa, Lillian Krantz, Eileen Delaney and Brett Litz, looks at the development of early interventions following a traumatic exposure and provides some insight into some of the developments of tools and techniques, emphasizing the importance of using techniques that have good evidence to support their effectiveness. Chapter 14 presents an integrated framework for supporting workers who are exposed to distressing material which has the capacity of causing secondary traumatic stress in the workers involved. The approach is based on a Health and Safety approach of risk assessment, management and review.

Part IV turns attention to the organisation and the need to take care of the organisation by building its resilience to traumatic exposures, so that it can operate healthily and productively. Sandra Bloom's second chapter (Chapter 15) describes an operating system, Sanctuary, which has been successfully adopted by a number of organisations wishing to create organisations that are open and supportive to the needs of employees and clients. Chapter 16 provides some ideas on the kinds of tools that can be used by employees to increase their mastery and understanding of the impact of traumatic stress. David Murphy, John Durkin and Stephen Joseph have demonstrated in Chapter 17 the importance of not being content with building resilience but seeking to transform traumatic experiences into opportunities for positive growth. Chapter 18, by Stuart McNab, turns the focus onto the trauma therapist and the need for this group of practitioners to engage in mindful supervision as a way of preventing the onset of compassion fatigue from their work with traumatized victims and organisations. The final chapter took a while to emerge; after considering the important contributions of all the contributors, there seemed to be a need to acknowledge the complexity of what faced workers, organisations and practitioners. Chapter 19, which looks at building resilient organisations in a complex world, is designed to open an ongoing debate on what else needs to be done to look after organisations and workers who are required to deal with situations which are traumatic.

A special thank you goes to all the contributors who have given freely of their time, knowledge and expertise in producing this wide-ranging and important book, which is essential reading for anyone involved in working in organisations.

Noreen Tehrani

Part I

The nature of organisational trauma

Chapter 1

Child protection social work and secondary trauma

Kate Richardson

Introduction

Although some of the issues discussed below may be relevant to other professionals, the term 'social worker' is used here to describe children and family social workers involved in child protection work.

This chapter focuses on the impact of child abuse on children and their families and how, in undertaking the safeguarding task, social workers can encounter experiences which contribute to compassion fatigue and burn-out. Social workers must probe and analyse the difficulties faced by children and families and communicate these issues to others. This work can involve significant contact with children and families in distress, a requirement to demonstrate empathy and a necessity to communicate the nature of another's pain and suffering in an understandable form; this can be through the written or spoken word, for example, report writing or testimony.

Often there are difficult decisions to be made on the balance between welfare and risk, each of these areas being potentially life changing and possibly life threatening to children. The consequences of making a mistake are part of the daily tasks facing a child protection social worker. Conflict with families, colleagues and wider society is an ongoing feature of safeguarding work, resulting in part from the emotionally charged subject matter of dealing with children at risk. Additional pressures brought by changing systems, individual and organisational responses to stress, scarce resources and lack of competence of others and confidence in oneself can bring further confrontation and stress.

Communications

Children need to be able to participate, wherever possible, in decisions relating to their future. Amongst other tasks, there is an obligation for social workers to establish the wishes and feelings of children, so that their participation is achieved. Communicating with traumatized children can be emotionally demanding, particularly as children adopt methods of coping with trauma that may limit their ability to communicate effectively and appropriately. Where the children are young or have additional or special needs, the task may be even more difficult. Sometimes the way in which children express their emotion can be challenging, for example with children being aggressive, severely distressed or withdrawn. Understanding and interpreting these behaviours and interpreting the underlying communications are key skills in working with children.

Balancing welfare and safety

Children are entitled to participate in decisions about themselves but may be in positions where what they want may compromise their welfare, for example, children may not wish to be parted from an abusive parent, even when no other course of action can protect them. Social workers must often balance children's wishes and feelings with their welfare and safety. In addition to ensuring that wishes and feelings are understood and the child's safety and welfare needs are met, social workers have the task of communicating these matters to others, including courts, professional groups and other family members. This must on occasion be managed in the face of minimization of risks of harm to children and a lack of ability or willingness to do something to improve their circumstances. When this occurs, social workers can feel responsible for the vulnerable child, yet unsupported by the systems that are there to protect children, such as courts, multi-agency groups and, sometimes, their own managers. This can be an isolating and frustrating experience for social workers, which must nevertheless be managed in order to provide the best possible service for a child. It is a core task to ensure that the appropriate response to situations is provided and that it supports the recovery of a child and prevents further harm. Understanding and communicating the child's circumstances to others is essential in securing that response. An example of this is the requirement to provide evidence of children's circumstances, wishes and feelings when presenting a case to court, to ensure appropriate legal remedy and effective care planning. It is particularly important that social workers feel that they have represented what they consider to be the best possible means of securing a good outcome for a child, as they are very aware of the consequences for a child of getting it wrong. This awareness is heightened on a regular basis through work with children where good outcomes have not been achieved.

Where harm has been experienced or there is a threat to a child, it is the role of the social worker to determine the nature of the harm and the potential or real impact. In understanding the impact, it is necessary for the social worker to understand the pain, upset and hurt caused to a child, and the social worker must engage and develop a trusting relationship with the child and family, including with the adult who presents the risk. Working with these two conflicting sets of needs demonstrates the challenge that social workers face from the outset. Research has shown that better outcomes for children and families in child protection are positively influenced by a good relationship with the social worker (Department of Health, 1995).

Dealing with the trauma

Children and their families can be angry and confused about the abusive incident(s) and also by the invasive process deemed necessary to protect a child. There can be complex issues when those in a responsible or caring position have abused a child, and dealing with the stigma of child abuse situations can be a challenge for service users and social workers. Some children are exposed to horrific levels of physical, sexual and emotional violence and neglect that most members of the public may never have to witness in their lifetimes. For social workers, there is regular contact with the most intimate details of these traumatizing events, and they have the task of translating the effects and taking action to prevent a repetition and to facilitate the recovery of the child. It may be important that social workers do not show certain feelings or responses during interactions, as this can affect children and young people, making them feel a sense of wrongdoing or shame. This can be particularly true when dealing with sexual abuse issues. On many occasions social workers need to suspend their personal feelings, or at least contain them, in order to effectively carry out the social work task, as it would be unhelpful for the child or family member in crisis to be met with someone unable to manage and deal with the potential for the feelings of disgust, shame and embarrassment that they feel about child abuse. There can be a consequence of hiding true feelings in order to achieve a professional goal (Theodosius, 2006).

Public reactions to child abuse

The understanding that society abhors child abuse and those responsible for it can exacerbate negative feelings. Even where these issues have an impact on other children, societal reaction can be overwhelming. The very tragic circumstances of 2 year-old James Bulger's murder in 1993 led to unprecedented outbursts of public anger against the 10 year-old boys responsible. Scenes of crowds attacking the transport that took the boys to court appeared on the news, with little coverage devoted to the impact upon them of such terrifying events. Following sentencing, petitions were circulated asking for the Home Secretary to intervene and exact more severe penalties. Anger and grief can drive this understandable need for demonstrative punishment and revenge. Our lack of understanding as to what motivates people to commit such terrible acts on the most vulnerable means that we are unlikely to ever find a punishment to fit the crime. This contributes to a level of frustration that in turn has a bearing on the need to find someone to blame. Where there has been social work intervention, which is charged with the protection of children, and this fails, the social worker can become the focus for some of the anger and the necessary means for the seeking of retribution. The call for social workers to lose their jobs and the media 'name and shame' is not unusual in high-profile cases.

The purported representation of the public view through a negatively critical media approach to child protection social workers is unrelenting. Media responses to high-profile cases have been almost overwhelmingly negative and aggressive in condemnation, even where other professions are considered to have missed opportunities to intervene. This has been particularly true when the death of a child may have been prevented by social care intervention. The media releases personal details of staff involved, photographs appear on newspaper front pages and television, and judgements are made on individuals' personal values and professional competence. One newspaper reporting in 2008 on the tragic death of Baby Peter in the UK ran a campaign and established a petition to sack the social workers involved; over half a million people signed the petition in the biggest ever response to a newspaper campaign (*The Sun*, 2009). The same newspaper advertised for people to tell their stories if they knew any of the social workers involved in the case.

Secondary trauma and the social worker

It is reasonable to assume that those directly involved in the aftermath of a tragic case will suffer some degree of trauma. It is also reasonable to assume that those indirectly involved, for example colleagues working in the same department, will suffer some level of emotional stress. For those not involved but working in the same profession, there is an almost daily reminder of the precipice on which they stand as they make decisions about intervening in the lives of children. The following case study gives an example of those indirectly involved.

A social work team in a local authority had been depleted by long-term sickness. There had been a number of cases made subject to serious case review, which occurs when death or serious injury has been caused to a child and inter-agency working needs to be examined. The more experienced staff in the team were able to take long-term sick leave, but the less experienced social workers had not worked long enough to be entitled to pay in any long-term sickness situation. The team was therefore staffed by the least experienced members. The level of stress and worry of what was to come for the day was so frightening that two of the social workers were vomiting on their way into the office on a regular basis.

The issues affect social workers in different ways and the relevant personal factors and circumstances need to be explored to identify how to assist individual social workers facing difficulties. The consequence of the majority of people's employment mistakes is unlikely to cause serious harm to a child, bringing about public castigation and media witch-hunt. The irony is that if children and families social workers were better supported, both publicly and professionally, they would be less likely to make the mistakes that create the environment in which they work.

Making difficult decisions

One of the most difficult areas of practice is the decision-making process involved in the removal of children from the family home. The benefits for children of staying with their families, and the benefits of their removal for short or longer-term periods must be acknowledged in the face of resistance by families and lack of appropriate resources to ensure good quality substitute care. Most decisions about children's circumstances are made with input from multi-agency professionals; however, frequently it is the social worker who has the responsibility for carrying out the decision.

Making the wrong decision when considering welfare and safety issues for children can have disastrous consequences for the child, the family, the social worker and their colleagues and families. This is a conscious thought for effectively functioning social workers on a daily basis.

A colleague had worked with a family where there had been serious domestic violence issues and a child had been injured. The child was removed from the family home but, after the couple separated, work was done with the mother to return the child to her care. The social worker had been proactive in the support of the mother and on her recommendation the care order was discharged. The social worker continued with family support work but the progress with the family deteriorated, with a number of visits being cancelled or postponed. On her last visit, the social worker attended and got no response from knocking at the door, but on leaving the property saw the child with a person she assumed to be the mother's ex-partner. She spoke to the adult, who stated that he was related to the child but did not identify himself as the ex-partner. The social worker spoke to the child, who she described as hesitant and reticent to talk. The social worker's 'hunch' was that this was the ex-partner, and the child's demeanour caused her concern that the child may be at risk of harm. Action to remove the child needed to be formal and coordinated. The social worker had to return to the office to contact police and other colleagues. It was discovered that the individual was the mother's ex-partner and the child was removed from the individual's care a couple of hours after the original visit. The social worker described her feelings at this time as being so terrified that something would happen to the child that she experienced physical symptoms of fear, including nausea and anxiety. Her genuine fear was that the ex-partner would harm the child, in part because he had been 'discovered' and the child may have been blamed, as the case history showed that the child had previously been injured as a result of that individual's frustrations and anger.

Managing these feelings during the incident is only part of the issue. The 'what-if?' question remains with social workers long after the event, despite there being little else in reality that could have been done other than follow carefully laid-out procedures, as occurred in this case.

Being too interventionist or not being interventionist enough – both of these behaviours cause a similar public response and add to an overarching perception of incompetence on the part of child protection social workers. It is arguable whether the perception of incompetence creates a self-fulfilling prophecy. Not to recognize the ability of social work staff to perform effectively means that there is no requirement to look for other answers to the problem of why children are not valued highly enough to ensure their safety, despite their general vulnerability. Not having answers to these difficult dilemmas means that the social work profession remains potentially ignorant of issues that could assist the ability to identify and protect the most vulnerable children. Constant criticism of professional behaviour, which is contradictory in its message as to what is expected, means that there is little focus on the reality which sees one or two children die each week in England and Wales as a result of child abuse and neglect (Coleman et al., 2007). Better focus on these issues could assist social workers in managing the difficulties and reducing the incidence of harm to children. Acknowledgement of the issues could possibly lead to increased understanding and therefore better support of child protection social work.

Burn-out and compassion fatigue in social work teams

In addition to the daily issues associated with direct work with families and a negative public perception, there are other factors that may affect social workers and contribute to burn-out and compassion fatigue. Morrison (1993) recognized the emotional impact of child protection work and described the process of 'professional accommodation syndrome', where social workers are unable to discuss the impact of their work on thinking, feeling and behaving. This denial results in feelings of helplessness and the attempt to appear to cope results in feelings beginning to emerge in irrational and dysfunctional ways. These unresolved issues lead to a perception that social workers are not coping, and denial of the existence of problems in turn compounds the inability to discuss the emotional content. It is arguable, then, that external and internal factors are inevitably connected, and that maintaining a perspective that both allows social workers to work effectively and continues to recognize the seriousness of the harm to children requires a mix of personal resilience and external support.

A dysfunctional reaction can manifest itself in conflict. One area for conflict is within the team environment, either with groups or individual colleagues. Social workers may incite conflict in teams or with colleagues as a result of compassion fatigue and burn-out. Constant and indiscriminate criticism of others' practice, aggressive and confrontational styles and undermining of other individuals should be considered indicators of concern that a social worker may lack empathy, an emotion required for recognizing issues for children and families.

Conflict with service users can occur in an environment where there is little support, sympathy or understanding. This can mean that workers develop individual methods of coping, including engaging in a confrontational manner, in a possible attempt to defend themselves.

A family was called into the local social work office to be told that the result of an assessment would be a recommendation to the court that their children should be removed and placed in the care of the local authority. The parents had a previous history of being aggressive and on one occasion had attempted unsuccessfully to attack the social worker. A colleague, jointly with the allocated social worker, had undertaken the assessment, in part to provide a safer working environment. As the parents were being given the news of the outcome of the assessment, their behaviour became increasingly agitated; they were shouting and swearing at the social worker and attempted to move towards her in an aggressive manner. They were asked to calm down by the colleague, at which point the father shouted, 'Look at her, look what she's doing'. While her colleague had been telling the parents about the outcome of the assessment, the social worker had been goading the parents by smiling smugly at them throughout the process. The behaviour had been witnessed by another colleague, who was present in the room due to the aggression previously displayed by the parents.

The social worker in this instance had been blatant in her behaviour, but many examples exist of less obvious methods of inciting conflict. Such behaviour leads to additional confrontation, adding further to the fear already perceived and possibly resulting in a cycle of high anxiety that is difficult to break. Working in this manner may be indicative of burn-out and compassion fatigue and can further compound associated difficulties. There is evidence to suggest that those who experience conflict with service users will fear similar violence occurring in the future, and this fear affects burn-out directly (Song, 2006).

Social workers must demonstrate empathy with individuals who, whether adult or child and whatever the circumstances, are people with needs and worries of their own. The depersonalization and objectification of children and their families is a symptom of compassion fatigue and burn-out. The inability to deal with others' emotions, or for those emotions to be masked by the stress of one's own concerns, leads to a lack of acknowledgement of the impact of harm. There is a distinct difference between maintaining a professional stance, demonstrated by the ability to identify and understand the emotions of service users and the impact on oneself, and detachment of all emotion from a fundamentally emotional task. It is arguable that the ability to make informed and positive decisions for children at risk of harm is reliant on the ability to comprehend the impact of harm and the impact of dealing with this on oneself. Social workers who are unable to manage this process can find themselves in a situation where they display uncontrolled emotion inappropriately. Social workers may also over-identify with the pain and grief that belongs to the service user.

In a case where a child had been tortured by the mother's boyfriend, a social worker found he was so unable to detach from the mother's point of view that he became personally abusive to colleagues who challenged his assessment. The strength of his viewpoint was such that he was unable to back down and the disciplinary proceedings that were instigated because of his behaviour resulted in his employment being terminated.

Minimization or over-personalization is not a substitute for management of feelings. Professionals may present as 'ultra-capable' or 'ultra-professional', delivering services in a detached manner and interpreting this as appropriate professional behaviour. Such individuals may be dismissive of the impact of issues of working in child protection, as this can be thought to denote weakness and therefore lack of capability. Dismissing the impact on oneself may indicate an inability to understand the feelings of service users. When this applies to children's situations, it means that the ability for appropriate decision making is compromised, as being unable to understand and express children's wishes and feelings and to articulate this to others is a fundamental part of child welfare service.

Professionals behaving in an emotionally inappropriate way on a regular basis should be considered to be having difficulties with managing the emotional component of child protection work.

Supervision and support

A number of studies point to the importance of effective supervision (Lloyd *et al.*, 2002; Kim, 2008), colleague support (Lloyd *et al.*, 2002; Collins, 2008) and autonomy in practice (Kim and Stoner, 2008; Kim, 2008) in providing social workers with positive working environments. The question that needs to be addressed is, can the social workers experiencing burn-out and compassion fatigue access the above?

Social workers can manage many demands as they experience high job satisfaction, particularly in the area of direct work with service users. Frustrations arise through such issues as organisational demands and lack of recognition (Collins, 2008).

Many teams work under significant resource pressure and, as in all areas of business, there are individuals who are less competent, less motivated and willing to leave the work to others. The social work profession has a strong commitment to equality, and as a consequence its reward strategy tends to be based on length of time served, rather than on performance-related recompense. There are also limited opportunities for progression whilst maintaining direct work with children and families, an area that provides substantial job satisfaction. A lack of explicit recognition of those who perform well contributes to a lack of value for competent and committed staff. It is an added pressure on social workers to deal with incompetent and lazy colleagues when they understand the implications for children of poor quality work.

Systems that have been brought in to assist with management of social work may compound the ability to depersonalize the issues for children and families, in addition to adding time pressure to services with high vacancy rates. Adopting a 'tick-box approach', which concentrates on ensuring that targets are met, does not always allow for the making of decisions in a holistic and individual manner. It could be argued that some systems increase stresses on social workers by adding to increasing workloads, curtailing the ability to understand and plan for individual circumstances, limiting professional autonomy and also supporting burn-out and compassion fatigue through objectifying children and families.

Supporting autonomous practice is important in valuing social workers; allowing for decisions to be based on the needs of children and families and to be made by experienced and competent individuals is a key component of effective outcomes. Measuring the quality of work is difficult, as the very nature of the work requires the success to be a negative. An example of how difficult this can be is the case of a young mother who had learning difficulties.

Her two very young children were removed from her care with a plan to rehabilitate them with significant initial support for the mother. The progress was very slow and a number of other more experienced social workers suggested that adoption at a very early stage would be most effective. The social work manager supported the social worker's view and the plan to rehabilitate. The children returned part-time to the care of the mother within 6 months but full-time unassisted care took a total of 4 years. Apart from the initial incident, which led to the children being removed, neither child suffered any abuse or neglect in the home; they remained in the care of their mother until adulthood, with no requirement for further intervention.

Calculating the benefits of productive social work is a difficult task. Over how long a period should benefits be calculated? Do we factor in the potential for placement breakdown of children removed from their families? Should we give a monetary value to what we are able to achieve, and if so, how is this to be done? The example above illustrates the reliance on sound practice decisions. Social workers must be supported to undertake their work and not hampered by a lack of understanding about how to evidence effective intervention.

Discussion

It is important to recognize that, of all the factors which have an impact on the stressful nature of child welfare and child abuse cases, the issue that causes most concern to social workers is the possibility of 'getting it wrong' and the effect that this will have on a child. If social workers establish relationships with children and families in order to promote the best interests of children and this is unsuccessful, it is difficult for this not to have a negative effect.

Social workers have to acknowledge the powerful emotive content so that they can work effectively with children and families. In order to acknowledge this, they must first confront the reality that child abuse is manifestly distressing. They should be provided with, and seek themselves, the necessary support to enable better outcomes for themselves and the children with whom they work.

Social work with children and families necessitates entering into other people's lives at a time when they are suffering stress and distress. Whatever the concerns presented, social workers need to engage with children who may be at risk of harm, often from those closest to them, and with those who present such risks. Social workers may be working with children and adults with profound needs and must make informed decisions as to the services required to meet those needs. The task requires skills, knowledge and experience and, most importantly, empathy and understanding of the human condition. The requirement to be open to others' experiences can expose social workers to accounts of violence and its impact on the most vulnerable members of society. A number of external factors influence this already stressful area of work and compound the difficulties associated with it. Social workers can be victims of secondary trauma, which can result in compassion fatigue and burn-out; this can be expressed through behaviour that may ultimately result in the inability to practice effectively and, in some cases, cause further harm to vulnerable individuals, as well as to the social worker themselves.

It is possible that the impact of emotional labour (employment requiring emotional skill) in such a highly emotive environment may lead to excessive distancing of oneself from the emotions in an attempt to remain unaffected by it.

There are numerous factors impacting on social workers, some of which have been explored in this chapter. As most of the work already involves dealing with significant levels of emotional trauma on the part of others, it is easy to fail to identify the signs and symptoms of compassion fatigue and burn-out on the part of affected social workers or their managers. What should be understood is that burn-out and compassion fatigue result in an inability to make effective decisions based on the best interests of children, and this inability is likely to compound the symptoms of compassion fatigue and burn-out. It is unlikely that those significantly affected will be able to access those traditional external or internal measures necessary to manage the consequences, and it is time to rethink the way in which support is offered to child protection social workers. Providing better support can only lead to benefit for professionals and the children and families with whom they work. There is scant research into the topic of secondary trauma in social work. Child protection is a difficult and demanding task, requiring robust and resilient individuals at all levels. Significant benefit would result from research into what creates and supports such robustness and resilience.

Acknowledgements

With grateful thanks to Elly Farmer, Miriam Rich and colleagues from CEOP and NSPCC for their assistance.

References

Coleman, K., Jansson, K., Kaiza, P., Reed, E. (2007) *Homicides, Firearm Offences and Intimate Violence 2006–2007* (supplementary vol. 2 to *Crime in England and Wales 2006–2007*). Home Office Statistical Bulletin

03/08: http://www.homeoffice.gov.uk/rds/pdfs07/hosb0207.pdf [accessed 21 October 2009].

Collins, S. (2008) Statutory social workers: stress, job satisfaction, coping, social support and individual differences. *British Journal of Social Work* **38**, 1173–1193.

Department of Health (1995) *Child Protection, Messages from Research.* London: HMSO.

Evans, S., Huxley, P., Gately, C., Webber, M., Mears, A., Pajak, S. *et al.* (2006) Mental health, burn-out and job satisfaction among mental health social workers in England and Wales. *British Journal of Psychiatry* **188**(1), 75–80.

Kim, H. (2008) A longitudinal study of job resources, burn-out, and turnover among social workers: implications for evidence-based organisational processes. *Dissertation Abstracts International Section A: Humanities and Social Sciences* **69**(6A), 2455.

Kim, H., Stoner, M. (2008) Burnout and turnover intention among social workers: effects of role stress, job autonomy and social support. *Administration in Social Work* **32**(3), 5–25.

Lloyd, C., King, R., Chenoweth, L. (2002) Social work, stress and burn-out: a review. *Journal of Mental Health* **11**(3), 255–266.

Morrison, T. (1993) *Staff Supervision in Social Care.* Harlow: Longman.

Song, K. (2006) Prevalence of client violence toward child and family social workers and its effects on burn-out, organisational commitment, and turnover intention: a structural equation modeling approach. *Dissertation Abstracts International Section A: Humanities and Social Sciences* **66**(9A), 3465.

The Sun (2009) Petition to Justice Secretary Jack Straw and Attorney General, 20 May 2009: http://www.thesun.co.uk/sol/template/v-1.0/module/petitionsPopUp.jsp?article=2443674 [accessed 21 October 2009].

Theodosius, C. (2006) Recovering emotion from emotion management. *Sociology* **40**(5), 893–910.

Chapter 2

Traumatic stress in the police service

Noreen Tehrani and Nicky Piper

Introduction

The police play a major role within society, protecting the public from crime, upholding the law, pursuing and bringing to justice law breakers, keeping the peace, protecting, helping and reassuring the community and acting with integrity, common sense and judgement (Home Office, 2007). Whilst this duty is accepted and promoted by police forces, the role places a heavy demand on the police officers and staff. This chapter examines the experiences of five police officers and a member of police staff working in fast response, firearms, body recovery, high-tech crime, family liaison and forensics.

It has been suggested that the level of stress-related mental ill-health in police officers and staff is higher than those found in other occupational groups (Collins and Gibbs, 2003) and that as a result police officers are more likely to commit suicide than other professional groups (Volanti, 2004). However, Berg *et al.* (2005) have challenged these views in a study that examined stress levels in police officers, which found that policing is not more stressful than other occupations. This chapter presents the results of a qualitative study that looked at the perceptions of police officers working in high-risk roles. Template analysis methodology was adopted in the study to capture the multiple dimensions of police officers' experience and because it is less prescriptive and time consuming than other qualitative methods (King, 2004).

The study

Officers from three policing organisations were interviewed for the study. The officers were engaged in high-risk roles, including family liaison (FL), forensics (FOR), high-tech crime (HTC; i.e. computer and mobile phone crimes), body recovery (BR), firearms (FA) and fast response (FR). The structured interviews were recorded and transcribed. In addition to demographic information, the interviews covered: (a) selection, induction and training; (b) difficulties in the role; (c) difficult or distressing incidents; (d) self-protection and relief humour; and (e) suggestions for improving support. The FR, FA and HTC officers had 3, 15 and 17 years of service, respectively, with each of the other participants having over 25 years of service. All the participants had been engaged in their high-risk role for a minimum of 3 years.

Selection, induction and training

All the officers apart from the FR officer had worked in other policing roles prior to moving to their current post, and all the participants apart from the FOR and FR were involved in training new recruits into their area of work. Looking back on their personal experiences of joining their policing discipline, most found themselves thrust into the role with little thought for their psychological suitability for the role. Although there is increasing evidence of the benefits of using psychological screening of police recruits (Burke *et al.*, 2006), this did not appear to play a major role in the recruitment of the police personnel involved in this study.

> There was a board and an application, and then effectively I had a chat with the DI and board for the job and you passed, you got in (HTC).

> . . . when I originally started to do the role there was no selection process, I was working on a racial crime team and told I was going out to do it. So I went out and did it for two years, there was no preparation, no discussion, I was not asked if I wanted to do it, I was told that I would be doing it. In fact I asked not to do it, but was told that I would be doing it (FOR).

All the participants expressed the view that the shock tactic of pushing people in at the deep end in the belief that they would 'sink or swim' was harmful, and that a gradual introduction to the more difficult aspects of the work enabled recruits to develop the essential skills required for the work.

All of the participants except FR had undertaken other roles within policing; the FR team is made up of uniformed police officers who are generally the first responders to an emergency call. Many FRs are in their 20s, newly out of training and may lack the life experiences to deal with some of the difficult and demanding issues which they face. FR officers are likely to find organisational hassles affecting their ability to deal with stress (Huddlestone *et al.*, 2006).

There was a lot of emphasis placed on physical exams – bleep tests, push-ups, pull-ups, sit-ups, etc. The other process was similar to any other job application you would give examples of how you are diverse, almost patronising questions . . . It is possible that it (a psychological assessment) was embedded within the questions but I cannot recall any specific psychological tests (TP).

So not only must they be professionally competent but they must have sufficient life skills . . . because it is a demanding role, psychologically as well (FLO).

A few of the participants had undergone training to help them recognize the symptoms of stress, burn-out and traumatic stress in them, and in colleagues this was rare.

We had quite a strong character, a former nurse (who did the training) she was very strict on personal health and well-being, we were trained to be team leaders and had to look out for signs of stress in our teams but equally she reinforced manual handling and being safe in the scene (BR).

Many officers do not want to share the more distressing aspects of their work with their colleagues, spouse or partner; as a result they experience the impact of unresolved trauma in their personal relationships. Occasionally the impact of untreated traumatic stress had a devastating effect when a traumatized officer becomes suicidal or violent (Volanti *et al.*, 2006).

He [a BR officer] had been to Lockerby and he had also done the *Marchioness* and he threatened his wife with a shotgun . . . she was in the job, there was domestic violence as a result of the trauma . . . she appealed for assistance from the job and no one would touch her, it [support] was all concentrated on her husband.

Difficulties in the role

The news, films and books often feature the police, and anyone applying to join the police will have formed an idea of the demanding nature of policing roles. However, the reality, whilst rarely as dramatic as portrayed in films, is nevertheless extremely demanding. In line with research (Brough, 2004), mundane aspects of the work, including adapting to shift working, dealing with the police culture, a lack of training and development and heavy workloads, were cited by the study's participants as major stressors.

> I would be turning out of bed at 2–3 a.m., my girl friend at the time said that instantly the phone goes you switch on and sound that you are fully awake . . . I have been at weddings, parties and family birthdays, where the pager goes off – and that's it, you are gone (FA).

Whilst, for experienced officers the strains of working for the police become part of normal life for new officers and staff the nature of the work can be more difficult; this is particularly true for the FR officers, where there is a pressure to respond to a high volume of emergency calls, the lack of recovery time prior to responding to the next call.

> You can start work at seven o'clock in the morning and can be called out immediately to a road traffic accident, it could be fatal, near-fatal or just a bump . . . with RTCs you don't even go back to the office to fill up the paperwork and can be immediately called to a sudden death, somebody passed away in a hospital a nursing home or at home . . . you arrive with the RTC still fresh in your mind . . . you know it you will be stripping and searching a body in front of hysterical family . . . as you are moving them [the body] around they are groaning and sloshing, just because bodies do stuff like that. You finish that and fill in your sudden death report, then you have a shoplifter or a burglary to deal with, you go back [to the police station] and finish the paperwork that you have accumulated over the day, go home, you are knackered, go to sleep get up and do it again (FR).

The media and the public's increasing use of mobile phones to pass photographs and film clips of crimes and disasters to friends, television and newspapers is having an increasing impact on the way incidents are handled.

> We were taking these people out at gunpoint, there were a lot of drugs and we were outside a parade of shops and a young girl videoed it on her mobile phone. We had not even left the scene when Sky News [were] on the phone asking about the incident because they had just purchased a video (FA).

> A friend of mine shot and killed someone and it was shown live by a local TV company by the time he got back, unloaded his guns, got into post-incident management, phoned his wife to let you know he had been involved in the incident. Her response was 'are you the murdering f****rs that have just shot someone?'. That is the effect that the media can have on you; when he got home and she was not there (FA).

The impact of members of the public filming criminal events is particularly relevant in high-tech crime, where images and films of disasters, child abuse, rapes, torture and murder are increasingly being filmed by participants, bystanders or witnesses. Rather than reading about a crime or seeing images of the aftermath, HTC are exposed to the secondary trauma of viewing images of crimes as they are being committed (Burns *et al.*, 2008).

> People are taking more immediate action films and videos [on their phones], so we are seeing submissions with current crime reports for rapes or murder or even assault where people have taken videos. The biggest issue for mobile phone technicians from a welfare point of view is that they end up seeing live action crime and having to deal with it live, as it could have happened a couple of hours earlier; there is that immediacy to what they are seeing (HTC).

Where there is a public interest, the press coverage can put even more pressure on the officers and staff working at the scene. This can result in additional pressure to protect the identity of the officer or member of staff. Inappropriate press coverage can also have a negative impact on grieving families and friends; while ethical journalists refrain from sensationalizing a disaster by not filming bodies and body parts, there are some who abuse their position (Mogensen, 2008).

They [press] always try to get onto the scene by any means possible. [In the Paddington rail crash] the British press seemed a lot more subtle and while we were removing the body we knew they would see it before we could get it into a bag. We put up a blanket; they knew something was going to happen. It caused a lot of activity; they would want a body bag shot rather than a body, but in the current climate with mobile phones and cameras it [images] will be on the internet in hours. It is not just the local but all the foreign press showing dead bodies in the streets and gory magazines where there are pictures of the dead; it is not fair on the families (BR).

I dealt with the Ben Kinsella murder in Islington . . . the media were unbelievable, they were at you all the time and these days of DNA you don't take your mask off – but if they photograph you smiling – you have to think about things like that (FOR).

There is normally a priority, if it is a train crash it would be the driver who has to go to toxicology, everyone wants to know if the driver was drunk, asleep, had a heart attack, on drugs. If an individual is further in the debris and you need cutting gear or time to get them out. It is distressing for the family if the press say that we did not recover a body for two days because they were black. We are unfairly targeted by the press for being racist when people of ethnic background were not recovered quickly (BR).

Distressing incidents

Each of the participants was asked to describe an event which he/she found particularly distressing. Two of the specialist officers graphically described their most distressing events as things that had happened when they were new recruits in the police. It is possible that the more vulnerable officers and staff leave the police service early or find roles that are less challenging. The interviews suggested that most of the police officers and staff had learnt how to deal with distressing events. However, there are occasions when even the most experienced officer or member of staff can become distressed by some aspect of their work.

It went through three phases for me; initially in the early days of my service I would not want to get too close. If it was a rape victim or a victim of severe domestic violence, I would not want to ask any questions that were too personal. In the middle phase I just did not seem to have any compassion and I don't know if I was purposely desensitizing myself; I would just say, your daughter is in there, she has unfortunately been raped by quite a few people, if you can wait here for a minute I will get you in when it is practical. That is no way to deliver a message. Towards the last phase I effectively broke down, becoming over-emotional towards incidents, the fight-or-flight would kick in and I would want to run away. But not when dealing with conflict; if I was policing a town and a big fight broke out, I would have no problem at all, but if a sudden death needed taking care of I would find any excuse not to do it.

Even the most resilient and experienced officers and staff experience trauma responses from time to time. These responses occur most frequently when there is something in the situation which is particularly meaningful causing the victims to become more real.

At the Paddington rail crash, a group of quite experienced police officers, we were lifting a heavy bloke who was impacted onto debris from the crash. Because he was heavy and was in a confined space it took a long time. As we pulled him his jacket opened and his wallet fell out and there was a picture of him and his family with young children and a wife. Everybody spontaneously stood up and held their arms up – we had now humanized the body we had been dealing with and, although we did not have any direct contact with the family, it made us think about this person as someone with a family – just like us (BR).

Several of the participants in the study talked about being shocked by something unexpected happening. If they knew what they were about to face, they were able to mentally prepare. Unfortunately, this is not always possible and having to face an unexpected danger or scene can be disorientating. Even for well-experienced officers who have dealt with dead bodies and violent incidents, they can be shocked when they are faced by something totally unexpected.

I remember one particular video, I switched it on and I remember seeing woman in a bikini with salsa music playing . . . she was dancing around and in the corner of the picture is this chap strapped to a chair. Suddenly, she picks up a chain saw, starts the chain saw – she is still dancing and the next thing she actually cuts off his feet first, then his hands. She is still dancing around and there is blood pouring out. It was that shift, between normal behaviour and abnormal, that really pushed me out of my comfort zone so that I stopped and literally walked away from it. Then I reassessed and after a large coffee I went back and carried on. I think for me it was seeing this appearance of normality and with an abnormal twist to it (HTC).

It was a Tuesday morning at 10 a.m. – coming out of the block of flats is this guy who is probably about 50, he didn't seem overly distressed, which was odd, what he said was, my wife is in the flat and she has been stabbed and that was it. As we go into the entrance lobby of these flats there was a door on the right which is slightly ajar and as we go in, the door on the left opened and the guy come out as cool as a cucumber, put his hands up and said 'I surrender, I think I have killed her'. 'What do you mean – killed her?' He said 'I cut her and the knife is in the bin'. There was a Stanley knife with a little bit of blood on it. As I enter the flat the room on the right was a bathroom and there are shower curtains across and I thought this is going to be like the exorcist. I backed in and I pulled the old shower curtain across and nothing. I kind of let my guard down, I came out of the bathroom and continued down the corridor and turned left and it was like a horror film, there was blood on the ceiling it was almost like stalactites hanging off and even now the smell makes me retch and the blood, it was a double bed. I can even smell it now . . . I look back and I think that I had set myself up that it is going to be behind the shower screen – then that's alright – I walked round the corner, bang, my guard was down, even though I was prepared emotionally my guard was down.

When a death is particularly tragic, avoidable or the victims are children, the magnitude of what has occurred can be more distressing.

Two children had been killed by their mother, the little girl was about two or three and the boy nine, the story was that the mother had denied that they were her children and believed that they had been swapped. The children were in the care of the father but social services decided that she should have them overnight so she could bond with them. The father very upset when he dropped the children off. She suffocated the little girl, the boy had woken up she chased him around the room. She hit him with a hammer and hammered him to death. When the father had arrived that morning to collect his children he found her sitting with the two dead children. It was distressing and a dreadful, dreadful experience for the boy because it was not quick (FOR).

Occasionally it is the police systems which fail, leaving officers and staff exposed to a traumatizing event for long periods of time without a break. Over-identification with victims or the families of victims can increase the experience of secondary trauma.

A family from Iraq had three daughters in their early 20s; one of them had dishonoured the family by having a relationship and was murdered, put in a suitcase and buried in the garden. We knew that it was somebody within the family who did the killing. The remaining sisters had become Westernized and they were living a similar lifestyle to their sister but hiding it from the family. As part of the investigation we needed to get information from the sisters about the killing. We had to be careful not to put the sisters in a position where they might suffer a similar fate. The FLO needed to make contact with the sisters on a daily basis to check that they were OK. It had to be done covertly by text messages, which meant that that the FLO had to manage the risk to the sisters on her own every day. Although at first she thought she could cope, as the investigation and trial lasted well over a year and she was on tenterhooks for hours if the contact was unsuccessful and worried on whether she needed to call the local police ask them to break the door down. The pressure started to get to her and in the end she had a breakdown (FLO).

Where the barriers or boundaries between the bereaved families, public and trauma scene are not maintained, there can be an increase in vulnerability. If FLOs see a disrupted body, it may be difficult for them to carry out their role with the family. On the other hand, it is difficult for BR officers to deal with bereaved families visiting the disaster scene, as it challenges the protective boundaries that the officers put in place to protect themselves.

> In the Tsunami we were a body recovery mortuary team and did not have any FLOs; people were in such distress weeks after they had lost whole families. They were desperate to find their loved ones; you are in a dream holiday and the next minute your family is wiped out. People come up to you and say 'this is a picture of – have you seen him?'. You could not tell them the bodies are a total mess, or how horrible the scenes were – it was not fair, they have already gone through enough already. I dealt with a Swedish family; the only one missing was a little lad, they had a picture of him they found on the internet – lying dead on the beach. I went to the other side and the bodies from that beach had come in but I had to try to tell them that it would not be a quick process. There is nothing to prepare anyone for that. I mean absolutely everywhere there were dead bodies (BR).

Self-protection and relief humour

Police personnel engage in a range of activities to help them deal with traumatic exposure. Individuals tend to develop their own set of coping skills, the most important being to establish the meaningfulness of the work and their reason for doing it (Wilson, 2006). Dealing with child abuse images is challenging, as the role involves the investigator trying to identify with the child being abused; helpful coping strategies include setting time limits on viewing (Burns *et al.*, 2008).

> I knew roughly what I was getting into but for me it was more of a technical challenge. I was a detective; I had come into this role with a computer leaning. It seemed the ideal job for me but I was not really prepared for the images or maybe the volume of the images. The way I got round it and certainly the way that I have passed on to my team is not to look at the pictures or dwell on

the pictures. It is sad that that event has occurred, but we are here to get the data behind that picture (HTC).

Having time to prepare and thinking through what one may need to do to meet a traumatically challenging event is helpful. This technique was used as a coping strategy by all those interviewed; however, having long periods of time thinking about what one may face can undermine resilience (Alexander and Wells, 1991).

I think that the moment you get a call, and they tend to happen more often than not on night duty, your mind is immediately overtaken with what you are going to do. The moment I get in the car and start driving I think, 'Is it a busy road? Will I have to get it cordoned? Am I going to need lights? Will I have to ring for a post-mortem?' Your mind goes into overdrive thinking about organisation, planning and dealing with what you are going to have to deal with (FOR).

When people come onto the scene of a disaster or murder, it is important to have something meaningful to do. Lacking the appropriate level of knowledge on how to handle a situation increases the stress and undermines confidence (Paton and Volanti, 2006).

My role [in dealing with sudden deaths] as a police officer was questionable to say the least. I am required to search the area and look for anything suspicious. What is suspicious? When you are in a cluttered bungalow in the dark, surrounded by smell and silence looking at an obviously deteriorating corpse and having the medical knowledge of a boy scout it is hard to fathom just what you should be looking for (FR).

What I generally try to do is give them [inexperienced staff] something to do, because it always helps if you are busy and you feel that you are useful when you are functioning, because that can justify it in your own mind. I normally try to keep talking to them, humour sometimes is required, but I mean that you have got to – leaving people hanging around with nothing to do does not help them (FOR).

Finishing a job was also seen as helpful, particularly when completing a job means that a family can regain some peace of mind by getting their loved one back. All the interviewees described times when they worked to reduce the distress of family members.

> I have seen people go against procedures to get a body moved quickly so it can be identified. In 7/7 [London terrorist attack] by rights we should have got cutting gear for an individual from under a train. One of the team went under to let the body drop onto them to roll them into a body bag. That was real dignity and respect, a really unpleasant job and . . . however, if we got all the cutting gear we would not have been able to remove the body until the next day. It is amazing – the officers want to get the bodies out and they want to get them identified. I don't like it as a word but it gives closure for the families (BR).

> One of my coping mechanisms is – I like to bag the bodies, seal them up and get them taken away by the undertakers. To me that completes something and I find that makes me more able to deal with it. I do not like walking away leaving a body out in the open, it distresses me. I know that they are dead but I think 'that's a mum and that is her little boy and she knows that he is lying there in that house overnight on his own'. I know that it is ridiculous logically but that means something to people (FOR).

Dealing with emotionally demanding situations increases emotional and physiological arousal. When in the middle of a disaster or crisis unexpected events, particularly those which involve dilemmas, incongruity or unexpected outcomes occur, the distressing event can take on the mantle of humour or farce. Relief humour (Critchley, 2002) occurs when there is a need to release pent-up energy. Humour can also be used to help people to detach from their immediate surroundings and enables situations to be reframed by letting people step back psychologically and adopt a different perspective on their work (Khan, 1989; Joyce, 1989).

> Black humour or morbid humour is incredibly important to the teams, but is not seen as entirely appropriate by other people. I would not want family members to see that inappropriate behaviour; however, it is an acceptable coping mechanism as it helps with the bonding of the teams. It is not that we don't treat the deceased with dignity and respect, it is just the banter you need to get on with the job (BR).

You are devastated for a family member in case they might have seen you laughing and joking – their lives have been devastated and we are laughing and joking. You feel guilty for doing that but at the back of your mind, especially as the supervisor, you appreciate that they need it, but there is a time and a place and our people need to be protected from it as much as the people need to engage in it (BR).

I was under a train, we were about to do a recovery and we needed a bit of equipment to remove the particular body. I had been left and weird things go through your mind that you feel that socially you must engage this dead person in conversation, 'Here we are' . . . which is weird. You know you can be uncomfortable in parties some time and you feel that you should make the effort, it was like the social pressure to engage this person because there are the two of us face to face – it is weird and it is perverse, like when people step accidentally on bodies and apologize to the body (BR).

Suggestions for improvements

When police personnel were asked about potential improvements to the way they were managed and supported, five main themes emerged: (a) the need for improved selection and induction; (b) training for managers and team members; (c) personal support/screening; (d) team working; and (e) organisational culture.

Selection and induction

There is a need to have a clearly defined selection process for all police roles which looks at technical, physical and psychological factors to help to identify interviewees who could undertake the particular role safely. There should be realistic information on what the job entails; this should not be designed to scare people, but rather to give them an opportunity to prepare themselves for the more difficult aspects of their work. There should be an induction programme that is constantly reviewed and updated, which gradually and systematically introduces police personnel to the more demanding aspects of their role.

Training

In addition to technical training, police personnel should have training in how to recognize stress, burn-out and trauma reactions in themselves and others. Line managers should be trained to help their teams to talk openly about the emotional impact of their work and to challenge negative behaviours within the team, including bullying and humiliation. Where officers and staff are infrequently deployed, then regular update training and assessment was seen as essential.

Personal support/screening

In the high-risk roles there should be regular screening which provides an opportunity for officers and staff to talk about their work with an independent person who is trained to identify the symptoms of stress and trauma. Records should be maintained to identify the number of traumatic incidents an individual has handled, where exceeding an agreed quota would automatically trigger an operational debriefing. Most of the interviewees also wanted to be able to seek confidential personal support from an occupational health nurse or counsellor, to deal with family issues which impacted on their ability to work, or when work issues were impacting on the family. Where a partner was directly affected by the impact of the policing work, consideration should be given to provide support/counselling.

Team working

The current trend in policing has tended to erode team working aspects in many of the policing groups. A few interviewees belonged to teams, but most would come together for a brief period of time and then return to their normal policing role. In these temporary groups it was seen as important for contact to be maintained after deployment, to ensure that the individual was coping and, where appropriate, a note sent to their line manager to alert them to possible reactions.

Organisational culture

Whilst humour is helpful in some situations, it can be used to cover up an emotional need. Being 'macho' and avoiding talking can result in emotional dissociation and a lost opportunity to learn and develop greater skills and resilience. Where police officers or staff are deployed as part of a larger team, for example to deal with a major incident or disaster, importance was given to the senior officers being aware of their roles and the needs of the specialist groups.

Discussion

This study gives some insight into the experiences of six police officers and staff members who were engaged in different roles. Despite the different stresses and strains of the work they undertake, there was a marked similarity in their reported emotional and psychological experiences. Although none of the findings was totally unexpected, the results indicated that the least experienced officers were engaged in the most demanding roles. New recruits in fast response teams, where they were put under a high level of pressure, had few opportunities to reflect on their experiences and seemed to have the least support and personal training available to them. The research also suggests that where police forces are introducing police staff into roles once occupied by police officers, there is a need to ensure that the staff members are fully aware of the nature of the work and that they go through an appropriate selection, induction and screening process. Whilst the police may get a bad press, the participants in this study appeared to be committed to their work and to be doing their best to achieve the Home Office's 2007 policing standard for acting with integrity, common sense and judgement.

References

Alexander, D.A., Wells, A. (1991) Reactions of police officers to body-handling after a major disaster – a before and after comparison. *British Journal of Psychiatry* **159**, 547–555.

Berg, A.M., Hem, E., Lau, B., Ekeberg, O. (2005) An exploration of job stress and health in the Norwegian Police Service: a cross-sectional study. *Occupational Medicine* **55**(2), 113–120.

Brough, P. (2004) Comparing the influence of traumatic and organizational stressors on the psychological health of police, fire and ambulance officers. *International Journal of Stress Management* **11**(3), 227–244.

Burke, K.J., Shakespere-Finch, J., Paton, D., Ryan, M. (2006) *Traumatology* **12**(3), 178–188.

Burns, M., Morley, J., Bradshaw, R., Domene, J. (2008) The emotional impact on and coping strategies employed by police teams investigating internet child exploitation. *Traumatology* **14**(2), 20–31.

Collins, P.A., Gibbs, A.C.C. (2003) Stress in police officers: a study of the origins, prevalence and severity of stress-related symptoms within a county police force. *Occupational Medicine* **53**(4), 256–264.

Critchley S. (2002) *On Humour*. London: Routledge.

Home Office (2007) The role of the police service: http://www.respect.gov.uk/members/article.aspx?id=8214 [accessed 30 April 2009].

Huddlestone, L.M., Paton, D., Stephens, C. (2006) Conceptualising traumatic stress in police officers, critical incidents and organizational influences. *Traumatology* **12**(3), 170–177.

Joyce, D. (1989) Why do police officers laugh at death? *Psychologist* **12**(9), 379–381.

Khan, W.A. (1989) Towards a sense of organizational humor: implications for organizational diagnosis and change. *Journal of Applied Behavioural Science* **25**(1), 45–63.

King, N. (2004) Using templates in thematic analysis of text. In Cassel, C., Symon, G. (eds), *Essential Guide to Qualitative Methods in Organizational Research*. London: Sage.

Mogensen, K. (2008) Television journalism during terror attacks. *Media, War and Conflict* **1**(1), 31–49.

Paton, J., Volanti, J.M. (2006) Policing in the context of terrorism: managing traumatic stress risk. *Traumatology* **12**(3), 236–247.

Volanti, J.M. (2004) Predictors of police suicide ideation. *Suicide and Life Threatening Behaviour* **4**, 277–283.

Volanti, J.M., Castellano, C., O'Rourke, J., Paton, D. (2006) Proximity to the 9/11 terrorist attack and suicide ideation in police officers. *Traumatology* **12**(3), 248–253.

Wilson, J.P. (2006) Trauma and transformation of the self: restoring meaning and wholeness to the personality. In Wilson, J.P. (ed.), *The Posttraumatic Self – Restoring Meaning and Wholeness to the Personality*. London: Routledge.

Chapter 3

Mental health problems in British veterans

Walter Busuttil

Introduction

In Britain, a military veteran is anyone who has served for at least 1 day in HM Forces (regular or reserve) or in the Merchant Navy in a vessel used in military operations. Very few medical discharges are for mental health problems, with only 150 of 1200 annual medical discharges being for mental health issues. It has been noted that many ex-service personnel report suffering from significant mental health problems while in the armed services but are reluctant to consult military GPs or access military mental health services (Hoge *et al.*, 2006). This reticence is linked to feelings of shame and guilt as well as stigma and the fear that their careers might be compromised or lost (Scheiner, 2008).

Military psychiatric services

Since 1948, the National Health Service (NHS) has been responsible in looking after the health of veterans. While serving in the military, physical and psychiatric health is the responsibility of the Defence Medical Services (DMS). In-service psychiatric care is currently organised into 15 multidisciplinary Departments of Community Mental Health (DCMHs) situated in the UK, with additional DCMHs situated in Germany, Cyprus and Gibraltar. There is rapid access to a high standard of mental health care. A hospital-based service contracted out to an NHS Consortium is also available. In combat zones, psychiatric field teams are staffed by uniformed community psychiatric nurses (CPNs), supported by military psychiatrists.

Currently, approximately 180 000 personnel serve in the UK

military. The DCMHs deal with around 5000 referrals each year, which equates to 4.5 referrals per 1000 personnel. Clinical audits indicate that common presentations include alcohol misuse (33%), depression (19%), anxiety (11%) and adjustment disorders (10%) (McMannus, 2009). Alcohol misuse in servicemen exposed to combat is at a higher level than that of a comparative civilian population, especially in the younger servicemen (Fear and Wesseley, 2009).

Studies have shown no significant differences between the rates of mental disorder between personnel deployed or not deployed in Iraq or Afghanistan, with the exception of post-traumatic stress disorder (PTSD) (Hotopf et al., 2006). The rates of PTSD reported in personnel serving in the British forces in Iraq and Afghanistan are 4–6.9% (Hotopf et al., 2006; Fear et al., 2010). These figures are low compared to other military organisations fighting in the same war zones, with the US and Australian military having higher rates of PTSD (Hotopf et al., 2006; Iversen and Greenberg, 2009). The reasons given for lower rates of PTSD is a lower dose–response effect; British soldiers are said to have been exposed to lower levels of psychological trauma, due to the tour of duty of the British soldiers being less than that of their American counterparts, where the US service personnel are expected to be in theatre of war for a year at a time, compared to the British, who have a 2 year break between their 6 month tours of duty. Where these guidelines are breached individuals have more problems, with particular difficulties in those whose tours are unexpectedly extended (Rona et al., 2007). Whilst the suicide rate in service is unremarkable, a study has shown that suicide rates for ex-servicemen aged under 24 years were two or three times higher than for their civilian counterparts (Kapur et al., 2009). Although the reasons for this are not clear, the researchers suggested three possible reasons: (a) they were more vulnerable to suicide before they had joined the forces; (b) they had trouble re-adjusting to civilian life; and (c) they had been exposed to more adverse experiences.

Occupational factors as causes of later mental health problems in veterans

Mental health problems seen in veterans can arise from a variety of causes related to military service. Many join up in order to escape difficult childhoods or life situations, including exposure to childhood abuse, attachment difficulties, poor childhood care giving, unhappy adoption, poor adult role models, poverty, poor housing, poor opportunities and deprivation (Novaco *et al.*, 1983; Iversen *et al.*, 2005; Busuttil, 2009).

Most people who join the military family adjust well and take the opportunity to reorder their lives, and consequently make good attachments that remain intact even after leaving the military (Iversen *et al.*, 2005). Some, however, have problems when leaving the military, particularly when they are forced to leave against their wishes, for example, if their contract has come to an end and, despite wishing to remain, they are forced to leave. Other military personnel apply for premature voluntary retirement (PvR) because they cannot cope with military service, due to undeclared mental health problems which they may have tried to mask by self-medicating with alcohol. However, alcohol misuse may result in a discharge from the military on disciplinary grounds, rather than for medical reasons. Leaving the military is a time of vulnerability and at this time psychological symptoms may increase, due to the breaking of attachments with the 'military family' and a need to relate to people in an alien civilian setting, including their wives, with whom they now have to spend an increased amount of time (Iversen *et al.*, 2005; Van Staden *et al.*, 2007).

Marital relations and family life can be adversely affected by the cycle of peacetime detachments, leading to 'intermittent husband syndrome', characterized by symptoms of anxiety, depression and sexual difficulties in wives and partners, which often leads to premature retirement. The psychiatric symptoms in spouses are increased if the partner is engaged in dangerous operational and combat zone service (Busuttil and Busuttil, 2001). Within the services there is also a reliance on social activities, revolving around the excessive use of alcohol in post-deployment and combat situations (Iversen *et al.*, 2007; Hooper *et al.*, 2008). Veterans are more likely to suffer physical disorders linked to their occupational service, such as orthopaedic problems, chronic pain and deafness (Busuttil, 2009). Additionally, US studies have demonstrated that those combat veterans who suffer chronic PTSD are more likely to go on to develop a variety of serious physical disorders, including cardiac disorders and diabetes, 10 years prematurely compared to those who have not suffered PTSD (Boscarino, 1997, 2004, 2008).

Combat zone mental breakdown: mechanisms and mitigation

The British military has been involved in an increasing number of operational commitments in recent years, including peacekeeping in the Balkans and active combat in Iraq and Afghanistan at a time when the number of service personnel has been reduced. War theatre mental breakdown or combat stress reaction (CSR) incorporates many features of acute stress disorder, which is recognized in DSM-IV and ICD-10. CSR can spontaneously resolve, resolve following early intervention or progress into long-term psychiatric illness, including PTSD. There is a dose–response relationship in the development of CSR (Noy, 1987, 1991; Shalev and Munitz, 1988). The development of the CSR is phasic. The *premonitory phase* includes: high arousal with a restricted field of interest; an inability to relax, shift attention, or concentrate; disrupted decision making; emotional dysfunction, with irritability, impulsivity; uncontrolled emotional discharge; diminished social interaction; withdrawal; isolation; loss of sense of humour and empathy; and sustained criticism and mistrust. Also present are physiological manifestations of anxiety, with diarrhoea, anxiety, tremulousness, weakness, cold, sweating, headaches, palpitations and unexplained physical complaints. These symptoms must be distinguished from normal fear reactions.

The *acute phase* occurs next. Often an additional traumatic event causes the shift into this second phase. This last event is often described as the cause of the CSR but careful enquiry reveals the premonitory phase before the onset of the acute phase. It should be noted that spontaneous recovery from the premonitory phase is also possible. In the acute phase, the functional deficit becomes total and overwhelming. Gross psychiatric symptoms occur. These include: cognitive impairment, comprising dissociative states, confusion and disorientation; impaired stimulus response, with hyperreactiveness to stimuli and inappropriate responses to minor events; and psychomotor symptoms, including restlessness, agitation, stupor and motor retardation; affective symptoms, including anxiety, panic, terror, sadness, guilt, shame, perplexity, stupefaction and shock; and conversion symptoms, with paralysis, blindness and muteness. It should be noted that a distinction from confusional states should be made.

The final phase is the *stabilization phase*, which develops over several days or weeks. It is often seen by medical officer at the end of military operation as the first manifestation of CSR in those who could handle the acute phase without medical help or in those whose CSR developed insidiously. It is often the case in soldiers whose position of command has not afforded the luxury of breaking down as long as active operations continued. It can also present at the first contact with the family at home and especially during the first leave after combat.

The symptom picture is midway between the acute phase and PTSD, characterized by affective symptoms (depression, guilt and shame), intrusive thoughts and vivid images of traumatic event(s), sleep disturbance, fatigue and irritability.

Risk factors for the development of CSR include primary and secondary factors

Primary factors have a dose–response relationship with the development of symptoms. They comprise the intensity of battle, including the unpredictability of the stressor, loss of the combat unit's social cohesiveness and the loss of the leader or poor leadership. Secondary factors include: psychological deprivations, with those who take a passive role (e.g. drivers, technicians) being more at risk; a lack of adequate (military) training for the actual role; an inability to sustain denial, for example, overexposure to casualties, atrocities, death of friend/relative; conflicts prior to combat, including stress following separation from loved ones. Secondary factors also include physical deprivations, with inadequate sleep, food and fluids, physical exhaustion and illness; poor weather conditions are also important; support deprivations, such as leadership failure, including death or replacement of the leader; the isolation from the basic unit; being a new soldier in a unit; lack of support from loved ones at home; and poor unit cohesion/*esprit de corps* all contribute to the development of CSR.

Prevention and mitigation of CSR and PTSD

Measures have been tried to reduce mental health problems before, during and after combat. There is little evidence that any of these prevent mental health difficulties; they include:

- *Screening*. Screening has mixed benefits. A study which looked at eliminating recruits with a history of psychiatric illness, including ASD or PTSD, found a reduction in subsequent psychiatric ill-health (McFarlane, 1989; Creamer *et al.*, 1993). Pre-deployment screening for mental health problems did not reduce subsequent morbidity or predicted PTSD in the short term (Rona *et al.*, 2006) and combat exposure and group cohesion affected mental health outcomes independent of previous mental health status, explaining why screening prior to deployment may be ineffective (Rona *et al.*, 2009).

- *Realistic professional training.* Realistic training equips soldiers and non-combat troops to counteract psychological threat. Training is helpful in forming supportive, cohesive groups (Novaco *et al.*, 1983; Busuttil, 1995).
- *Stress inoculation training (SIT).* This has been used by police body handlers (Miller, 1989). These strategies can be utilized by military personnel who become involved in body handling following atrocities. SIT used in relation to nuclear, biological and chemical (NBC) warfare training has been shown to improve resilience (Carter and Cammermeyer, 1989).
- *Induction training.* Induction training helps military personnel to cope with expected adversity. It enables and facilitates open peer discussion. Induction training is used before individuals are exposed to a traumatic situation, reinforcing SIT techniques and taking the form of briefings or lectures delivered by commanders or military mental health workers in collaboration with the chain of command (Srinivasan, 1993).
- *Prophylactic medications.* If medication were to be used to prevent the onset of CSR and PTSD, it would have to be safe, efficacious and cause no performance or cognitive impairments to personnel. Whilst research is sparse, there is some evidence to support the usefulness of prophylactic medications (Foa *et al.*, 2009).
- *Leadership, cohesion and buddy–buddy care.* Maintenance of social support networks and buffers is essential. Good leadership includes good communication and measures taken to prevent deprivation. In many military tasks, each man has a buddy for mutual practical help in carrying out duties and many necessary drills are double-checked in this way. Buddies usually become close friends. It is not entirely unexpected, therefore, that pairs of buddies will attempt to talk about their feelings before and after going into a stressful situation. The benefits of the intimate support provided by buddy–buddy care have

been noted during the Vietnam War. Those who had buddies and were affected by CSR who came for treatment were rehabilitated more quickly than those with no buddy (Strange and Arthur, 1967).

Proximity, immediacy, expectancy and brevity (PIE B)

Since World War I, the treatment of CSR has comprised crisis intervention, delivered as close as possible to the front line, incorporating the principles of PIE B. These interventions aim to replenish depleted physical and psychological needs by satisfying the lack of sleep, food and drink for a few days in relative safety. Minimal psychological intervention is attempted. Following this, the expectation is that the soldier will want to return to the front line. If symptoms persist, evacuation to a middle zone facility is undertaken; if there is a failure to respond, evacuation out of the battle zone completely for prolonged psychiatric intervention is arranged. It has been argued that this approach itself decreases the numbers afflicted by later PTSD (Solomon and Benbenishty, 1986). Nowadays the principles of PIE B are implemented by the field psychiatric teams but, because of the nature of modern conflicts, there is a lack of clear front, middle and rear battlefield zones. Aero-medical evacuation procedures now mean that the transition time from front line to a home psychiatric facility has been greatly diminished.

Psychological debriefing (PD) and critical incident stress debriefing (CISD)

Because of growing concerns that PD and CISD might not be effective in 2000 within the UK military, the Surgeon General banned the use of single-session PD. Following a Cochrane review (Rose *et al.*, 2001) and the development of National Institute for Clinical Excellence (NICE) guidelines in 2005, it was advised that single PD sessions should not be offered, as it was thought that this could be harmful at worst and have no effect at best. The effects of phasic CISD are still unclear and much research is required to evaluate this further, although users find it helpful (Tehrani, 2002). Further discussion about these techniques and other similar putative preventative measures can be found in Chapter 13.

Trauma risk management (TRiM)

Initially starting in the Royal Marines in the late 1990s, TRiM has been rolled out across all three services. TRiM training aims to equip non-medical junior manager personnel to manage the psychological aftermath of a traumatic incident. TRiM is defined as:

> ... a proactive, peer group delivered management strategy that aims to keep employees of hierarchical organisations functioning after traumatic events, to provide support and education to those who require it and to identify those with difficulties that require more specialist input (Greenberg *et al.*, 2005, 2008).

TRiM does not aim to prevent PTSD; it aims to reduce stigma associated with mental health issues and to help the early identification of those who suffer psychological decompensation following exposure to traumatic stress. It can be seen as an extension of buddy–buddy support, a peer support network within a hierarchical structure. The evaluation of TRiM is still awaited (Creamer *et al.*, 2009).

Transfer to war and home from war: pre-deployment briefings and psychological decompression

The British military adopted pre-deployment briefings, including mental health education; however, no empirical evidence exists to show that this reduces medium-term psychological ill-health (Sharpley *et al.*, 2007). A period of psychological decompression after leaving the combat zone has also been adopted in which personnel will defuse with rest and relaxation and psycho-educational briefings for a few days before returning home. While there is no empirical evidence to show that this prevents subsequent mental health problems, it is believed to enable a better re-entry into the family (Hacker Hughes *et al.*, 2008). Support by the public to military personnel on return home, including welcome parades and respect for the uniform, helps to mitigate psychological reactions to combat (Figley, 1978).

Many of the techniques mentioned above have been adopted by the US military and incorporated into the framework of Battle Mind USA. Battle Mind's effectiveness is currently being evaluated (Jarrett and Barnett, 2007).

Assessment of need: veteran population studies

There is a need to undertake population studies to produce a picture of the bio-psychosocial needs of veterans, which would help in service planning, investment and targeting the delivery of care. Without these data, service planning is difficult. It is estimated that there are five million veterans in the UK and seven and a half million first-degree dependents. Even small percentages of veterans with complicated mental health needs would amount to very large numbers. Military at-risk population studies have been most conducted in US Vietnam war veterans, with the gold standard set in 1990 by the National Vietnam Veterans Readjustment Study (NVVRS). Before this study was performed, assessment and treatment facilities for veterans in the USA were dispersed, variable and inadequate. Following the study, the US Veterans' Agency was able to plan and deliver appropriate level of mental health services to their veterans.

The NVVRS estimated that 1.7 million veterans (or 50% of all who served in Vietnam) suffered partial or full PTSD at some time since discharge from military service, and that 828 000 did so at the time of the study. The study revealed high PTSD co-morbidity, with 50% of those suffering from PTSD also suffering from at least one other diagnosable psychiatric disorder. The percentage lifetime and current co-morbidity findings in the NVVRS study found that depression, alcohol and substance misuse were the main co-morbid features. High levels of divorce, unemployment, accidents (including road traffic accidents) and suicide were also demonstrated (Kulka et al., 1990).

In Britain a study conducted by the King's College Hospital military psychiatry research team, into a population of military personnel who participated in the invasion and war in Iraq (Operation TELIC), found that serving military personnel commonly suffer depression, anxiety disorders, substance misuse (mostly alcohol) and psychological trauma-related disorders, including PTSD. In time it is hoped that this study will evolve a longitudinal study including veterans as the servicemen end their military careers. Approximately 25% of the original population are now veterans, having left the military (Hotopf et al., 2006; Iversen and Greenberg, 2009).

The rates of PTSD in Operation TELIC personnel who are still serving are reported as low, with 1% and 8% levels being reported from recent conflicts. However, it is likely that late-onset clinical presentations can be expected, based on the finding of the mental health charity Combat Stress, which finds that, on average, veterans ask for help 14 years after they leave military service (Busuttil, 2009). A study conducted in veteran populations claiming war pensions showed that veterans were twice as likely as civilians to develop delayed-onset PTSD, and that 43% of veterans who suffer from delayed-onset PTSD developed it within the first year of leaving the services (Andrews and Brewin, 2008). The Scottish Government has recently funded a study to look at the feasibility of undertaking a veterans' population study. The feasibility study will be undertaken by Robert Gordon University, Aberdeen, in collaboration with Combat Stress, the veterans' charity. It is possible that similar projects will be undertaken in Wales and England.

Clinical presentation: special needs and lack of access into care

The true mental health needs of the British veteran population are unknown, as no record is kept by NHS primary or secondary carers about patients with a military service background. It is not known what proportion of veterans access the NHS for their mental health needs or the outcome of any treatments provided. Charities such as Combat Stress are contacted by a large number of veterans with chronic complex mental health problems. Clinical audits demonstrate that 80% of a group of 608 veterans tried to get help through the NHS, but that for a variety of reasons the NHS could not meet their needs (Scheiner, 2008; Busuttil, 2009). Many veterans felt misunderstood by clinicians who had never served in the military or could not understand the mentality, culture and language of ex-servicemen. For many veterans, being put on long waiting lists was frustrating, resulting in many impulsively removing themselves from NHS waiting lists (Scheiner, 2008).

The Ministry of Defence has worked jointly with Combat Stress and other agencies to set up six pilot projects, embedded in NHS services across Britain, to attempt to signpost veterans into mainstream NHS care. The efficacy of these pilots is awaited. It is also hoped that the setting up of the initiative Improving Access into Psychological Therapies (IAPT) will capture veterans' needs, although it is difficult to see how IAPT alone will provide treatment for the more complex needs cases that present. The government has also set up two Medical Assessment Programmes, based at Chilwell

Barracks in Nottinghamshire for reservists and at St Thomas's hospital for veterans.

The mental health charity Combat Stress

Combat Stress, the only mental health charity of any size specializing in treating veterans, was set up in 1919 after World War I. For years it provided residential respite care. Over the past 5 years, radical changes have taken place. It increasingly provides multidisciplinary mental health treatment within the community and within a residential setting. Combat Stress is partly funded via the Ministry of Defence (MOD) through the War Pensions system and partly funded through charity (60%). The British government has decided that the NHS will take over MOD funding in the near future, as is the case in Scotland from 1 April 2009.

In the past 90 years the charity has helped over 90 000 veterans and their families. Currently there are 4190 veterans actively receiving care, either in the community or attending residential treatment services or both. In a further 5617 passive cases in the process of accessing care or who have already accessed care, the intervention is completed but the cases have not yet been discharged from care. Referral rates have increased by 65% in the last 5 years, with 1257 new referrals being received in the last year compared to rates of 300–400 new referrals/year before this time, when the average age of the veteran was 60 years, with many being veterans of World War II. Currently the average age is 43 years and falling. Ex-army veterans account for 81.5%, with the remainder equally shared between the Royal Navy and RAF, with a very small number of ex-Merchant Navy seamen. Female veterans account for around 3% of the total. 92% of veterans have served in multiple operational tours of duty (Busuttil, 2009), with combat exposure being extremely common, particularly service in Northern Ireland.

Clinical audits supported by a comprehensive psychometric data conducted between 2005 and 2009 on over 600 patients have shown that 75% of new cases suffer from PTSD as their primary diagnosis, and that 62% of these have complex co-morbid presentations, most commonly depressive disorders and alcohol disorders, including dependence and severe abuse. Many also suffer from chronic physical illnesses, including high levels of orthopaedic problems and chronic pain; however, significant numbers have cardiac disorders or diabetes. Isolation, social exclusion, social withdrawal, unemployment (including multiple episodes of unemployment), inadequate housing, multiple house moves, multiple employment episodes and employers, and multiple marriages and relationships are characteristic. Behavioural disorders, including anger, are common. Many have been homeless for long periods of time and significant numbers have been in prison (Fletcher, 2007; Busuttil, 2009).

Commonly, referral is precipitated by a family, relationship or marital crisis and in many of these cases the veteran is being given an ultimatum to get better by his spouse or girlfriend; 50% are self-referrals, including referral by family members, especially wives, girlfriends, or partners; 11% are referred through the NHS, social services and military service discharge boards. Service charities, welfare organisations, veterans' associations and the Service Pensions Veterans Agency account for 31%.

Clinical services offered by Combat Stress include community, outpatient and residential treatments. Community services are divided into 16 regions across Britain and Eire. Each region has a Regional Welfare Officer (RWO) and is managed by a desk officer, who coordinates the work of the RWO and liaises and supports the veterans by telephone. Currently, regional multidisciplinary teams (MDTs) are being set up, each with a psychotherapist, community psychiatric nurse and support worker delivering sessional psychiatric and psychology clinics. The RWO is a retired military officer, not formally trained in mental health but with knowledge of mental health problems. The RWO is the main entry point into care for the veteran, as issues of stigma, shame and other civilian barriers can be broken down by the RWO, who comes from a similar culture to the veteran. Once referred, the veteran receives an initial RWO home visit. The RWO provides welfare advice, such as helping the veteran to apply for benefits and a war pension and to access other ex-service charities as required. If a mental health problem exists, with their GPs' written consent, veterans are offered a multidisciplinary residential 5 day mental health assessment. Assessments can also be conducted on an outpatient basis. Each assessment produces a multidisciplinary Care Programme Approach (CPA), a meeting report and a psychiatric report.

Combat Stress has three residential treatment centres, each with 30 beds, including some double rooms for carers to attend with the veteran. They are based in Ayrshire, Shropshire and Surrey. Each is run by an MDT, comprising occupational therapists, psychotherapists, registered mental health nurses, nursing assistants, psychiatrists and psychologists. These centres have a therapeutic milieu that is highly supportive and sensitive to a military culture. Some, but not all, staff are ex-military. Peer support is encouraged but this is directed by staff.

One of the main aims of intervention is to help veterans to access NHS mental health services wherever possible. Clinical management may be taken over by the NHS or joint management undertaken, depending on the clinical presentation and the veteran's own wishes. The community MDTs work closely with local NHS services. Welfare needs are also managed and access to work retraining is encouraged wherever possible.

Because of the chronic nature of many of the veterans' mental health illness, the main therapeutic aims are to improve function, maintain wellness and treat psychiatric symptoms. A phasic rehabilitation model of care has been adopted, in keeping with the recovery model and in keeping with presentations of complex PTSD (Herman, 1992).

The first phase is a *preparatory phase*. This includes: RWO assessment; a multidisciplinary team referral meeting; information gathering from the GP and NHS team; and active preparation for initial assessment admission, including NHS detoxification from alcohol and drugs.

The second phase comprises *stabilization and safety*. This includes: a 5 day MDT residential assessment; prescription of appropriate medications; establishing trust and safety within a therapeutic milieu; and subsequent further admissions (current practice). Care planning, liaison with GPs and other treating agencies, and treatment of co-morbid disorders, such as chronic pain, depression and alcohol dependence, is given before trauma work is undertaken. There are psycho-education groups for PTSD, alcohol and illicit drugs, coping, anxiety and anger management.

The third phase comprises *disclosure and working through* of the traumatic material. This utilizes individual trauma-focused therapies, including trauma-focused cognitive-behavioural therapy (CBT) and eye movement desensitization and reprocessing (EMDR) (Shapiro, 1995). Psychodynamic therapies are also used for attachment problems (Foa *et al.*, 2009).

The final phase is *rehabilitation and reintegration*. This utilizes occupational therapy interventions, including: normalizing activities of daily living and healthy living and OT run exercise programme; welfare support; and reintegration within society and work retraining.

Veterans are currently offered three 2 week residential admissions or six 1 week admissions over a 1 year period before their care plans are reviewed. Many are offered outpatient support and treatment by Combat Stress and the NHS between residential admissions. It is hoped that community MDTs will be able to offer more local group and individual interventions.

In the future, Combat Stress will deliver more community assessments and will be reorganising its residential bespoke treatment programmes in line with those run by the Australian veterans rehabilitation services and the VA of the USA. The programmes will be a mixture of residential and community-based phases and will be targeted more specifically at individual need. These will comprise: an intensive 5–6 week programme for relatively recent-onset PTSD; a PTSD substance misuse psycho-education programme; a PTSD treatment-resistant programme, which will commence in a residential setting but then will transfer to the community; an old age programme; an upgraded rolling programme; and a respite care programme, which will include summer camps, allowing the individual to have a holiday as well as offering respite to carers (Creamer *et al.*, 1999; Ready *et al.*, 2008). Carers' groups similar to those established in the Australian veterans mental health services are already offered in treatment centres as well as in the community. These will be expanded to be more widely run. The groups help, educate and support the family members of the veteran accessing the care of Combat Stress. Veterans also have access to a comprehensive website, which they can access at any time, together with advice from the welfare desk during normal working hours and nursing stations after working hours. It is hoped that a bespoke helpline will be set up in conjunction with the Samaritans, the confidential emotional support service available to anyone in the UK and Ireland.

Conclusions

While it is impossible to prevent trauma-related mental illness in a military setting, education and the reduction of stigma may well allow more to admit that they have problems without shame or the loss of their careers. However, the needs of veterans in Britain are not fully understood or acknowledged, as there are no reliable statistics on the level and nature of the need to allow proper service provision across for ex-military personnel. The development of mental health problems in veterans appears to be related to the nature and intensity of military service experiences. While innovative preventative interventions are being utilized, evidence for their efficacy is not yet established. Earlier efficacious interventions are likely to improve prognosis. At this time the third-sector charity Combat Stress is leading the way in Britain in the management of veterans' mental health. Better interagency collaboration is required. With the current level of world unrest and the level of British military commitments, it is likely that there will be many more psychological casualties in the future. Efficacious occupational measures, as well as longer-term treatment programmes, are required to contain this increasing morbidity.

References

Andrews, B., Brewin, C. (2008) The development of delayed-onset PTSD in UK servicemen. Presentation at the 24th International Society for Traumatic Stress Studies Annual Meeting, 'Terror and Its Aftermath', Palmer House Hilton, Chicago, IL, 13–18 November 2008; abstract 154.

Boscarino, J.A. (1997) Diseases among men 20 years after exposure to severe stress: implications for clinical research and medical care. *Psychosomatic Medicine* **59**, 605–614.

Boscarino, J.A. (2004) Posttrauamtic stress disorder and physical illness. Results from clinical and epidemiologic studies. *Annals of the New York Academy of Sciences* **1032**, 141–153.

Boscarino, J.A. (2008) A prospective study of PTSD and early-age heart disease mortality among Vietnam veterans: implications for surveillance and prevention. *Psychosomatic Medicine* **70**, 668–676.

Busuttil, W. (1995) Interventions in Posttraumatic Stress Syndromes: Implications for Military and Emergency Service Organizations. Master's Thesis, University of London, Faculty of Science, Department of Psychology.

Busuttil, W. (2009) Psychometric Data Analyses and Clinical Audit Data for Combat Stress 2005–2009. Internal publication, Combat Stress, Tyhritt House, Leatherhead, UK.

Busuttil, W., Busuttil, A.M.C. (2001) Psychological effects on families subjected to enforced and prolonged separations generated under life-threatening situations. *Sexual and Relationship Therapy* **16**(3; Special Psychological Trauma Edition), 207–228.

Carter, B.J., Cammermeyer, M. (1989) Human responses to simulated chemical warfare training in US Army reserve personnel. *Military Medicine* **154**, 281–288.

Creamer, M., Burgess, P., Buckingham, W., Pattison, P. (1993) Posttrauma reactions following a multiple shooting. A retrospective study and methodological inquiry. In Wilson, J.P., Raphael, B. (eds), *International Handbook of Traumatic Stress Syndromes*. New York: Plenum; 201–212.

Creamer, M., Morris, P., Biddle, D., Elliott, P. (1999) Treatment outcome in Australian veterans with combat related posttraumatic stress disorder: a cause for cautious optimism? *Journal of Traumatic Stress* **12**(4), 625–641.

Creamer, M., Moreton, G., Lyng, H., Greenberg, N., Richardson, D. (2009) Peer support and practical guidelines. Presentation at the 11th European Conference on Traumatic Stress, European Society for Traumatic Stress, Oslo, 15–18 June 2009.

Fear, N.T., Jones, M., Murphy, D., Hull, L., Iversen, A.C., Coker, B. *et al.* (2010) What are the consequences of deployment to Iraq and Afghanistan on the mental health of the UK armed forces? A cohort study. *Lancet* **375**, 1783–1797.

Fear, N., Wesseley, S (2009) Combat exposure increases risk of alcohol misuse in military personnel following deployment. *Evidence Based Mental Health* **12**(2), 60.

Figley, C.R. (ed.) (1978) *Stress Disorders Among Vietnam Veterans: Theory, Research and Treatment*. New York: Brunner Mazel.

Fletcher, K. (2007) Combat Stress (the ex-servicemen's Mental Welfare Society) and war veterans. In Lee, H., Jones, M. (eds), *War and Health: Lessons from the Gulf War*. London: Wiley.

Foa, E.B., Keane, T.M., Friedman, M.J. (eds) (2009) *Effective Treatments for PTSD: Practice Guidelines from the International Society for Traumatic Stress Studies*, 2nd edn. New York: Guilford.

Greenberg, N., Cawkill, P., Sharpley, J. (2005) How to TRiM away at post-traumatic stress reactions: traumatic risk management – now and in the future. *Journal of the Royal Naval Services* **91**, 26–31.

Greenberg, N., Laughton, V., Jones, M. (2008) Trauma risk management (TRiM) in the UK armed forces. *Journal of the Royal Army Medical Corps* **154**(2), 121–126.

Hacker Hughes, J.M., Earnshaw, N.M., Greenberg, N., Eldridge, R., Fear, N.T., French, C. *et al.* (2008) Use of psychological decompression in military operational environments. *Military Medicine* **173**, 534–538.

Herman, J. (1992) *Trauma and Recovery. The Aftermath of Violence – From Domestic Abuse to Political Terror*. New York: Basic Books.

Hoge, C.W., Auhterlonie, J.L., Milliken, C.S. (2006) Mental health problems use of mental health services, and attrition from military service after returning from deployment to Iraq or Afghanistan. *Journal of the American Medical Association* **295**(9), 1023–1032.

Hooper, R., Rona, R.J., Jones, M., Fear, N.T., Hull, L., Wesseley, S. (2008) Cigarette and alcohol use in the UK armed forces and their association with combat exposures: a prospective study. *Addictive Behaviours* **33**, 1067–1071.

Hotopf, M., Hull, L., Fear, N.T., Horn, O., Iversen, A., Jones, M. *et al.* (2006) The health of UK military personnel who deployed to the 2003 Iraq war: a cohort study. *Lancet* **367**, 1731–1741.

Iversen, A., Dysen, C., Smith, N., Greenberg, N., Walwyn, R., Unwin, C. *et al.* (2005) 'Goodbye and good luck': the mental health needs and treatment experiences of British ex-service personnel. *British Journal of Psychiatry* **186**, 480–486.

Iversen, A., Greenberg, N. (2009) Mental health of regular and reserve military veterans. *Advances in Psychiatric Treatment* **15**, 100–106.

Iversen, A., Waterdrinker, A., Fear. N.T., Greenberg, N., Barker, C., Hotopf, M. *et al.* (2007) Factors associated with heavy alcohol consumption in the UK armed forces: data from a health survey of Gulf, Bosnia and era veterans. *Military Medicine* **172**(9), 956–961.

Jarrett, T.A, Barnett, J.S. (2007) Combat Stress Prevention: Warrior Resilience. Internal publication, Womack Army Medical Center, Department of Social Work, Fort Bragg, NC.

Kapur, N., White, D., Blactchley, N., Bray, I., Harrison, K. (2009) Suicide after leaving the UK armed Forces a cohort study. *PLoS Medicine* **6**(3), 01–09.

Kulka, R., Schlenger, W.E., Fairbank, J.A., Hough, R.L., Jordan, B.K., Marmar, C.R., Weiss, D.S. (1990) *Trauma and the Vietnam War Generation.* New York: Brunner Mazel.

McFarlane, A. (1989) The aetiology of post traumatic morbidity: predisposing, precipitating and perpetuating factors. *British Journal of Psychiatry* **154**, 221–228.

McMannus, F.B. (2009) Accessing defence psychiatric services: clinical pathways to the NHS and other agencies on leaving the military. Presented at a meeting of the Royal College of Psychiatrists, BT Convention Centre, Liverpool, UK, 2–5 June 2009.

Miller, I. (1989) Preparation for disaster: trauma inoculation training for police disaster victim identification teams. Presentation at the World Federation for Mental Health, Auckland, New Zealand.

Novaco, R., Cook., T.M., Sarason, I.G. (1983) Military recruit training. An arena for stress-coping skills. In Mietchenbaum, D., Jaremko, M.E. (eds), *Stress Reduction and Prevention.* New York: Plenum; 377–417.

Noy, S. (1987) Stress and personality as factors in the causation and prognosis of combat reactions during the 1973 Arab–Israeli war. In Belenky, G.L. (ed.), *Contemporary Studies in Combat Psychiatry.* Westport, CT: Greenwood Press; 21–29.

Noy, S. (1991) Combat stress reaction. In Gal, R., Mangelsdorff, A.D. (eds), *Handbook of Military Psychology.* Chichester: Wiley; 507–530.

Ready, D.J., Thomas, K.R., Worley, V., Backscheider, A.G., Harvey, L.A.C., Baltzell, D., Rothbaum, B.O. (2008) A field test of group based exposure therapy with 102 veterans with war related posttraumatic stress disorder. *Journal of Traumatic Stress* **21**(2), 150–157.

Rona, R.J., Hooper, R., Jones, M., Hull, L., Browne, T., Horn, O. *et al.* (2006) Mental health screening in the armed forces before the Iraq war and prevention of subsequent psychological morbidity: follow-up study. *British Medical Journal* 333, 979–980.

Rona, R.J., Fear, N.T., Hull, L., Greenberg, N., Earnshaw, H., Hotop, M., Wesseley, S. (2007) Mental health consequences of overstretch in the UK armed forces: first phase of a cohort study. *British Medical Journal* 335, 571–572.

Rona, R.J., Hooper, R., Jones, M., Iversen, A., Hull, L., Murphy, D. *et al.* (2009) The contribution of prior psychological symptoms and combat exposure to post-Iraq deployment mental health in the UK military. *Journal of Traumatic Stress* 22(1), 11–19.

Rose, S., Bisson, B., Wessely, S. (2001) *A Systematic Review of Brief Psychological Interventions ('Debriefing') for the Treatment of Immediate Trauma-related Symptoms and the Prevention of Post-traumatic Stress Disorder – The Cochrane Collaboration* (database on-line and CDROM); updated issue 3. Oxford: Update Software.

Scheiner, N.S. (2008) Not 'At Ease': UK Veterans' Perceptions of the Level of Understanding of Their Psychological Difficulties Shown by the National Health Service. Doctoral Thesis, City University London, Department of Psychology.

Shalev, A., Munitz, H. (1988) Psychiatric care of acute stress reactions to military threat. In Ursano, R.J., Fullerton, C.S., Dixon, M.S., Doran, E.S. (eds), *Groups and Organizations in War: Disasters and Trauma.* Bethesda, MD: USUHS; 107–119.

Shapiro, F. (1995) *Eye Movement Desensitization and Reprocessing: Basic Principles, Protocols, and Procedures.* New York: Guilford.

Sharpley, J.G., Fear, N.T., Greenberg, N., Jones. M., Wesseley, S. (2007) Pre-deployment stress briefing: does it have an effect? *Occupational Medicine* 58(1), 30–34.

Solomon, Z., Benbenishty, R. (1986) The role of proximity, immediacy and expectancy in frontline treatment of combat stress reaction among Israelis in the Lebanon war. *American Journal of Psychiatry* 143, 613–617.

Srinivasan, M. (1993) *Mind at War.* Army PTSD Video. Paper presented at the Defence Medical Services Military Psychiatry Conference, Royal Army Medical College, Millbank, London, 13 October 1993.

Strange, R.E., Arthur, R.J. (1967) Hospital ship psychiatry in a war zone. *American Journal of Psychiatry* 124(3), 281–286.

Tehrani, N. (ed.) (2002) Psychological debriefing. Professional Practice Board Working Party, British Psychological Society, Leicester.

Van Staden, L., Fear, N.T., Iversen, A., French, C.E., Dandeker, C., Wessely, S. (2007) Transition back into civilian life: a study of personnel leaving the UK. Armed forces via 'military prison'. *Military Medicine* 172(9), 925–930.

Chapter 4

Compassion fatigue and human resource professionals

Noreen Tehrani

Introduction

In the mid-nineteenth century, following the introduction of the Factory Acts, employers were required to comply with legislation controlling the working hours and employment of children (Gray, 2002). The introduction of company-built towns, such as Bournville and Saltaire, was largely driven by enlightened self-interest, with such arrangements allowing for a high level of paternal direction with the banning of public houses and the monitoring of lifestyles. Some organisations conscious of the personal and social difficulties facing some of their employees introduced the role of welfare officer (CIPD, 2007). Initially this role focused on protecting the health and well-being of workers; however, as the usefulness of a welfare officer as a resource to deal with a range of employee-related activities emerged, the role was widened to include recruitment, training, absence management and pay negotiations. Over the next 100 years the role evolved, a situation that has been reflected in the changing role names: 'personnel officer', 'industrial relations manager' and 'human resources manager'. From the beginning there have been tensions within the role arising from the difficulties in balancing the needs of the employee with those of the organisation. These tensions have not diminished over the years, with today's human resource professionals (HRP) sitting Janus[1]-like, uncertain of whether to look forward to become a strategic partner, fully integrated with business, creating people strategies with tangible financial and organisational benefits (SHRM, 2002a), or to return to their origins as an advocate

---

1 Janus: the two-faced god of gates, doorways, beginnings and endings, a symbol of change and transition.

for ethical management of the workforce (Foote and Robinson, 1999). Balancing these competing tensions is not without cost; in this chapter we will look at the price paid by HRPs who, as a regular part of their role deal with employee distress, unethical behaviours, organisational dilemmas and heavy workloads, together with their other roles of strategic development, culture and diversity, recruitment and selection, training and development, performance evaluation and management, compensation and benefits (Tsui and Wu, 2005).

What are the difficulties of working in human resources?

The suggestion that anyone can work in HR underestimates the true nature of the role. Whilst many of the repetitive HR administration tasks are being outsourced or undertaken by line management, there is an increased requirement for HRPs to respond to the complexities of business, requiring a higher level of knowledge and competence. To be respected by a business partner, it is not enough for an HRP to know about or apply HR knowledge and processes; what organisations want is an HRP who understands and responds to the requirements of the organisation, the wider community, employees and legislation (Losey, 1997). In recent years there have been a number of business scandals in which senior managers have been found to be acting out of self-interest rather than considering the needs of their employees, customers or community (Anon., 2009). It could be argued that one of the roles of an HRP is to act as an honest broker, balancing the needs of all parties within the strategic decision-making process,. However, by taking this role HRPs should be prepared to put themselves at risk in order to manage the competing interests; this is particularly true when the issues are complex or where double standards may occur, for example, when a senior manager seeks to protect his pension whilst cutting the pensions of his workers. Whether the HRP wishes to take on the role of moral standard bearer or not, he/she will need to deal with a wide range of moral, ethical and personal dilemmas.

The bearer of bad news (e.g. redundancy, benefit cutbacks or reduced job security)

Over recent years the bond between employer and employee has shifted from a long-term relationship involving loyalty and commitment to one involving a simple economic exchange; an employee is engaged to perform short-term and well-defined duties in exchange for a set of performance-related rewards and a reduced level of job security. In addition, many organisations have opted to outsource non-core work, increasing their use of temporary and part-time employees and contractors and eroding the range and value of employee benefits, such as pensions, sickness benefits and training. This move towards under-investing in employees is not an easy message for HRPs to convey to a workforce, particularly when it is allied with the demand for improved employee engagement.

> It was my first job; I could not have been more than 23. We were split into groups and I was given a bunch of mainly older ladies, and I remember being quite uncomfortable talking to them. What makes dealing with redundancy and change situations especially stressful is being at the front line of implementing decisions that you do not always agree with (Carol Hosey, quoted in Tehrani, 2006, p. 37).

Supporting an employee who had developed a terminal health condition

HRPs are required to make practical and strategic decisions based on a full understanding of how these decisions will have an impact on employees. However, when the business decision has a serious implication for an employee suffering from a life-threatening health condition, this can be difficult to handle. The need to empathize and support an employee at a time when the organisation is going through structural change and redundancies is challenging, and finding a solution that is sensitive to the needs of the sick employee whilst applying organisational decisions requires courage, wisdom and flexibility (Meisinger, 2005).

> Maggie had been one of the most popular and positive members of the team. When she developed breast cancer we all thought that she would recover. As the months went by we supported her to return to work but it then became obvious that the cancer was spreading. She kept positive and talked about the future and her children. Although I knew she was dying, when it happened it really hit me hard. I suppose it did not help that my mother had died of cancer the year before (Tehrani, 2006, p. 36).

Having to be responsive and even-handed when dealing with employees in conflict

Dealing with bullying and harassment can cause difficulties, particularly when the bully or harasser is a senior manager, a top-performing sales executive or someone with specialist skills or relationships where inappropriate behaviours may be excused rather than investigated (Prost, 2007). The primary role of the HRP in any interpersonal conflict is to achieve a resolution of the difficulty, increase the interpersonal understanding and sensitivity of everyone involved in the conflict, and identify how similar problems can be prevented in the future. Unfortunately, bad behaviours tend to go unchallenged and escalate until working relationships are totally disrupted, to such an extent that an informal resolution is impossible. In the following account, an HRP describes some of the difficulties she has experienced when dealing with bullying investigations:

> I have come to dread dealing with bullying cases. People think that the investigation process is straightforward but it is never that simple. I usually deal with two or three cases a year. I have met employees who are extremely distressed, not eating or sleeping, unable to leave their house or answer the phone. It is clear that they are unwell but when I investigate there may be insufficient evidence to demonstrate that the behaviour that they experienced was bullying. It is not easy telling them the results of an inconclusive inquiry. On the other hand, I have had other cases where the 'victim' continually phoned and e-mailed me, complaining or bombarding me with more and more information. In the end I feel that they are bullying me. You have to have broad shoulders to do this job, as in most cases it does not matter what result emerges, no-one is happy and everyone holds you responsible (Dignity at Work Investigator).

Maintaining confidentiality

HRPs have a duty to protect the privacy of employees' personal and health information. Employees have the right to expect that any personal information passed to HR remains confidential and is not disclosed without their explicit permission. Breaches in confidentiality can be a result of carelessness, where an HRP discloses confidential information unintentionally, for example, discussing cases where they can be overheard or leaving personal information showing on a computer screen. It may involve an HRP seeking unauthorized access to confidential material, such as unnecessary viewing of a senior manager's salary or health records, to the most serious breach, where the HRP is persuaded to provide confidential information to a third party without authorization or justification (Duke, 2006). The pressure on HRPs to divulge confidential information can be extreme; in a survey (Schramm, 2003) it was found that 47% of HRPs had felt pressure from managers or other employees to compromise their ethical standards in order to achieve a business objective.

> The problem that I have with HR getting closer to the business is that the boundaries become blurred. Some managers do not see why I cannot tell them what is in a GP's report, particularly when an absence is having an adverse impact on productivity, or there is a belief that the employee is 'swinging the lead'. At times I feel totally alone, having to deal with difficult situations which I cannot share with anyone. For example, if I hear rumours or speculation about people that I know to be untrue, it is difficult to remain silent (Absence Coordinator).

Dealing with a disaster

Although disasters are uncommon events, when they do occur they can challenge the emotional resilience of the strongest HRP. Whilst most organisations have business continuity management plans which include HR, the reality of dealing with the real traumatic event can be very different. Within the first few hours of the disaster the HRP may be required to account for missing employees, setting up a help-desk for distressed employees and their families, brief line management, supporting bereaved families, in addition to liaising with the crisis management team and continuing to support business operations. This is particularly difficult for young HRPs, who may have no experience of dealing with death in their own lives.

> It was my job to return the personal belongings of the dead employee. I remember driving to her home with a box of personal effects in the boot of the car. All the way I tried to think of something to say to her parents. When I got there the whole family was sitting in the lounge, her parents, brother and boyfriend. I handed over the box and said how sorry I was for their loss.

They were all very calm, I was offered a cup of tea; it felt strange being treated as a guest. The parents talked about their daughter and I listened, making the occasional comment. This was one of the most difficult times of my life. After I left, I drove to the nearest parking place and sobbed for half an hour before I was able to drive back to work (HR Manager).

People, practice and pressure

There is a cost to engaging with the stories and lives of distressed or traumatized people, which can result in the HRP experiencing symptoms of shock, disbelief and horror similar to those of the people they are trying to support. These negative experiences have been described as 'compassion fatigue' or 'secondary trauma' (Figley, 1999) and are viewed as a natural consequence of helping or wanting to help distressed people. Some of the effects are subtle and involve a gradual change to an individual's underlying beliefs, values or assumptions at a pre- or unconscious level. These changes have been explained by social construction theories (Piaget, 1971), which suggest that people build a framework or cognitive schema consistent with their beliefs and values and informed by their past responses and experiences. For HRPs, the continual exposure to employee distress, fear, anger and anxiety can result in their feelings, attitudes and beliefs being changed, affecting the way they view the world (Janoff-Bulman, 1989). Where an employee's story or experience is particularly intense or has significance to the life of the HRP, the disruption to the HRP's beliefs about him/herself and the world may be sudden and dramatic (Janoff-Bulman, 1992).

HRPs have to face some of the most challenging ethical dilemmas in business (Schumann, 2001); however, unlike most other professions, where the practitioner is obliged to achieve a prescribed level of competence in order to register with the professional body, there is no compulsory professional registration for HRPs and no legal protection of the HR job titles. Nevertheless, HR professional bodies in most countries provide their membership with codes of professional standards, conduct and ethics. Whilst most people are unaware of the philosophical underpinning of their ethical beliefs, they will find that most are based on four moral principles:

1   *The utilitarian principle*, i.e. the maximization of the positive and minimization of negative outcomes to everyone affected.

2   *The rights principle*, i.e. of the upholding the moral rights and responsibilities people have for each other.
3   *The distributive duty principle*, i.e. the fair distribution of costs and benefits to all stakeholders.
4   *The virtue principle*, i.e. the identification of the virtues or vices involved in a particular action or activity (Schuman, 2001).

A survey of HRPs in the UK (Foote and Robinson, 1999) identified the ethical stance taken by a group of senior HRPs. The study found that, whilst some HRPs saw ethical standards as fundamental and that they would rather resign than work unethically, others regarded ethics as an expensive luxury, which they left at the door when they went to work. The largest group of HRPs described themselves as honest brokers, engaging in difficult and challenging discussions with directors and line managers in order to find a solution which would mitigate or remove the unethical issue. The ethical dilemmas faced by HRPs can be seen in those working in Enron, World Com and similar organisations where HRPs have become whistle-blowers; however, whistle-blowing is rare, as few HRPs are willing to risk the consequences of being shunned for disloyalty or to face having their job terminated (Beatty *et al.*, 2003).

There is evidence to show that over the past few years HRPs have been working increasingly long hours (CIPD, 2008); a survey of over 6000 HRPs found that almost 70% were working more than their contracted hours and 56% were working 40–45 hours, a 20% increase over the previous two years. The survey also showed that HR directors were the worst offenders, with 82% working more than 40 hours a week. The situation in the USA was found to be similar, with two-thirds of HRPs reporting feeling burned out and 80% finding the pace of their work to be very fast (SHRM, 2002b). It is suggested that HRPs are also experiencing high levels of stress due to being so busy fixing things for other employees that they do not have time to take care of themselves (Grensing-Pophal, 1999).

The survey

A survey which looked at the impact of work on personal beliefs, values and well-being (Tehrani, 2009) involved 276 caring professionals and included HRPs, occupational health advisors and employee counsellors. The participants completed a survey which included the short form of the Carers Belief Inventory (CBI; Tehrani, 2007) and asked questions on supervision, support and coping strategies. A clinical anxiety/depression scale was also included (Goldberg *et al.*, 1988; Gann *et al.*, 1990). The results showed no significant difference between the negative attitudes and beliefs recorded by the HRPs and those of the other two professional groups. However, the HRPs had a significantly lower level of positive attitudes and beliefs, suggesting that HRPs were either less able to cope with their negative experiences or unable to translate their negative experiences into learning or feelings of competence. There was no significant difference in the levels of anxiety or depression between the groups, with 14% of HRPs suffering high levels of anxiety and 18% high levels of depression. One of the major differences between the HRPs and the OHAs and counsellors was in the levels of organisational support provided. HRPs received very little supervision, with only one in five having access to professional or management supervision, compared with 91% of counsellors and 53% of occupational health nurses. Over 80% of the professional groups talked to friends and colleagues, with 66% of HRPs talking to their families compared with around half of the other professional groups. There were large differences in the way that coping mechanisms were used by the three professional groups. HRPs did not look after themselves as well physically or spiritually as the other two groups, scoring significantly lower in their use of meditation or prayers, exercise, hobbies and healthy eating. An analysis of the combined data from the caring professionals identified the methods of support and supervision that were most closely associated with personal growth. The results showed no significant benefit from talking to friends and colleagues or family in terms of positive attitudes or beliefs. The greatest positive impact was associated with professional and peer supervision, which were related to increased learning and competence as well as a feeling of doing a good job and being fulfilled. Management supervision did not improve the professional's feelings of competence, learning or fulfilment; however, it positively influenced the feeling of doing a good job. Taking exercise and engaging in hobbies were positively related to the four positive growth items, and praying, healthy eating and spiritual and religious beliefs were associated with improved learning. Whilst anxiety and depression were associated with a lack of fulfilment and job satisfaction, they were not related to a reduced opportunity to learn.

Can HR professionals afford to care about the workers?

In a study involving 300 companies, representing 20 industries within 25 countries, Mercer (2007) found that the HR function was going through considerable change in order to align itself with business requirements. Organisations are increasingly requiring HR professionals to become competent in a wide range of skills, including business strategy, finance, cost analysis, vendor management, process management and business understanding. In addition, HR is still expected to deal with those activities that are more readily recognized as belonging within the HR domain, including change management, employee engagement, business continuity management, health and well-being, benefits, training and development, disability, sickness absence, bullying and harassment and many other HR activities. With the major emphasis being concentrated on the bifurcation of HR into strategic and transactional functions (Mercer, 2007), there is a possibility that HR will become disconnected from its primary purpose of representing the moral and ethical values of the profession and the business community. Although rarely mentioned as essential HR skills, the ability to speak up for ethical standards and to care about people and their contributions are key characteristics of a good HR professional; these skills should never be undervalued or minimized by those who choose to see them as old-fashioned or irrelevant. Having the courage to model ethical behaviour, and expecting it from others, is good for business (Meisinger, 2005) and relevant, whether contributing to business strategy, financial management and cultural change or dealing with sickness absence, distressed employees and bullying. If HRPs do not take up this essential role of promoting ethics and caring, this will diminish the importance of HR as a profession (Armstrong, 2007).

Keeping the heart in HR

There is every indication that HRP will continue to move towards a more strategic business-driven role; however, HR holds a pivotal position in recognizing and reflecting the needs of all their business partners and stakeholders. However, with the current HR emphasis on acting and doing, rather than considering, reflecting and responding, HRPs have neglected the unique role they hold within the organisation, which provides them with the opportunity to observe and translate their experiences in dealing with relationships, conflicts and challenges into professional knowledge, competence and learning. It is suggested (Mockler, 2009) that HRPs have undermined their key organisational function by continually asserting that HR needs to be more strategic and to have a seat on the board, whilst having few of the essential skills necessary to operate at this level. The research reported in this chapter (Tehrani, 2009) demonstrates that, unlike the other caring professions who use their difficult and demanding experiences to learn and grow, HRPs have chosen to disregard their humanistic experiences and, as a result, they fail to gain professional competence and achievement. As the evidence is showing, HRPs are becoming more vulnerable to stress, burn-out and compassion fatigue (Andrews, 2003) and unless something is done to address the fundamental issues affecting the profession, the health and well-being of HRPs will deteriorate. The HR professional bodies could be more open in expressing their views on the pressures being placed on their members by their employers by disregarding the essential values of the profession and perhaps being more pro-active in identifying good and bad ethical practice in organisations. The professional bodies could also commission research to look at the benefits of HRPs' role in providing an ethical compass for organisations. If organisations are to get the best out of their HRPs, they need to consider the unique contributions that can only be made by HRPs. This is likely to mean that there will be a greater need for training HRPs in more aspects of business strategy and operations, not to usurp the roles of the business specialists but to allow HRPs to express well-informed opinions and offer competent advice and guidance on the key business areas of finance, operations and systems. However, many of the barriers to HRPs becoming healthier and more effective rest with themselves. They appear to be resistant to taking the advice they offer to the workforce. For example, they need to make sure that they establish a positive work/life balance, eat healthy food, take exercise and enjoy a good social life. If they are unable to organise and protect their own health and well-being, it is difficult to see how they will be able to persuade others. HRPs have developed a culture within their profession which overvalues stoicism. Whilst there are numerous papers and articles on the health and well-being of most professions, very little has been written or discussed within the HR community. It would appear that HRPs are so busy administering stress audits and introducing healthy living campaigns that they forget to include themselves.

I cannot say that I am optimistic about the future of the role as a whole but I am sure of one thing. Unless we introduce a greater degree of reflective practice into the HRP role, the present drive towards sub-specialization will accelerate and the prospect of HRPs becoming true strategic thinkers, safeguarding humanitarian values at the core of a business, will evaporate (HR Director).

References

Andrews, L.W. (2003) Avoiding HR burnout: dealing with the human side of business. *HR Magazine* **48**(7), 1–2.

Anon. (2009) Who taught them greed is good? *The Observer*, 8 March 2009.

Armstrong, M. (2007) *Human Resource Management Practice*, 10th edn. London: Kogan Page.

Beatty, R.W., Ewing, J.R., Thrap, C.G. (2003) HR's role in corporate governance: present and prospective. *Human Resource Management* **42**(3), 257–269.

CIPD (2007) *People Management: A Short History*. Wimbledon, UK: CIPD.

CIPD (2008) *Code of Professional Conduct and Disciplinary Procedures*. Wimbledon, UK: CIPD.

Duke. (2006) *Confidentiality*. Durham: Duke Human Resources.

Figley, C.R. (1999) Compassion fatigue: towards a new understanding of the cost of caring. In Hudnall Stamm, B. (ed.), *Secondary Traumatic Stress: Self-care Issues for Clinicians, Researchers and Educators*, 2nd edn. Lutherville, MD: Sidran Press.

Foote, D., Robinson, I. (1999) The role of human resources manager: strategist or conscience of the organization. *Business Ethics: A European Review* **8**(2), 88–98.

Gann, M., Corpe, U., Wilson, I. (1990) The application of a short anxiety and depression questionnaire to oil industry staff. *Journal of Society of Occupational Medicine* **40**, 138–142.

Goldberg, D., Bridges, K., Duncan-Jones, P., Grayson, D. (1988) Detecting anxiety and depression in a general medical setting. *British Medical Journal* **297**, 897–899.

Gray, R. (2002) *The Factory Question and Industrial England, 1830–1860*. Cambridge: Cambridge University Press.

Grensing-Pophal, L. (1999) HR heal thyself: recognising and conquering on-the-job burnout. *HR Magazine* **44**(3), 82–88.

Janoff-Bulman, R. (1989) Assumptive worlds and the stress of traumatic events: applications of the schema construct. *Social Cognition* **7**(2), 113–136.

Janoff-Bulman, R. (1992) *Shattered Assumptions*. New York: Free Press.

Losey, M.R. (1997) The Future of HR Professional: competency, buttressed by advocacy and ethics. *Human Resource Management* **36**(1), 147–150.

Meisinger, S.R. (2005) The four Cs of the HR profession: being competent, curious, courageous and caring about people. *Human Resource Management* **44**(2) 189–194.

Mercer (2007) *HR Transformation v. 2.0: It's All About the Business.* London: Mercer Human Resource.

Mockler, J. (2009) HRPs and compassion fatigue [personal communication].

Piaget, J. (1971) *Psychology and Epistemology: Towards a Theory of Knowledge.* New York: Viking.

Prost, M. (2007) Fighting workplace bullying: http://www.hreonline.com/ HRE/printstory/ [accessed 22 June 2009].

Schramm, J. (2003) A return to ethics. *HR Magazine* **48**(7), 114.

Schumann, P.L. (2001) A moral principles framework for human resource management ethics. *Human Resource Management Review* **11**, 93–111.

SHRM (2002a) The future of the HR profession. Virginia, Society for Human Resource Management: http://www.shrm.org/about/pressroom/ Documents/future_of_hr.pdf [accessed 21 October 2009].

SHRM (2002b) Senior human resource professionals feel 'burn-out', but are satisfied with their jobs and feel valued within their organizations: http:// www.eepulse.com/documents/pdfs/Final_Senior_HR_Professionals _073102.pdf [accessed 25 June 2009].

Tehrani, N. (2006) Bad news bearers. *People Management* **12**(14), 36–39.

Tehrani, N. (2007) The cost of caring – the impact of secondary trauma on assumptions, values and beliefs. *Counselling Psychology Quarterly* **20**(4), 325–339.

Tehrani, N. (2009) Compassion fatigue and caring: experiences in occupational health, human resources, counselling and the police. *Occupational Medicine* **60**(2), 133–138.

Tsui, A.S., Wu, J.B. (2005) The new employment relationship versus the mutual investment approach: implications for human resource management. *Human Resource Management* **44**(2), 115–121.

Chapter 5

Critical incident stress and the prevention of psychological trauma in air traffic controllers

Jörg Leonhardt and Joachim Vogt

Introduction

This chapter deals with critical incident stress and preventive measures in air traffic control (ATC). There are several special characteristics in ATC that influence the kind of critical incident stress and how to cope with it. ATC service providers are high-reliability organisations (HROs) with the twin goals of maintaining a safe operation with minimal risk of accidents and an efficient work flow. HROs are faced with a working environment where safe operations have to be achieved in an environment of constantly changing circumstances and conflicting priorities. There is a need to maintain control of the safety of the aircraft and its passengers despite constant time pressure, cost cutting and staff shortages. In this working environment, critical incidents occur and the ATC operators (ATCOs) are central to the resolution of these incidents. A critical incident in ATC does not need to be an accident or an event of which members of the public would be aware. A critical incident can be the infringement of the agreed separation space between two or more aircraft, a near miss, or a runway incursion by an unauthorized aircraft or vehicle. These critical incidents are clearly defined with respect to temporal and/or spatial distances between aircraft, which are dependent on the airspace and operational procedures that the aircraft operate within. The normal separation between aircraft in cruising altitude is five nautical miles horizontal and one thousand feet vertical. Occasionally, this separation falls below this distance and in most cases – even the very significant ones – nothing untoward happens to the pilots or passengers, no one gets injured or killed and most passengers are unaware that the critical incident has occurred.

However, the situation for ATCOs is quite different, as it is their role to control the passage of aircraft within three-dimensional space and the fourth dimension of time in order to prevent incidents and accidents occurring. The ATCOs are directly involved in the development of incidents and construct vivid images of what could happen had the critical incident actually caused a collision. Their knowledge of the potential devastation which can occur allows for the creation of a vivid construction of an aircraft disaster of such intensity that it can cause them to experience critical incident stress reactions (CISRs). The intensity of these responses is increased by the feelings of responsibility and guilt felt by the ATCO who did not foresee the separation loss or unintentionally took the actions which have caused the critical incident to occur. Where there is inadequate support for the ATCOs following a critical incident, these initial CISRs can develop into chronic traumatic stress. This chapter will discuss the nature of ATC trauma and outline the special requirements for crisis intervention. A peer model of crisis intervention is described, together with the clinical and cost benefits of the programme.

Trauma, incident or traumatic event

The popular usage of such words as 'disaster', 'trauma', 'psychological trauma' and 'crisis' has led to their use in almost any situation considered as traumatic. Whilst it might be expected that the physical and psychological reactions or symptoms would determine diagnosis, the public tend to be interested in the nature of the preceding traumatic event or disaster. The inflationary use of words like 'disaster' and 'trauma' creates a folk model of trauma without a real understanding or common definition or description of the features of the traumatic event or essential responses. People may be labelled as being 'traumatized' because they were involved in a particular event that had the potential to be traumatizing, whether or not they are actually experiencing trauma symptoms. Howarth and Leaman (2001) emphasize the importance of considering the reaction rather than the precipitating event, as being labelled as traumatized has a negative impact on those people who are exposed to a traumatic event but do not develop CISRs, with the result that people feel that there is something wrong with them if they do not develop CISR. It is helpful to describe the differences between some of the terms related to critical incidents in order to develop a language which is congruent with the actual reactions and responses of the people involved.

It is important to define the nature of the traumatic exposure; for example, was the individual a primary victim and directly exposed to the impact of the event, or a secondary victim involved as a rescuer or eyewitness? Was handling or being exposed to the traumatic event a normal part of an individual's work or profession? Are there any personal relationships with those involved as primary victims? ATCOs can become secondary victims of a traumatic event because they, like rescuers, have a professional role and responsibility in critical aviation incidents.

Traumatic events cause a direct threat to the primary victim's life, psychological or physical integrity. This may involve being raped, taken hostage, tortured or violently attacked. During the traumatic events, the individual may be unable to escape from a threat to his/her life. Traumatic events can lead to a number of traumatic stress reactions which can develop into post-traumatic stress disorders if untreated. Post-traumatic stress can disrupt normal living, relationships with family members and ability to plan for the future. The trauma victims will need to readjust their beliefs after the traumatic experience in order to reframe the negative event into one in which they are survivors. In contrast, a critical incident is a situation in which an individual has a secondary involvement in a traumatic incident as an eyewitness, relative to a primary victim, rescuer, ATCO or pilot. Exposure to a critical incident can cause CISR, similar to those experienced by the primary victims of a traumatic event. Human brains have a lot in common in the reaction to critical incidents; however, the professional role of an ATCO influences the intensity and quality of this reaction. Feelings of guilt and doubts of professional capability, for example, have a significant impact, in contrast to primary aviation victims who had no control over the situation. Whether the exposure to the traumatic event is direct or indirect, there is no difference in the reactions of the brain. This does not minimize the experiences, feelings, emotions, reactions and disturbances of the primary victims. However, no matter whether directly or indirectly involved, the limbic system, one of the oldest parts of the brain, triggers the autonomic nervous system response, described by Cannon (1914) as the 'fight-or-flight response'. The fight-or-flight response provides the energy for physical activity aiming at fighting or escaping the situation in which control is threatened. The sympathetic nervous system activates the adrenal glands to release adrenaline, which increases the heart rate, respiration rate, blood pressure and blood sugar concentration for the energy supply of muscles (Selye, 1936, 1950). The stress response is dominated by adrenocortical hormones released by the pituitary gland, which cause the adrenal cortex to release corticosteroid hormones. These hormones cause the individual to enter a state of inactive endurance as control over the situation is lost. The Cannon and Selye survival mechanisms have been integrated into a single model (Henry and Stephens, 1977). The arousal involved in the fight-or-flight response can be positive (eustress) when it allows the individual to deal with high demands; however, when it becomes overwhelming, it is experienced as distress and out of control (Selye, 1936, 1950). Reactions to autonomic arousal can be observed in the individual's physiological, cognitive, emotional and behavioural processes. Physiologically, the typical reactions are increased heart rate and blood pressure. Emotionally, there may be feelings of guilt, anxiety or anger. Cognitive outcome may be impaired mental abilities, resulting in poor decision making, mental inflexibility and difficulties in planning, with the result that the individual begins to behave in a confused and disorientated manner. Comprehensive lists of reactions are given, for example, in Leonhardt and Vogt (2006a, 2006b).

ATCOs are likely to notice their physiological reactions during or after a critical incident, but their impaired cognitive performance may remain hidden until they are required to work under a high level of work pressure. By this time, however, it may be too late to cope with their cognitive impairment and fulfil their ATC tasks. This lack of cognitive resource can jeopardize aviation safety, and it is for this reason that it is essential to identify those ATCOs who are having difficulties and to provide effective support following critical incidents in ATC. This is made more difficult as responses to critical incidents can be found to appear over time, sequentially or be delayed.

Where an individual is exposed to a traumatic event, the impact may involve the development of post-traumatic stress and have long-term consequences on the person's life; whilst the effects of being exposed to a critical incident may be less intense, they can result in changes to the individual's values and beliefs or world view. The ATCOs' involvement in a critical incident may alter their belief and trust in their equipment, operational procedures or organisation and they may choose to work in a way that suits their values and allows them to challenge unreasonable management demands. Vogt *et al.*

(2007) reported that ATCOs who experienced a critical incident and were not provided with CISM (Mitchell, 2006a) used more aircraft separation than prescribed in the aviation rules.

ATCOs have a tendency to minimize their reactions to critical incidents and to be unwilling to accept support from anyone other than a peer. Without a CISM programme and peers to explain that CISRs are normal reactions to abnormal situations, and that an incident can be critical even when there are no casualties, ATCOs may falsely believe that there is something wrong with them. The comparison of their reactions with those of primary victims may create feelings of not being normal or that 'something is wrong with me', which is not a helpful outcome. ATCOs may also compare their reactions to critical incidents at work to those of primary trauma victims and be unable to recognize that their reactions to critical events, whilst not post-traumatic stress, are still disabling CISRs. The secondary trauma involved in the CISR which is experienced by ATCOs is caused by the cognitive modelling and the ATCO's imagination of the potential disaster which could have happened.

In addition to the features of the critical incident and how these are appraised, CISRs are also determined by the individual's coping abilities and their mental and physical well-being. Leonhardt and Vogt (2006a) use the metaphor of a battery to describe ATCO resilience. Whereas one operator may have a nearly full 'battery' (e.g. 90%) and can be relied upon to deal with the work demands and to cope with critical situations, another operator may be experiencing stressful life events such as illness, divorce, debt or work-related stress and, as a result, may have only 30% of his/her mental coping capacity available to deal with work-related challenges. The two operators, having different coping capabilities as a result of personal circumstances, are likely to react in different ways to the same critical incident. Therefore, it is not only the traumatic event that determines the magnitude of the CISRs, it is also the strength of personal coping and resilience available to overcome them. In a resilient operator, a potential trauma event may be downgraded to a critical incident when the operator feels capable and competent to handle his/her CISRs effectively.

In ATC the coping abilities of the operators have been found (Leonhardt, 2006; Leonhardt and Vogt, 2006a) to be dependent on a number of factors, including:

- Mental and physical health.

- Relationships with supportive family/friends.
- Support provided by a trained peer.
- Positive attitudes and beliefs before the incident.

Observations and interviews of ATCOs have shown the importance of recognizing and mobilizing their inherent coping abilities in dealing with critical incidents (Vogt *et al.*, 2007). Depending on the ATCO's coping abilities and the success of the CISM intervention, the operations room supervisor has to decide – ideally after consulting the CISM peer – when and at what position the ATCO can return to work, as to fail to undertake this risk assessment would be gross negligence in ATC.

In addition to the personal characteristics of the ATCO, there are features of the individual impact of the incident. The following features tend to increase the incidence of CISRs occurring:

- Feelings of helplessness/powerlessness.
- Feelings of guilt.
- Massive personal shock.
- Degree of identification.
- Intensity of the event (e.g. disasters).
- Direct threat to body and life.

The nature of critical incident stress reactions in air traffic control

Critical incidents happen in aviation. They mainly involve violation of the aircraft separation rules between flying aircraft, or runway incursions on the ground, in which a vehicle or other aircraft crosses the path of an aircraft engaged in landing or lifting off. The nature of the psychological impact will be related to the appraisal of the situation and the professional self-concept of the ATCO required to control air traffic movements and to foresee air traffic situations by planning aircraft movements and anticipating what will happen in the near future. This professional self-concept is severely challenged when a critical incident occurs or, despite the ATCO's best endeavours, there is a near miss or other form of critical incident. At this time the ATCO will typically experience feelings of failure, guilt and creation of an image of what could have happened had the crash occurred. In a blaming culture, an investigation focusing on individual failure and criticisms of colleagues or managers will add to this unhealthy process (Dekker, 2006); however, these attitudes are not common in ATC. Where there is no CISM programme, it is not unusual for ATCOs to regard CISRs as abnormal. The introduction of CISM, where a peer will support the individual ATCO and normalize the CISR as normal and understandable reactions, is very helpful, as despite separation losses occurring, they are still abnormal critical incidents. It is the normal autonomic and cognitive reaction to the critical incident, and not the incident itself, that needs to be normalized. The common, yet harmful, view that just because no one was injured or killed nothing happened, and therefore the reaction to the 'non-event' is unreasonable or inappropriate, fails to recognize the real distress experienced by the ATCO. It is for this reason that the peer model of crisis intervention is vital to ATC. An ATCO–CISM peer understands how CISRs resulting from what may appear to be an insignificant event can be experienced by an ATCO.

The ability of ATCOs to use their imaginative capacity in conceptualizing events in three dimensions makes the ATCOs more vulnerable to experiencing CISRs, as they are masters in creating images and therefore it is not difficult for them to construct an air disaster which triggers their autonomic fight-or-flight response. Imaginative thinking is a powerful traumatizing factor and should never be underestimated, as human beings are programmed to complete a story or a picture; even when the visual stimuli do not provide a complete picture, the gaps will be constructed in the brain (Kanisza, 1979). However, this can cause confusion to an ATCO, who might be thinking, 'I know that nothing has happened and I know that the aircraft have not collided, so why do I feel so bad, am I crazy?' In their planning, ATCOs not only consider spatial dimensions, they also anticipate the temporal situation 3–4 minutes ahead; thus, they are primed to make the future real and respond to that imagined future in their actions. Damasio (1999) explains that mental images include all sensory modalities and shows that the orbito-frontal cortex of the brain plays a key role in the ability to adjust behaviour to such anticipated emotional consequences (Damasio, 1994).

How these responses differ from symptoms found in emergency services personnel

Emergency service personnel are often confronted in a direct aftermath of an accident, a disaster or other traumatic events. Something has happened and the accident is real; the firefighters, police officers or paramedics are exposed to a multitude of sensory impressions. The exposure to the accident is combined with the smells, sounds, images and physical sensations of the traumatic environment, which may cause them to become overwhelmed by these impressions. The emergency service workers therefore have a wide range of sensory triggers, related to their traumatic exposure, that are held in the amygdala of the brain (Fanselow and LeDoux, 1999). The trauma memories tend to exist as fragments of their sensory components and can be reactivated whenever exposed to a trauma reminder (Van der Kolk and Fisler, 1995). The fact that some of the sensory information is held in the amygdala and not in the conscious memory means that some people will find themselves reacting to sensory cues, even when they are unaware of the connections between cues and the original traumatic exposure. ATCOs are rarely exposed to direct sensory stimuli, as only ATCOs working in the air traffic control towers at the airports, in good weather conditions, have a direct view of air traffic movements. Most ATCOs see something on their radar screen that represents a real flight, which may be occurring miles away from their workplace. Tower ATCOs may see an aircraft moving into an occupied runway or their colleagues responsible for the upper airspace observe a near miss of two aircraft on the radar screen. Despite the potential danger of an incident, nothing happened, it was a near miss, maybe it was close but there was enough space to prevent the collision happening. ATCOs react with very similar responses to emergency service workers, but this time their reactions are triggered by their imagination and not by direct sensory stimulation. This is a major difference between the experience of the emergency service worker and that of the ATCO, and the reason why it is essential to organise support from peers who are aware of the nature of the cognitive constructions involved. Only a fellow ATCO could visualize or understand the magnitude of distress caused at discovering that the 5 nautical miles of separation has been inadvertently reduced to 4 nautical miles. During the critical incident, the ATCO will experience a range of physical and cognitive response which can continue for some time; some ATCOs begin to believe that they are going crazy, because they cannot understand why they are having nightmares about something that never happened and still feel guilty despite being told that the near miss was not their fault. Because of the unique nature of the ATC roles, the only people capable of providing credible support are peers; it is for this reason that the role of ATC–CISM peers was established. The ATC–CISM peers understand the technical terms; they can imagine the situation and identify with the reactions and fears. Where external support is required, the psychologist or counsellor needs to understand the nature of the ATCOs' world. In the past, external supporters have become confused by the reactions of ATCOs and have tried to provide comfort, causing the symptoms to intensify due to the ATCOs believing that they must be ill.

Central to peer support is the normalization of the physical and psychological responses to the near miss. The psychological effect of explaining that the responses to the critical incident are adaptive and protective helps to facilitate the integration of these rational beliefs in the restructuring of the whole experience as a cognitive success, rather than a failure.

Normalization of the reactions is important to recovery (Leonhardt, 2006). Following an exposure to a critical incident, it is normal to have difficulty in sleeping, to have an increased pulse rate, to feel frightened or concerned about the stressful experience. For the affected person these reactions may not feel normal but, in the context of the neurobiology of fight-or-flight responses, the responses make sense. Unlike physical threats, today's critical situations do not require high levels of energy supplied to fuel a fight-or-flight response. However, it is extremely helpful for ATCOs to have an explanation by their CISM peers in order to integrate their reactions into their self-concept and finally to sustainably overcome them. Thus, education and understanding the reason for their responses helps ATCOs to return to normal functioning. When the new learning is established and an understanding of the elements of the CISRs is clear, the individual aspects of the trauma response begin to fit together and recovery begins.

Everyday example of the might of imagination

ATCOs can suffer from CISR because they experience an unforeseen separation loss between aircraft as personal failure and they have a professional role in this. Their role and responsibilities alter their relationship to the incident, compared with that of merely hearing of bad news about a major accident or incident. To be involved in a nearly missed accident, be it direct or indirect, with or without damage, facilitates strong responses. In order to illustrate this phenomenon, the following story of a car accident is used, since it may be easier to understand, as more people will have operated a car rather than a plane.

A woman was in a hurry to buy food in a supermarket. Coming back to her small car, she began to load the items into the boot and on the back seat; she finally sat in her car, starting the engine, and started reversing to leave the car park. Whilst reversing, a truck hit her from behind. Nothing serious happened, no one was injured and the vehicles were not damaged. She was shocked, in a hurry and stressed by all the things she had to do – the crash was too much. She was cared for by the people in the supermarket, the truck driver and later by family and friends. She found it impossible to overcome the stress reactions, including bad dreams, crying, sad feelings and fear of driving the car. Everyone told her that nothing had happened and that there was no reason to be sad or afraid. It is easy to imagine that the sympathy began to ebb away after people had tried several times to convince her that she must be fine. After some years, PTSD was diagnosed and she declared herself crazy.

From the perception of a CISM peer, we see that she was not in a good mental and physical condition when the accident occurred; her 'battery' was almost flat. This needed to be understood from the beginning, and then she needed to understand that her responses were normal. A crisis intervention directly after the accident would have found that, as she looked in her rear-view mirror and saw two big shining headlights, the cue stimulus she formed was an intense impression that the lights were huge, the speed was high and the first thought coming into her mind was that this was the last second in her life and she would never see her children again. These strong thoughts connected with the imagination of getting killed, and in the next second triggered the fight-or-flight reaction.

The role of the CISM peer needs to be clearly defined. The provision of comfort is not helpful and may prevent or displace the distress caused by the imagination and increase the feelings of failure and overreaction to a situation where nothing happened. The role of the CISM peer will explore and validate the cognitive and physical responses to the imagined disaster. Despite the obvious benefits of using an ATCO peer, there can be some contagion between the ATCO and the CISM peer who may find that his/her own imaginative functions are engaging with the features of the critical incident; as a result, the CISM peer begins to experience the autonomic and psychological reactions present in the person being supported. CISM peers need to be trained and continually be reminded of the importance of checking their own responses to supporting their colleagues, and to remember the importance of accepting and normalizing reactions, providing appropriate information and education and avoiding being comforting. CISM peers need appropriate training and support if they are to help their colleagues recover from their critical incident experiences.

The psychological cost of critical incidents as a basis for evaluation of the intervention

A pilot study to investigate the introduction and evaluation of a CISM programme was undertaken in the German Air Traffic Control Services (Deutsche Flugsicherung, DFS) (Vogt *et al.*, 2004). The study showed that it was possible to relate business benefits to the deployment of CISM. The pilot study was followed by the main study, based upon 309 questionnaires from ATCOs, 39 interviews with operations room supervisors, and 11 interviews with senior managers (Vogt *et al.*, 2007). The main study, which looked at recovery time following a near miss, showed that ATCOs who went through the CISM programme, and who had the opportunity to go off operations for the rest of the day, were less risk-averse when they returned to their operational role the next day. Instead of needing to leave increased gaps between aircraft, they felt comfortable with aircraft flying within the normal safety limits. The financial benefits related to the reduction in the overcautious behaviour and the increase in air traffic control efficiency; the benefits significantly exceeded the costs of the programme. The use of CISM peer support, in combination with encouraging the ATCO to go off operations for the rest of the day, brought about a significant reduction in the CISRs. Without CISM support, the magnitude of the impairment following a critical incident was considerable, creating additional critical incidents, freezing or slowing down of the air traffic system. Figure 5.1 shows the mean reduction in ATCO functioning, with the standard error, where 0 was taken to be the normal functioning level. The differences in behaviours marked with * were statistically

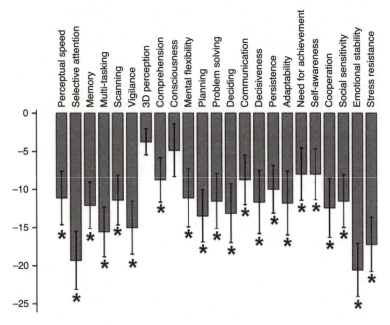

Figure 5.1 The average reduction in ATCO self-esteem and performance following a critical incident (*$p < 0.05$).

significant in a one-tailed *t*-test with α < 0.05 adjusted for multiple testing (Krauth, 1988)

In addition, the CISRs were also found to have a negative impact on the ATCOs' self-esteem and performance, leading to difficulties in workload management, information assessment and planning. Pilot requests would be rejected and aircraft movements reduced. Figure 5.2 shows the reduction in the mean scores, with the standard errors, for the ATCOs' perceptions of their self-esteem and perform-ance following a critical incident compared to their normal ability (0) before the critical incident. The differences marked * were statistic-ally significant in a one-tailed *t*-test with α < 0.05 adjusted for multiple testing (Krauth, 1988).

ATCOs cannot undertake their roles with any significant reduc-tions in their essential skills, and exposing a distressed ATCO to having to handle another critical incident is not acceptable in a high-reliability organisation. In the German Air Traffic Control it is common practice after a critical incident to replace the ATCO, and

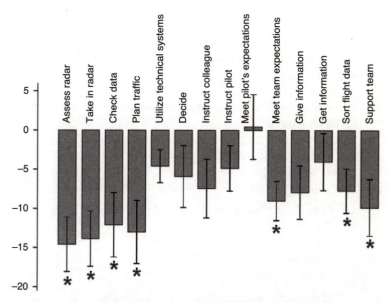

Figure 5.2 The average reduction in ATCO work-related behavioural competency following a critical incident (*$p < 0.05$).

for the supervisor to arrange for a meeting between the affected ATCO and a CISM peer (Vogt *et al.*, 2007).

Intervention method: critical incident stress management (CISM)

The CISM approach (Mitchell, 2006a) was established in the 1980s. Initially the programme was named 'critical incident stress debriefing' (CISD), with a focus on emergency personnel. CISM is a comprehensive and multi-component programme and includes multiple methods for crisis intervention. In aviation (Mitchell, 2006b), CISM was first used following the Sioux City air crash in the late 1980s and is currently being used by airlines, airports and air navigation services (Leonhardt and Vogt, 2006b).

The aim of CISM is to support people after an acute crisis to establish their normal functions and to start the recovery process; it is not psychotherapy or a substitute for professional psychological care. Mitchell (2008) recommends three to five CISM peer contacts and a referral to psychosocial services where necessary: in the German Air Traffic Control programme, one peer contact is normally sufficient.

The CISM programme for air navigation service providers or airlines should adhere to ICISF (2005) standards and involve the following elements:

- A programme structure on how the programme is to be established and applied.
- A statement and support from senior management.
- A CISM-trained programme manager.
- A peer selection process.
- Peer education, containing the following courses:
  - Individual crisis intervention and peer support.
  - Group crisis intervention.
  - Advanced group crisis intervention.
  - Strategic response to crisis.
  - Update courses.
- CISM should be embedded in the organisations.
  - Training and education programme.
  - Crisis and disaster plan.
- Training programme for supervisors and operational managers.
- A crisis intervention team led by a mental health professional.
- Programme evaluation.

The importance of using a peer model of support

When considering these requirements, it is essential for ATC to use peers, as they understand the technical aspects of the work and are aware of the different incidents which could occur; more importantly, they understand the reactions to potential events. This basic understanding is important to allow the focus to remain on the crisis intervention and the reduction of the stress reactions. Normalization of the CISRs is easier for peers, due to their experience and knowledge of the role. Peers are also available, as they are normally working within in the operations room or available within a short period. In a study with ATCOs (Vogt *et al.*, 2004, 2007), the most frequent CISM intervention was a one-on-one individual treatment (SAFER-R), involving stabilizing the person, acknowledging the crisis and admitting emotions, facilitating normalization of the reaction, encouraging adaptive coping, recovering normal functions/abilities, and referring to other professional help if there was no improvement after a couple of peer contacts.

The backbone of the CISM process is peer education, which consists of the four CISM courses:

1 Individual crisis intervention and peer support.
2 Group crisis intervention.
3 Advanced group crisis intervention.
4 Strategic response to crisis.

Peers should be trained by an approved and experienced instructor, and training should be embedded in the programme's structure and include the whole team, involving standard procedures, rules, supervision and refresher trainings. The peer education never ends, as update courses, refresher trainings and practical experience are essential.

The need for international standards in providing support

The aviation industry works across borders and cultures. The more international a business is, the more often employees from different countries and cultures are found within these organisations. Critical incidents in aviation may occur outside the country in which the ATCOs are located and involve people from other countries who need support. Although the neurobiological response to critical incidents is largely universal, the cultural differences in dealing with crises are wide (Leonhardt and Boege, 2008) and must be considered in crisis management programmes, especially in cross-border incidents.

Occasionally an air traffic disaster is of such a magnitude that the CISM peers will become over-identified with the accident and the involved colleagues and the organisation find that they are unable to apply the interventions. In the catastrophe of Überlingen/Lake Constance described in Leonhardt et al. (2006), the CISM peers and the responsible MHP recognized a strong identification between the CISM peers and their Swiss colleagues. Where cross-border and cross-culture assistance is required, international standards are essential (Gaber and Drozd, 2006; Leonhardt, 2006). Peers and MHPs in the field of CISM need to speak the same language regarding the method, they need to know what to do when something has already been done, and they need clear procedures and protocols to act. International standards, approved, applied and evaluated across cultures, countries, languages and professions, are available through the ICISF. Networking between professions and nations is a good basis for cooperation when disaster strikes. For this reason, the European Office of the ICISF organises European and regional conferences (Vogt *et al.*, 2009).

Conclusions

The message of this chapter is two-fold:

1   ATCOs are a special target group for crisis intervention because they are highly selected, highly trained, continuously monitored for mental and physical health, their critical incidents usually are not accidents and do not involve direct sensations. Planning ahead and thoughts play an important role; they may impair basic work abilities and without special attention these cognitive impairments would be recognized too late in high-demand situations.
2   CISM is the method of choice to prevent the special kind of trauma ATCOs may experience in their professional lives. The CISM programme must be peer-based; peer training, continuous development and quality assurance are most important.

ATCOs are selected and trained to acquire a four-dimensional mental picture of air traffic on the basis of the two-dimensional radar picture, with altitude information (third dimension) and the flight plan data providing time as the fourth dimension. They plan 3–4 minutes ahead and this facilitates strong thoughts and emotions with respect to unforeseen separation losses. ATCO peers can immediately comprehend the criticality of such events on the basis of their own ATC qualifications and experience. They need, however, a solid and continuous education with respect to CISR, neuropsychological processes and healthy and unhealthy coping processes, to understand the cognitive–emotional responses and to support sustainable coping. They also need supervision and annual conferences for exchange of what is going on in the organisation about handling critical incidents and what new developments in CISM are achieved worldwide. Finally, supervisors and senior managers (Riedle, 2006) have a key role in supporting CISM within their areas of accountability. They are the key persons to create a sound safety culture as a basis for the professional handling of critical incidents and accidents, including the proper treatment of staff and the public, because such events can happen as long as we fly.

References

Cannon, W.B. (1914) The emergency function of the adrenal medulla in pain and major emotions. *American Journal of Physiology* **33**, 356–372.

Damasio, A.R. (1994) *Descartes' Error*. New York: Grosset/Putnam.

Damasio, A.R. (1999) *The Feeling of What Happens. Body and Emotion in the Making of Consciousness*. New York: Harcourt Brace.

Dekker, S.W.A. (2006) *The Field Guide to Understanding Human Error*. Aldershot, UK: Ashgate Publishing.

Fanselow, M.S., LeDoux, J.E. (1999) Why we think plasticity underlying Pavlovian fear conditioning occurs in the basolateral amygdala. *Neuron* **23**, 229–232.

Gaber, W., Drozd, A. (2006) Critical stress incident management at Frankfurt airport (CISM Team Fraport AG). In Leonhardt, J., Vogt, J. (eds), *Critical Incident Stress Management (CISM) in Aviation*. Aldershot, UK: Ashgate Publishing; 109–124.

Henry, J.P., Stephens, P.M. (1977) *Stress, Health and the Social Environment*. Berlin: Springer.

Howarth, G., Leaman, O. (eds) (2001) *Encyclopedia of Death and Dying*. London: Routledge.

ICISF (2005) Peer Education, International Critical Incident Stress Foundation, 10176 Baltimore National Pike, Unit 200, Ellicott City, MD 21042, USA: http//www.icisf.org [accessed December 2005].

Kanisza, G. (1979) *Organization in Vision: Essays on Gestalt Perception*. New York: Praeger.

Krauth, J. (1988) Distribution-free statistics: an application-oriented approach. In Huston, J.P. (ed.), *Techniques in the Behavioral and Neural Sciences*, vol. 2. Amsterdam: Elsevier; 37.

Leonhardt, J. (2006) CISM intervention methods. In Leonhardt, J., Vogt, J. (eds), *Critical Incident Stress Management (CISM) in Aviation*. Aldershot, UK: Ashgate Publishing; 53–63.

Leonhardt, J., Boege, K. (2008) Kulturelle Unterschiede im Umgang mit Krisen. In Boege, K., Manz, R. (eds), *Traumatische Ereignisse im interkulturellen Kontext*. Heidelberg: Kröning/Asanger.

Leonhardt, J., Vogt, J. (2006a) Critical incident, critical incident stress, post traumatic stress disorder – definitions and underlying neurobiological processes. In Leonhardt, J., Vogt, J. (eds), *Critical Incident Stress Management (CISM) in Aviation*. Aldershot, UK: Ashgate Publishing; 43–52.

Leonhardt, J., Vogt, J. (eds) (2006b) *Critical Incident Stress Management (CISM) in Aviation*. Aldershot, UK: Ashgate Publishing.

Leonhardt, J., Minder, C., Zimmermann, S., Mersmann, R., Schultze, R. (2006) Case Study Lake Constance (Überlingen). In Leonhardt, J., Vogt, J. (eds), *Critical Incident Stress Management (CISM) in Aviation.* Aldershot, UK: Ashgate Publishing; 125–143.

Mitchell, J.T. (2006a) *Critical Incident Stress Management (CISM): Group Crisis Intervention,* 4th edn. Ellicott City, MD: International Critical Incident Stress Foundation.

Mitchell, J.T. (2006b) Critical incident stress management in aviation: a strategic approach. In Leonhardt, J., Vogt, J. (eds), *Critical Incident Stress Management (CISM) in Aviation.* Aldershot, UK: Ashgate Publishing.

Mitchell, J.T. (2008) *Critical Incident Stress Management Refresher Training Course, December 2008.* Langen, Germany: DFS.

Mitchell, J.T., Eggert, W., Leonhardt, J., Vogt, J. (2008) Gestion du Stress lié à un incident critique; critical incident stress management (CISM). Une approche flexible et une stratégie adaptative à l'intervention de crise. *Stress et Trauma* **8**(3), 163–175.

Riedle, R. (2006) Importance of CISM in modern air traffic management (ATM). In Leonhardt, J., Vogt, J. (eds), *Critical Incident Stress Management (CISM) in Aviation.* Aldershot, UK: Ashgate Publishing; 5–11.

Selye, H. (1936) A syndrome produced by diverse nocuous agents. *Nature* **138**, 423–427.

Selye, H. (1950) *The Physiology and Pathology of Exposure to Stress.* Montreal: Acta Inc.

Van der Kolk, B.A., Fisler, R. (1995) Dissociation and the fragmentary nature of traumatic memories: overview and exploratory study. *Journal of Traumatic Stress* **8**(4), 505–525.

Vogt, J., Gasche, V., Muris, J., Leonhardt, J., Mitchell, J.T. (2009) A report on the evaluation of the First European Conference on Critical Incident Stress Management, organised by the European Office of the International Critical Incident Stress Foundation. *International Journal of Emergency Mental Health* **11**, 111–119.

Vogt, J., Leonhardt, J. (2009) Critical incident stress m(CISM) bei richtiger Anwendung ohne Nebenwirkungen [CISM – no negative side effects if correctly applied]. Trauma und Gewalt. *Trauma and Violence* **3**(3), 261–266.

Vogt, J., Leonhardt, J., Köper, B., Pennig, S. (2004) Economic evaluation of the critical incident stress management program. *International Journal of Emergency Mental Health* **6**(4), 185–196.

Vogt, J., Pennig, S., Leonhardt, J. (2007) Critical incident stress min air traffic control and its benefits. *Air Traffic Control Quarterly* **15**(2), 127–156.

Chapter 6

The impact of disasters on schools and the school community

Tom Lowe

Introduction

Each day children go to school to learn and meet their friends; at the same time, they, their families and the whole school community assume that they will be safe from harm and distress. Yet each day, somewhere in the UK, a school will be faced with a critical incident of a type and severity that will significantly disrupt the functioning of the school and everyone attending as a pupil or member of staff. The press and television reports of disasters involving children and schools are particularly memorable. Whenever one is asked about school traumas, most people can recall a number of headline traged-ies involving the death of children or school staff. Events such as the abduction and murder of Holly Wells and Jessica Chapman by a school janitor, and the sinking of the cruise ship *Jupiter*, are some British examples of large-scale school disasters. Internationally, there has been the killing of 32 students at Virginia Tech, USA, and the Finnish student who shot and killed 10 students before turning the gun on himself.

However, there are many other events which can cause just as much distress within the school environment that do not get the same level of media coverage, for example a child killed in a road traffic crash or the death of a child from a terminal illness.

School and communities

Today, schools vary in terms of their size, the age range of the children, the ability and additional support requirements for gifted children, and the cultural diversity of staff, the children and the local community. Local and national educational policies, priorities and initiatives tend to increase this diversity. Within the schools, there are equally diverse groups of people. In addition to the headteachers and other teaching staff, most schools have a number of ancillary workers, including janitors, clerical and catering staff, and also may involve community and project workers. A typical Scottish high school catering for around 1000 pupils will have a number of people providing a range of inputs and interventions to support pupils. Given the size and complexity of the educational environment, the school and external staff need to be well organised and coordinated to enable them to undertake their roles effectively. At the time of an incident, the communication and coordination in a busy school campus can be demanding and problematic (see Table 6.1).

While schools may at first appear to be similar, individual schools have unique characteristics. They may be staffed by experienced or recently qualified teachers; they can differ in size, ranging from village schools at the heart of their community to urban technology colleges taking pupils from a large catchment area. They may have an excellent or failing reputation. The relationship between different schools in a local education authority area may be close, due to the creation of academic and social contacts, networking and joint projects, with the result that during a crisis it is often possible to call on or receive offers and support within this network. Pupils may also have brothers, sisters and close friends attending other local schools, so that when a disaster strikes there can be a contagion of distress, with the traumatic event having an epicentre in one school but a strong resonance within many of the other local schools. Therefore, when teachers and other school staff are considering the impact of a traumatic event on the children from their school, they should also liaise with other schools to identify what may be required in order to meet the unique needs of each of the affected schools. This need can be illustrated in a situation where the death of a pupil or member of staff is deeply felt at their own school, but has an even greater impact in another school, for example, if the deceased pupil was a popular member of a sports team involving other schools, or where a deceased secondary school teacher had spent time leading a community drama group where the children came from a number of primary schools.

Major disasters

In Britain there have been a number of school-related disasters; a few stand out in terms of their local, national or international impact. One of the most memorable disasters occurred on 21 October 1988, when the cruise ship *Jupiter* was struck by an Italian tanker and sank within 45 minutes. On board the *Jupiter* were 415 students and 60 teachers from 30 different British schools. Although only one teacher and one pupil were lost, presumed drowned, two rescuers were killed and many of the children saw their bodies (Yule and Gold, 1993). The impact of this event still had a profound effect on many of those involved 20 years later (Campion, 2008). The Dunblane massacre of children occurred in 1996, when Thomas Hamilton entered the primary school, walked to the school gym and began shooting at the children. He killed 16 children and their teacher in an attack that lasted 3 minutes. He then turned the gun on himself. The staff at Dunblane School were strongly affected and found a gulf between the meaning that the event had for them and the meaning created by children with whom they were working. Finding a way of bridging this gulf was challenging and demanding (Tomlinson, 2004). Internationally, there have been similar incidents (Infoplease, 2009), with the hostage crisis in Beslan being one of the most traumatic of recent incidents. This event, in 2004, resulted in the deaths of at least 334 hostages, of whom 186 were children. UNICEF set up a rehabilitation programme to support these children and their families, the operation of which has recently been taken over by the local government in North Ossetia (UNICEF, 2005; UNESCO, 2009).

Critical incidents

Major disasters are not the only traumatic events that have an impact on schools. Indeed, the smaller-scale and less publicised critical incidents can have a profound impact on the whole school community. Whilst the likelihood of a school needing to respond to a major disaster is relatively small, critical incidents occur regularly and have the potential to cause serious distress to school staff and pupils. The kinds of event that have a direct impact on a school are numerous and may involve the following:

• Sudden death of a pupil or member of staff from a road traffic accident, drug overdose, asthma attack, heart attack or other health problem.
• Suicide of a pupil, ex-pupil, parent or member of staff or their immediate family.

- Serious accidental injury to a pupil.
- Serious assault on a pupil by another pupil(s) or a member of staff.
- Disaster affecting the school building, including fire, arson or flood destroying the school, particularly with a loss of personal treasures.
- Deaths or injuries on school journeys.
- Refugee children joining a school, having been uprooted from their country of origin.
- Female genital mutilation.
- Child abuse (sexual, physical or psychological).
- Bullying and intimidation.

Working in critical incident support work, there are occasions when one is required to deal with pupils who have become severely injured in front of fellow pupils and their teachers. Generally the school staff instinctively respond to a crisis by contacting the emergency services, helping the pupil concerned, supporting the witnessing pupils whilst carrying on the educational programme for other pupils. Their support involves not only in dealing with the emergency but also in providing help over subsequent days and years. In some cases, their involvement may extend to visiting the pupil in hospital or at his/her home. Most of the school staff feel positive about their contributions at difficult times during the incident, but others become unnecessarily self-critical, feeling that they should have done more or better. The traumatic impact sometimes continues for years and is related to the resilience and training of the members of staff, their level of exposure and the nature of their involvement in the incident (Lowe, 2004).

Differences between child and adult responses to trauma

While there has been a long history and in-depth research into trauma in adults, it is only in recent years that attention has turned to children and young people. At first, the research sought reports and information from adults, usually parents (Dalgleish et al., 2005). More recently, research strategies and models have been developed to allow researchers to work with children and young people (Lustig et al., 2004). However, this research has tended to focus on a few areas, such as sexual and physical abuse, bereavement and loss and the impact of road traffic accidents. There has been less attention given to the impact of school traumas on pupils (Dalgleish *et al.*, 2005).

In addition to the various factors that influence the effect of an incident on adults, it is important to consider how pupils' developmental stage affects their understanding, response and recovery from an incident:

> Children, for several reasons, are particularly vulnerable to the impact of trauma. Children do not deny trauma: rather, they tend to record its full impact and horror. Trauma terrorizes children, making them feel helpless and unprotected. Their coping skills have not yet matured. They are still in the process of developing their own personality and traits (Poland and McCormick, 1999, p. xiv).

We are now aware that children and young people are particularly susceptible to the emotional, psychological and physiological sequelae of trauma experiences. Young adolescents, who may be struggling with psychological and physiological developmental changes, are particularly at risk. The impact of trauma experiences on children and young people, including babies and toddlers, can result in significant short- and long-term changes in their psychological and physiological behaviours. Sudden, one-off events are more likely to have short-term effects, while the sustained and repeated experience of trauma is likely to be long-term in its impact (Terr, 2003). Neuropsychological studies have identified the negative effect that such traumas can have on early brain development; these changes affect the ability of children to concentrate, learn and behave appropriately, with their behaviour appearing as unpredictable and emotionally labile (NCTSN, 2003). Teachers and other school staff need the knowledge and skills to recognize, understand and respond to the complex needs of these pupils (Massachusetts Advocates for Children, 2005).

As children progress from the toddler stage to adulthood, their ability to understand a situation, to communicate distress and engage in healing activities becomes more complex and sophisticated. Those identified as being at the epicentre of a trauma will usually be identified and offered support by adults. However, children may not be aware that the changes in their moods and behaviours are related to the traumatic exposure and fail to recognize their need to seek help. This problem is not unique to pupils; there are accounts of adults recognizing some time after an event that a trauma was still having a significant impact on their ability to function (Renaud, 2008). It is important that school staff are aware that these changes in mood and behaviour can signpost hidden traumatization.

Generally, children will be able to cope with the help of their parents and other caring adults, and young people will also benefit from support and understanding of their peers. However, some children may be at risk of more extreme reactions. The severity of children's reactions will depend on their specific risk factors, which include the nature of their exposure to the actual event, real or perceived personal injury or loss, elevated estimates of future harm, any pre-existing risk factors, such as earlier traumatic experiences or psychological, health or physical problems, as well as the level of support from others. How children and young people react depends on their age and developmental stage, but for all there will be some notable change in mood and behaviour. These changes can include:

- *Pre-school children (less than 5 years)*. Thumb sucking, bedwetting, clinging to parents, sleep disturbances, loss of appetite, fear of the dark, regression in behaviour and play, and withdrawal from friends and routines.
- *Primary school children (5–12 years)*. Irritability, aggressiveness, clinginess, nightmares, school avoidance, poor concentration, withdrawal from activities and friends, and impaired memory and concentration.
- *Secondary school pupils (12–18 years)*. Sleeping and eating problems, irritability, increase in conflicts, physical complaints, risk-taking behaviours, and impaired memory and concentration.

Any of these responses can disrupt a pupil's ability to cope at school, academically and socially. While such changes are generally transient, some can persist for some time, as found in the children and staff involved in the Dunblane and the *Jupiter* disasters (Galea *et al.*, 2004).

Community disasters

The disaster does not have to occur within the school to cause a traumatic impact. When school janitor Ian Huntley was identified as the murderer of Holly Wells and Jessica Chapman, children in other schools started to be nervous about their safety at school and sought reassurance from their parents and teachers that their janitor would not harm them. Clearly, the pupils were able to imagine what had happened to the murdered girls and this undermined their feelings of safety. Similar problems arose in January 2004, when a fire swept through the Rosepark Care Home at Uddingston, near Glasgow, and 14 elderly residents were killed. Many of these elderly people had extensive family and social connections in the wider Lanarkshire area, with the result that a number of schools had to support pupils distressed by the death of a loved family member. Indeed, some of the children who had not lost a relative also became upset as they realized that such disasters might also occur in the care homes where their grandparents lived. In both cases, the trauma ripples had not been anticipated and school staff had to respond quickly to deal with the distress experienced by the children.

The way school staff and community respond to an event has implications well beyond the immediate crisis. Responses can affect the long-term relationships within the school community, building bonded groups or leading to fragmented angry subgroups, creating or destroying trust, fostering a sense of security, hope and optimism or shattering these core beliefs. Epidemiological studies have shown the rates of exposure and post-traumatic stress disorder (PTSD) in children and adolescents. These studies have mainly been undertaken in the USA, with results being similar to those in the adult studies, with 15–43% of girls and 14–43% of boys having experienced at least one traumatic event in their lifetime (McDermott, 2007). Where children and adolescents have had a traumatic experience, 5–100% of the children were diagnosed with PTSD. Similar to adults, most children and young people tend to be resilient, coping and experiencing post-trauma growth following their traumatic experience. Nonetheless, the research reinforces the need to provide longer-term support to traumatized individuals and school communities, as those with post-traumatic symptoms can continue to be affected for many years after the event (Galea *et al.*, 2004). Even for those who cope and recover from the crisis, the journey may take time and involve periods of emotional struggle and disillusionment.

Wise before the event

Schools are part of the local community and benefit from the experience of colleagues in neighbouring schools. Many educational authorities have introduced critical incident training and critical incident support teams. In 2009, the results of a survey sent by the author to educational psychological services (EPS) revealed a mixed pattern of critical incident support teams. At one extreme, a local authority had a multi-agency team, led by an officer from the education department or a psychologist; at the other extreme there was no planned response in place. Most had a Critical Incident Support Team (CIST), managed by the EPS and staffed by educational psychologists (Lowe, 2009b). Whilst in the past external consultants have provided support to schools experiencing a critical incident, organised crisis intervention in schools is a more recent development (Lowe, 2009a; Nickerson and Heath, 2008).

It has been possible to transfer some of the strategies and intervention developed for use in wars and civil disaster, but there has been a need to make adjustments and adaptations to make them appropriate for delivery by school staff for school children. School and crisis support staff require training, coordination and support. In the USA, these systems have been in place for many years. The National Association for School Psychologists (NASP, 2009) provides information and advice to its members and the general public and recently has established a National Emergency Assistance Team (NEAT) to provide trained and experienced school psychologists to deal with emergencies, including those following the shootings at Columbine High School and Virginia Tech. NASP has also organised training programmes to prepare school psychologists as critical incident responders and to provide trained and experienced psychologists to support staff and students.

Critical incident support for pupils and staff

In recent years, British education authorities have identified and trained school staff to provide critical incident support. Originally, post-incident support was provided by an external trauma expert who was given the task of managing the crisis, taking over the responsibilities of the senior staff in the school. The problems with this approach were quickly identified and current approaches involve external critical incident support, consultants working alongside the school management and wider school community who maintain the overall responsibility for responding, coping and recovering from the incident. Generally, these external staff come from the local community and are familiar with the school, local networks and staff. The key principle is that the school remains responsible for identifying and organising the post-incident support and identifying where additional external resources may be necessary. There has been a move towards mobilizing trained and coordinated multi-agency trauma support teams with a range of skills, resources and capacity to help schools during times of crisis and in the following weeks, months and occasionally years.

As part of their emergency planning, many areas within the UK have introduced major incident support teams (MISTs), which include personnel from the emergency and social services. For schools, Educational Psychology Services have taken on the responsibility for training the critical incident support team (CIST) and preparing school staff to deal with incidents. Some areas have integrated the MIST and CIST, while other areas have chosen to respond on an ad hoc basis with school staff, with external staff being involved on request. Where an established CIST exists, there are a number of key components to the critical incident response (MacNeil and Topping, 2007); these are summarized in Table 6.2.

Interventions

In the late 1990s, a number of psychological interventions were developed, primarily for use by emergency services, to help emergency service personnel deal with a crisis (Jimerson et al., 2005). Efforts to explore how these interventions could be used with school children and staff began relatively recently. There has been a reluctance in schools to engage in psychological interventions, including psychological debriefing, judging them as inappropriate for children and young people and reacting against the medicalization of trauma responses. Schools tend to adopt the stance that the behaviours of children and young people following a traumatic exposure are normal, given the abnormal circumstances of the trauma. Recent work with refugee children in war zones and children affected by natural disasters has shaped and informed the models and strategies that are now emerging in UK schools (IFRC, 2009; Lowe, 2009a). This work has also provided research tools and approaches that facilitate and encourage school-level interventions and research into trauma issues (Fazel et al., 2009). The current CIST approach is a more planned and staged support strategy, with an emphasis on psychosocial care by the school community rather than an approach that depends upon outside trauma experts and counsellors. Typically,

Table 6.1 Staff involved and typical duties during a critical or major incident

Staff involved	School-level critical incident (exemplar duties)	Major incident with impact on school (exemplar duties)
Major incident support staff (MIST)	Not directly involved but could be contacted for information, advice and support to CIST	Implement, coordinate and revise the appropriate contingency plan as the assessment of the incident progresses Set up, staff and manage rest centres and information systems Direct the appropriate services to the scene(s) Liaise and support school management staff, CIST and other professional staff working in the school
Critical incident support team (CIST)	Provide information, advice and support to school management team and pastoral support staff Enable school staff to normalize and validate stress reaction to the crisis Help school staff to provide coping assistance to pupils Provide direct psychosocial support to pupils and staff, if required Facilitate the identification of those who need immediately, or later will need, enhanced psychosocial support or psychological interventions Provide information leaflets appropriate to the event	Liaise with MIST staff and school management team to organise and deliver support to the children and young people affected, and to provide information and advice to their families Facilitate the identification of those who need immediately or later will need enhanced psychosocial support or psychological interventions Provide information, advice and support to school management team and pastoral support staff Provide direct psychosocial support to pupils and staff, if required Provide information leaflets appropriate to the event

School management team	Help school to return to the security of the standard school routines Ensure that support is provided to staff and pupils affected Ensure that information is shared and is accurate and up-to-date Liaise with CIST, local authority staff, press officer, etc. Liaise with e.g. hospital staff and police	Liaise with MIST staff Support establishment and running of rest centre in school Help school to return to the security of the standard school routines Ensure that support is provided to staff and pupils affected Ensure that information is shared and is accurate and up-to-date Liaise with CIST, local authority staff, press officer, etc. Liaise with e.g. hospital staff and police
Pastoral support in schools	Support sense of safety and security and facilitate emotional processing Provide psychosocial support and psycho-educational input Comfort, reassure, and listen to pupils' concerns and questions Arrange and support 'sanctuary' rooms. Provide one-to-one or small group sessions for pupils needing enhanced support or 'time-out' of timetable Identify and offer support to pupils significantly affected by the incident. Continue to monitor their progress and difficulties Liaise with families and other staff, providing advice and information required for good support to all affected but especially to any vulnerable pupils	
Teaching and classroom support staff	Reinstitution of familiar roles and routines and provide, even for short period, distractions to ease the psychological and emotional impact of the crisis Continue the standard timetable Provide support to pupils finding it difficult to settle to classwork Remain alert to pupils who need enhanced support	
Ancillary staff, particularly administrative and reception staff	Answer calls from families, other schools, and local authority staff Pass calls from media to press officer	Answer calls from families, other schools, local authority staff and MIST staff Pass calls from media to press officer

it is the CIST who works with school, the staff and families, ensuring that they have the understanding, skills and information to provide appropriate and effective help to pupils, members of staff and family members. Additional supports, including psychological interventions where necessary, may be considered for those pupils and staff members who have been identified as requiring this level of input (Figure 6.1).

Initially, the strategy of the CISTs was to take over, manage the incident and then leave. This approach deskilled and marginalized the school staff, with their depth of knowledge of the school, pupils, its staff and its routines. Currently, the critical incident support staff work alongside school staff, bringing their expertise and knowledge to work in collaboration with that of the school staff for as long as they are required. In this approach, the school staff continue to manage their school but are also able to build up their own experience and expertise in responding to critical incidents and in helping pupils and staff cope with the impact of a trauma. Similar to the

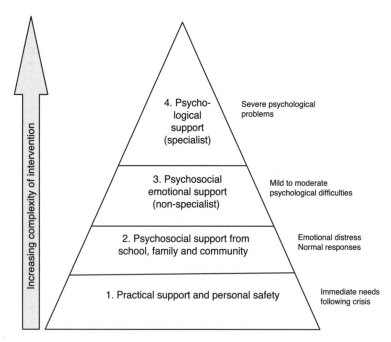

Figure 6.1 Levels of support following a traumatic exposure. Adapted from the Intervention Framework (IASC, 2007).

Traumatic Risk Management Model (Greenberg, 2006), a key contribution of CIST is to facilitate the development of internal support systems that are managed and delivered by school staff.

On arriving at a school, the CIST will work with school staff to establish some clear priorities, making sure that basic safety and physical needs are met and that the traumatic situation has been stabilized. There is a need to create an understanding of the crisis and provide reassurance that it is being managed. Pupils and staff need to make sense of what has happened and be provided with supportive information to promote social cohesiveness within the school and wider community. There is a focus on problem solving, involving pupils and staff recognizing issues and developing solutions and plans. Where individuals have a need for psychosocial support, this should be provided with the goal of re-establishing normality for the individual and the school community. An overview of the process, including an outline of the contributions of the key groups, is shown in Table 6.1, with the left-hand column focusing on a critical incident that is local to the school, such as the suicide of a member of staff or a minor road traffic incident injuring a few pupils; the right-hand column considers a major incident that directly or indirectly affects the school.

Compassion fatigue in teachers

CIST members exposed to traumatic events on a regular basis need to engage in a programme of continuous development and screening, with the aim of helping the team to improve their skills in dealing with crises and creating a positive atmosphere for growth. Part of the development should be to help the CIST to increase their coping skills and strategies (Saakvitne and Pearlman, 1996). CISTs should also be aware of the signs and symptoms of burn-out, compassion fatigue and secondary trauma, which is particularly prevalent in people involved in supporting children (Meyers and Cornille, 2002). Team members should also be alert to the warning signs of compassion fatigue in others and, where necessary, have easy access to mental health interventions. It is important that the climate within the educational establishment and the CIST is receptive to the fact that compassion fatigue and secondary trauma are the hazards of supporting distressed and traumatized children, and that recognizing the signs of it is a measure of professional competence, rather than a failure or inadequacy. Unfortunately, such

Table 6.2 Key components of a critical incident response

Mitigation and prevention	Preparation or readiness	Response (crisis phase)	Recovery (post-crisis)
Disasters, natural or man-made, are unpredictable	Provide staff with the opportunity to undertake training	This period of a crisis is pivotal to the process of providing support	Schools return to the longer-term priorities, which will involve resuming familiar timetables and activities
It may not be possible to prevent them	Help them become aware of the crisis support resources	School staff and CIST assess the nature and severity of the crisis	Staff maintain vigilance over the ability of pupils and staff to recover from the trauma
Provide programmes to develop resilience, social problem solving and social connections in pupils	Enable them to become more confident in responding and more able to work with the critical incident support team	Marshall the appropriate practical and psychosocial resources	Some who have been earlier identified as requiring enhanced help may continue to need this help
Programmes are provided to e.g. reduce the likelihood of suicides	In this way they can provide better managerial and psychosocial support for their colleagues and the pupils in their school	Support coping and emotional processing	Most are now able to manage independently
These programmes help pupils and staff to be better able to cope with, respond to and recover from a traumatic event		Coordinate school and external staff	Psychological interventions may be required for some of this group and others who are newly identified

policies and frameworks are in their infancy, although they are being made explicit in some CIST team publications (Cook, 2006: North Lanarkshire Psychological Service, 2009).

Teaching is not an easy profession, and whilst most of the emphasis in this chapter has been on those teachers and other educational staff who choose to provide support for distressed and traumatized children, the normal stresses and strains of the role can be exhausting. A report on the level of sickness absence (CIPD, 2009) shows that educational sector employees take an average of 7.4 days off work sick each year, at an annual cost of £684 per employee, with stress and other mental health conditions being cited as a major cause of absence. While not all teachers see themselves as having a pastoral remit, in general, teachers and other staff who choose to work in schools do so because they want to help pupils to learn and progress. They have a fundamental bias towards understanding and meeting the academic, emotional and psychological needs of the pupils in their care. In addition, especially in the early years and in smaller specialist schools, staff work very closely with their pupils and, indeed, with their families, and begin to develop strong, personal relationships with their charges. Managers in schools feel that they have to wear the mask of the headteacher, requiring them to exude professional warmth at the same time as they are struggling with a personal or school-related crisis. Research into the impact of trauma on therapists and counsellors highlights the empathetic relationships, placing individuals at increased risk of compassion fatigue. However, unlike workers in emergency services, mental health, psychologists, counsellors and therapists, where personal supervision is a professional requirement, teachers and other school staff are unlikely to receive any training on compassion fatigue and therefore may be unaware of the warning signs, the protective actions or the services available to them. Moreover, they may not have the opportunities to develop protective coping mechanisms or the professional and social networks and supports that provide the essential emotional and psychological buttresses to help them deal with the impact of a crisis. Whilst critical incident support teams may plan post-incident debriefing and supervision for their members, it is rare for schools to provide teachers and other staff with any training in pre- or post-trauma training or support. It is important that this gap is recognized and that there is a move to extend personal trauma support to all school staff and to educate them in the importance of accepting this help.

Similarly, pupils and school staff are no different to CISTs, with some who develop feelings of guilt or shame over the way that they have behaved during the crisis. These feelings are rarely grounded in reality and are often experienced by those who were recognized to have made a major contribution during the incident, but still feel that they:

• Caused the event or made it worse by their actions or inactions.
• Are less traumatized than other people.
• Have no right to enjoy themselves, given what has happened.
• Are bad because they feel glad or relieved when someone has died after a long period of suffering.
• Need to be helped to understand and accept the 'normality' of their beliefs and help in achieving a more positive re-framing of them.

Discussion

The way schools respond to and support pupils has a major impact on how well and quickly pupils are able to adjust to the trauma, return to their studies and, more generally, return to positive functioning. The size and type of school tends to be less of an issue than the ethos and support strategies established before the crisis (McDermott, 2007). Whatever the approach and the strategies adopted, they need to be tailored to the needs of the individual pupil and school, for while the return to a normal routine has therapeutic value, if pupils believe that their distress is being minimized or they are being rushed back to school, regardless of their feelings, further distress can be caused (Dyregrov, 2004). Adolescents may be particularly reluctant to admit to having problems and accept a referral to a mental health professional, and there may be difficulties in persuading parents to engage in an educational process which will provide them with the psychosocial information and advice that would enable them to support their children. The experience of school staff working with traumatized children and staff suggests that psychosocial interventions are better provided in the community, rather than expecting pupils and their families to attend a mental health professional working in a clinic.

While most of this chapter has focused on the vulnerabilities of staff and pupils, it would be remiss to ignore initiatives aimed at developing the psychological resilience and improving the mental health and well-being of pupils. These imaginative programmes correspond to level 1 in Figure 6.1. In Scotland, the 'Curriculum for Excellence' (LTS, 2009) aims to ensure that 'our young people become successful learners, confident individuals, responsible citizens, and effective contributors'. At the same time, the Scottish Government's (2008) 'Getting It Right for Every Child' programme aims to improve collaborative working among professionals in statutory and voluntary services, to ensure that they are skilled and effective at assessing and meeting the needs of children and young people. Both programmes are involved in supporting pupils to develop greater resilience and better social problem solving skills, and to be more effectively supported and empowered by the adults working with them. If these programmes are successful, then pupils will be better prepared to deal with traumas in their lives and more ready to seek out and accept help from their peers and adults. In addition, professional staff should become more confident and effective in their ability to work with and support children and young people when a crisis occurs. The impact of trauma should become less painful and long-lasting for pupils, school staff and the critical incident support teams.

References

Campion, M. (2008) A cruise to disaster. Presentation at the When Disaster Strikes in Education Conference, Bracknell Forest, UK, November 2008.

CIPD (2009) *Absence Management: Annual Survey Report 2009*. Wimbledon, UK: CIPD.

Cook, E. (2006) *Crisis Support Worker Handbook* [internal document]. Crisis Support Team, Essex, UK.

Dalgleish, T., Meiser-Stedmand, R., Smith, P. (2005) Cognitive aspects of posttraumatic stress and their treatment in children and adolescents: an empirical review and some recommendations. *Behavioural and Cognitive Psychotherapy* 33, 459–486.

Dyregrov, A. (2004) Educational consequences of loss and trauma. *Educational and Child Psychology* 21(3), 77–84.

Galea, S., Nandi, A., Vlahov, D. (2004) The epidemiology of post-traumatic stress disorder after disasters. *Epidemiologic Reviews* 27(1), 78–91.

Greenberg, N. (2006) In conversation – TRiM. *Counselling at Work* **Summer**, 5–8.

Fazel, M., Doll, H., Stein, A. (2009) A school-based mental health intervention for refugee children: an exploratory study. *Clinical Child Psychology and Psychiatry* 14(2), 297–309.

IASC (2007) IASC guidelines on mental health and psychosocial support in emergency settings: http://www.humanitarianinfo.org/iasc [accessed 17 July 2009].

IFRC (2009) Psychosocial interventions: http://www.ifrc.org/psychosocial [accessed 17 July 2009].

Infoplease (2009) Timeline of world-wide shootings: http://www.infloplease. com/ipa/A0777985html [accessed 30 April 2009].

Jimerson, S.R., Brock, E., Pletcher, S.W. (2005) An integrated model of school preparedness and intervention. *School Psychology International* **26**(3), 275–296.

Lowe, T (2004) The impact of a school-based trauma on school staff [unpublished research].

Lowe, T. (2009a) Supporting school communities during a critical incident. Presentation at North Lanarkshire Psychological Service Meeting, The Theory and Models Underpinning the Critical Incident Response by Educational Psychologists, Coatbridge, UK, August 2009.

Lowe (2009b) Critical incident support provided by local education authorities and educational psychology services in the UK [unpublished research].

LTS (2009) Learning and Teaching Scotland: curriculum for excellence: http://www.ltscotland.org.uk/curriculumforexcellence/> [accessed 17 July 2009].

Lustig, S., Kia-Keating, M., Knight, W.G., Geltman, P., Ellis, H., Kinzie, J.D. *et al.* (2004) Review of child and adolescent refugee mental health. *Journal of American Child Adolescent Psychiatry* **43**(1), 24–36.

Massachusetts Advocates for Children (2005) Helping traumatised children learn: http://www.massadvocates.org/uploads/gg/hS/gghS4PIVtMYt7u BhJ2Embg/Help_Tram_Child-Med.pdf [accessed 22 August 2009].

McDermott, B. (2007) Child and youth post-disaster emotional responses. Paper presented at Psychosocial Response and Recovery Symposium, Brisbane, Australia: http://www.disasters-psychosocial.org.au/uploads/ Brett_McDermott.pdf [accessed 15 August 2009].

MacNeil, W., Topping, K. (2007) Crisis management in schools: evidence-based prevention. *Journal of Educational Enquiry* **7**(1), 64–94.

Meyers, T.W., Cornille, T.A. (2002) The work of working with traumatized children. In C.R. Figley (ed.), *Treating Compassion Fatigue*. New York: Brunner/Mazel.

NASP (2009) National Emergency Assistance Team (NEAT), National Association of School Psychologists: http://www.nasponline.org/ resources/crisis_safety/NEAT.aspx [accessed 25 September 2009].

NCTSN (2003) Complex trauma in children and adolescents: http:// www.nctsnet.org/nccts/asset.do?id=478 [accessed 22 April 2009].

Nickerson, A.B., Heath, M.A. (2008) Developing and strengthening school-based crisis response teams. *School Psychology Forum* **2**(2), 1–16.

North Lanarkshire Psychological Service (2009) Critical Incident Handbook [internal document].

Poland, S., McCormick, J.S. (1999) *Coping with Crisis: Lessons Learned.* Longmont, CO: Sopris West.

Renaud, E. (2008) The attachment characteristics of combat veterans with PTSD. *Traumatology* **14**(3), 1–12.

Saakvitne, K.W., Pearlman, L.A. (1996) *Transforming the Pain.* New York: W.W. Norton.

Scottish Government (2008) Getting it right for every child: http://www. scotland.gov.uk/Topics/People/Young-People/childrensservices/girfec. [accessed 15 August 2009].

Terr, L.C. (2003) Childhood traumas: an outline and overview. *Focus American Psychiatric Association* **1**(3), 322–333.

Tomlinson, P. (2004) *Therapeutic Approaches in Work with Traumatized Children and Young People: Theory and Practice (Therapeutic Communities).* London: Jessica Kingsley.

UNESCO (2009) Summary of midterm reviews of country programmes: http://www.unicef.org/about/execboard/files/E-ICEF-2009-PL25-CEE-CIS-MTR-E.pdf [accessed 26 August 2009].

UNICEF (2005) 1 year after siege, Beslan's children still need help: http://www.unicef.org/infobycountry/russia_28072.html [accessed 26 August 2009].

Yule, W., Gold, A. (1993) *Wise Before the Event: Coping with Crisis in Schools.* London: Calouste Gulbenkian Foundation.

Chapter 7

The incidence of secondary traumatic stress in workers dealing with traumatizing materials, victims and perpetrators

Noreen Tehrani

Introduction

Over the past 30 years there has been an increasing recognition that workers in the armed forces, emergency services, nursing and social work professions are expected to deal with the immediate horror of death and injury as an integral part of their work, and that as a result they can develop responses to their work, including symptoms of post-traumatic stress, major depression and anxiety (Shalev and Yehuda, 1998; Tehrani, 2004). Less well recognized is the impact of indirect exposures to death, pain and injury through supporting victims (Steed and Bicknell, 2001), reading or analysing accounts of the traumatic events (Vrklevski and Franklin, 2008) or viewing images of traumatic events (Burns *et al.*, 2008). Exposure to distressing or traumatic information in the form of pictures, films, statements or materials is challenging (Cornille and Meyers, 1999). Whilst there is evidence that many police officers, social workers, nurses and others involved in this kind of work have been found to be resilient and able to cope with the demands of their roles, some have found themselves succumbing to a range of psychological conditions, including anxiety, depression, burn-out and secondary traumatic stress (Alexander, 1999; Mitchell *et al.*, 2000). This chapter presents an analysis of a psychological assessment of 182 workers. Those assessed included crime analysts, intelligence officers and others in roles where the workers were indirectly exposed to testimony and other materials relating to child abuse, serious sexual attacks, murders and other traumatic crimes.

Secondary traumatic stress

It has been established that traumatic events not only impact on those directly involved but also affect those people who come in contact with distressed victims through being a family member, nurse, counsellor or carer (Figley, 1995). However, recently it has been recognized that similar symptoms can be found in workers with little or no direct contact with the traumatic incident or the primary trauma victim, including crime analysts (Burns *et al.*, 2008), lawyers (Vrklevski and Franklin, 2008) and insurance workers (Ludick *et al.*, 2007), where exposure to the traumatic incident or victim is only through artefacts, images, auditory records and written testimony. The development of symptoms in those directly and indirectly involved with the primary victims of trauma has been variously named as empathetic strain (Wilson and Lindy, 1994), compassion fatigue (Figley, 1995) and vicarious traumatization (Saakvitne and Pearlman, 1996). However, in this chapter the term 'secondary trauma' will be used, as it most closely describes the situation of workers who are indirectly involved in dealing with traumatic incidents. It is suggested (Wilson and Thomas, 2004) that workers develop secondary traumatic stress as a result of becoming empathetically attuned to the experiences of a trauma victim or victims through interactions with trauma material; this process is intensified when some aspect of the traumatic material has a particular meaning or resonance with the worker's own life and experiences. For example, when the name or appearance of a trauma victim is similar to that of a close friend, an emotional/cognitive link may be formed and the worker begins to experience distressing emotions, as though the trauma victim was his/her friend. Equally, where the location of the traumatic event is familiar to the worker, that knowledge of the area can place the trauma within a familiar context, allowing personal memories of the place to become entwined with the case information. This process of identification makes it difficult to separate personal experiences and feelings from those connected to the traumatic incident. Despite the lack of any direct involvement with the traumatic incident and its victims, it is possible for workers dealing with trauma cases to begin to experience symptoms similar to those found in the actual victim of trauma. These secondary trauma responses include symptoms of post-traumatic stress, together with elevated levels of anxiety and depression (Shalev and Yehuda, 1998). The pressure of working within investigatory and crime-related roles often involves high levels of demand together with a lack of control over the way that the work is undertaken. In this demanding environment, it is not unusual for senior management, the public and others to develop unrealistic expectations of what can be achieved, leading to high levels of stress and burn-out in this group of workers (Maslach and Jackson, 1981).

The assessments

The original purpose of assessing secondarily traumatized (ST) workers was to help their organisations meet their duty of care to the ST workforce by understanding the levels of pressure and strain they were facing during the course of their work. The assessments were designed to identify opportunities to increase resilience and, where necessary, provide support. Over the course of a year, the number of assessments undertaken increased, and the opportunity occurred to use the data to identify latent themes or patterns of secondary trauma within this group of workers (Hanson and Roberts, 2006). The organisations involved in this study required their workers to engage with a range of materials, including viewing images of children being sexually abused, reading and viewing testimonies relating to sexual crimes, viewing pictures of scenes of murders and post-mortems and other equally demanding aspects of crime investigations and analysis.

Included in the analysis were 192 ST workers, of whom 101 were female and 81 male, the average age of the women (34.2) being almost 10 years younger than that of the men (42.1). The men also were generally more experienced in this type of work, with 46% of men having less than 2 years experience, with the number rising to 61% for the women. The level of long-term experience also differed, with 33% of men and 13% of women having worked in this kind of work for 6 or more years.

The assessment process involved each worker completing a set of questionnaires. Included in the assessment pack was a description of the purpose of the assessment, which explained that the statistical information gained from the completed questionnaires would be used to monitor the psychological well-being of the workers and to identify ways to improve the support provided. Workers were also told that they would be given a personalized copy of their results, together with any recommendations for improving their physical and psychological health and well-being. The assessment procedure involved a structured interview, which established the workers' current state of well-being, family history, relationships, personal style, education, employment and current stresses. This was followed by a sharing of the results from the clinical and occupational questionnaires, allowing time for the workers to gain some personal insight into the nature and reasons for their responses and an opportunity to comment on the findings. Well-being information and guidance was also provided, which was tailored to the needs of the worker; however, where workers were found to be experiencing psychological difficulties, offers of counselling or other support were made.

Psychometric tools

Three clinical questionnaires were used in the study. The Goldberg short-form was used to measure the levels of anxiety and depression (Goldberg *et al.*, 1988; Gann *et al.*, 1990), the extended Impact of Events Scale (IES-E), to measure the level of traumatic stress (Tehrani *et al.*, 2002), and the Maslach Burnout Inventory (MBI; Maslach and Jackson, 1981) was used to identify symptoms of burn-out. Each psychometric tool had been chosen because it had been validated within a working population. In addition to the clinical tools, five occupational questionnaires were administered. These were chosen to reflect factors previously identified as predictors of resilience in emergency services (Paton *et al.*, 2003). The tools included a lifestyle survey, a locus of control questionnaire (Rotter, 1966), a coping skills questionnaire (Tehrani *et al.*, 2007), a measure of emotional awareness (Steiner and Perry, 1999) and the EPI, a personality test (Eysenck and Eysenck, 1987). This set of occupational tools had been used within a number of workplace settings for over 10 years (Tehrani *et al.*, 2007). The demographic data from the structured interviews and scores from the psychometric tests were input into an SPSS statistical analysis package for analysis.

Clinical questionnaires

Anxiety/depression

The Short Anxiety and Depression Questionnaire was created and validated using patients visiting a GP's practice (Goldberg *et al.*, 1988); however, when the questionnaire was revalidated using onshore and offshore workers for Shell (Gann *et al.*, 1990), it was found that the cut-off level used to predict a level where there was a 50% probability of developing a clinically significant condition was set too low. Gann and co-workers raised the cut-off level for anxiety from five to six and for depression from two to three. Tehrani *et al.* (2007) used the questionnaire with workers in the financial sector and found the cut-off level for depression was still too low. and increased the cut-off level to five.

In the assessments of the ST workers, 17% of male and 12% female workers scored 6 or more for anxiety and 16% male and 20% of female workers scored 5 or more for depression, the mean scores being 3.9 (anxiety) and 2.8 (depression) for women and 3.2 (anxiety) and 2.4 (depression) for men. These results are only slightly higher than those found in a study (Parslow *et al.*, 2004) involving 927 men and 1024 women in regular employment, where the mean scores were 3.6 (anxiety), 2.44 (depression) for female employees and 2.44 (anxiety), 2.21 (depression) for male employees.

Traumatic stress

The traumatic stress questionnaire IES-E (Tehrani *et al.*, 2002) was used to assess the level of traumatic stress experienced by postal workers being taken hostage, involved in armed raids or physically attacked. This questionnaire has been used in commercial organisations and emergency services to screen for traumatic stress (Tehrani *et al.*, 2001; Tehrani, 2008). A score of 50 on the IES-E is indicative of the presence of PTSD. Epidemiological studies (Breslau *et al.*, 2008) show the incidence of PTSD in a US population to be 11.0%. The percentage of the ST workers with IES-E scores of 50 or more was 20% males and 28% females. These levels were similar to those found in Swedish ambulance workers (Sterud *et al.*, 2006) but higher than for firefighters involved in the Oklahoma City bombings (North *et al.*, 2002), where the combined male/female scores were 21% and 13%, respectively.

Burn-out

Burnout was assessed using the Maslach Burn-out Scale (Maslach and Jackson, 1981), which involves three symptoms: emotional exhaustion (EE), depersonalization (DP) and lack of personal achievement (LPA). Maslach tested workers in a number of professions and established the following cut-off levels: EE more than

27; DP more than 13; and LPA less than 31. In the assessment of ST workers, the percentage of workers above the cut-off level was: EE 14% female and 19% male; DP 6% female and 6% male; and LPA 18% female and 19% male. A study of male and female lawyers (Jackson *et al.*, 1987) found the mean scores to be: EE 31; DP 14.4; and LPA 38. In ambulance personnel (Alexander and Klein, 2001), the mean scores were: EE 17.2; DP 8.4; and LPA 34.5. The mean scores for the ST workers were: EE 17.2 female and 16.2 male; DP 3.8 female 4.9 male; and LPA 36.0 female 37.8 male. These results indicate that the ST workers are generally not experiencing high levels of emotional exhaustion, that they have reasonably high levels of personal achievement and that they have lower levels of depersonalization than the other workers.

Occupational questionnaires

Personality

Although a number of personality variables have been identified, there is wide agreement on the importance of two personality dimensions, namely the extroversion–introversion variable and emotional stability–instability variable. Studies have shown that there were two variables accounting for most of the variance in individual behaviour (Tedeschi and Calhoun, 1996). Eysenck identified two further dimensions, psychoicism or tough-mindedness and social desirability. Table 7.1 shows the scores for the ST workers together with the norms developed by Eysenck and Eysenck (1987). The results (Table 7.1) show that the female ST workers were more extroverted than their male colleagues and that both male and female ST workers were less neurotic than the Eysenck norms, but that the females were more neurotic than the males. Both male and female ST workers had lower levels of psychoticism than anticipated by the Eysenck norms. The mean lie scale score for males was found to be higher than those of their female colleagues and similar to the Eysenck norm for females.

The analysis of variance scores between the female and male ST workers showed no significant differences between males and females apart from the neuroticism scores, where the female workers were significantly higher scoring: $F(1,125) = 6.67$ $p < 0.01$.

Table 7.1 Comparison between EPQ norms and means scores for the ST workers

Sex	Personality factor	Secondary trauma		Eysenck norms	
		Mean	SD	Mean	SD
Female	Extroversion	13.05	4.96	12.60	4.83
	Neurotic	11.17	5.51	12.74	5.20
	Psychotic	2.18	1.97	2.63	2.36
	Lie/social desirability	7.56	3.60	7.73	4.18
Male	Extroversion	12.36	5.32	13.19	4.91
	Neurotic	8.77	6.12	9.98	5.18
	Psychotic	2.36	2.13	3.78	3.09
	Lie/social desirability	7.74	3.36	6.80	4.14

Lifestyle

Maintaining a healthy lifestyle has been shown to protect workers from secondary trauma and burn-out (Yessen, 1995). The lifestyle questionnaire was scored using a three-point scale: 3, good; 2, average; and 1, poor. There were eight lifestyle items, which included eating patterns, caffeine, nicotine and alcohol consumption, levels of exercise, sleep, hobbies/interests and socializing. The maximum score on this questionnaire is 24. Individuals drinking in excess of the recommended unit levels of alcohol (NHS, 2008) were separately identified. The mean score for the workers was 18.7 (SD 2.7). It was also found that 16 men (18.5%) and 9 women (8.8%) were drinking alcohol in excess of the NHS units of alcohol limits.

Coping skills

The term 'coping' is used to describe a range of responses for dealing with everyday hassles and stressors. Much of the research into how people deal with stress has been based on the work of Folkman and Lazarus (1980). In this assessment, the coping skills questionnaires measured the usage of practical coping skills (Tehrani *et al.*, 2007). The coping skills questionnaire measures eight common coping skills: time planning; physical well-being; psychological well-being; assertiveness; social support; involvement; problem solving; and relaxation. The mean scores for 100 workers in a financial sector organisation and 20 retail managers were compared with the scores of the ST workers in Table 7.2. Scores above 10 are indicative of a reasonable level of the use of skill.

When compared with the other two groups, the ST workers appear to have a good level of coping skills; however, over 16% of ST workers were not using mental fitness coping skills and over 13% were not using relaxation as a coping technique.

Emotional awareness

The Emotional Awareness Questionnaire was developed by Steiner and Perry (1999) and adapted for use with the ST workers. Emotional literacy requires the worker to recognize, accurately translate and respond to their emotional responses. For workers involved in emotionally demanding work, gaining an understanding of their emotional experiences provides a mechanism for reducing the impact of distressing and destructive material (Damasio, 2003). The adapted Emotional Awareness Questionnaire measures seven areas of emotional awareness: *dissociation* involves the creation of a protective barrier between ST worker and the person or material they are handling; *primary physical awareness* involves the awareness of a physical reaction a worker has to a person or material; and the *primary emotional response* is a feeling or hunch which attracts the worker's attention without being fully understood; *sensory awareness* is the recognition and ability to describe an emotional response; *empathy* is the sharing of emotional responses experienced by others; *interpersonal sensitivity* is the ability to anticipate how one's own emotional states may interact with that of others; and *emotional resilience* is an ability to continue working or operating in difficult or demanding situations without becoming distressed. The maximum score for each of the emotional awareness levels is 6. Table 7.3 shows the mean scores for male and female ST workers.

The results of the ANOVA showed that men were significantly more dissociated [$F(1,125) = 16.13 < 0.001$] and emotionally resilient ($3.9 < 0.5$) than women. However, women are more aware of their emotions [$F(1,125) = 6.22 < 0.014$] and empathetic ($8.78 < 0.004$) than men. Inspection of the means showed that neither group was particularly aware of primary physical or emotional responses.

Table 7.2 Comparison between levels of coping skills for finance sector employees and ST workers

Coping skill	Retail workers (n = 20)		Finance workers (n = 173)		ST workers (n = 182)		Scores (%) > 5
	Mean	SD	Mean	SD	Mean	SD	
Time planning	10.27	3.319	10.80	4.841	12.53	4.271	8.9
Physical fitness	9.55	4.009	9.37	4.871	11.34	4.827	6.7
Mental fitness	10.27	2.054	8.38	4.109	10.13	4.484	16.7
Assertiveness	12.36	4.739	10.02	4.738	11.91	4.435	8.9
Social support	11.91	4.505	11.22	5.233	12.46	5.232	9.4
Involvement	13.55	5.241	9.15	4.756	11.44	4.129	8.3
Problem solving	13.82	3.545	10.73	5.046	13.10	4.556	5.6
Relaxation	10.27	3.319	8.06	4.143	9.94	3.791	13.3

Table 7.3 Comparison of male and female mean scores for emotional awareness

Emotional awareness	Female (n = 69)		Male (n = 58)		ANOVA	
	Mean	SD	Mean	SD	F	p
Dissociation	2.57	1.57	3.66	1.47	16.13	0.000
Primary physical	1.49	1.51	1.00	1.16	4.14	0.044
Primary emotional	1.58	1.89	1.40	1.36	0.38	0.530
Sensory awareness	4.62	1.07	4.14	1.12	6.22	0.014
Empathy	3.57	1.44	2.88	1.11	8.78	0.004
Interpersonal sensitivity	4.43	1.36	4.38	1.39	0.05	0.941
Emotional resilience	4.14	1.54	4.67	1.46	3.90	0.051

Factor analysis

Whilst the data gathered provide some insight into the nature of responses experienced by ST workers, they are not easy to understand. It was therefore decided to reduce the data by undertaking an exploratory factor analysis, from which an underlying coherent model of secondary trauma responses might emerge (Tabachnick and Fidell, 1996). The pre-analysis checks on the number of subjects and the nature and number of variables indicated that the data gathered in the assessments were suitable for exploratory factor analysis (Ferguson and Cox, 1993). Factors with eigenvalues greater than 1 were extracted from the correlation matrix using principle component analysis and varimax rotation. Six factors emerged which accounted for 62.87% of the variance. The six factors were inspected and, following consultation, the following names emerged: secondary trauma, personal well-being, healthy living, task focus, burn-out and engaged. These factors are illustrated, together with their components, in Table 7.4.

Discussion

The analysis of the results of the assessment of the ST workers has its limitations; it only provides a snapshot of the well-being of the workers, it was only possible to undertake an exploratory factor analysis and these findings need to be confirmed with another group of workers. However, the results do raise a number of new questions, some of which are identified below. Some of the findings were surprising: based on previous research, it had been expected to

Table 7.4 Factors relating to the assessment of workers dealing with secondary trauma

Factors	Eigenvalue	Variance (%)	Components – assessment results
1. Secondary trauma	6.776	28.23	Anxiety, depression, trauma, neurosis, primary physical awareness, primary emotional awareness, low emotional resilience, and younger age
2. Personal well-being	2.286	9.53	Personal achievement, mental fitness, assertiveness, social support, involvement
3. Healthy living	1.896	7.90	Lifestyle, physical fitness, relaxation
4. Task-focused	1.485	6.19	Internal locus of control, time planning, problem solving
5. Burn-out	1.423	5.93	Emotional exhaustion, depersonalization
6. Engagement	1.222	5.09	Empathy, interpersonal sensitivity, extroversion

find ST workers to be more anxious, depressed and suffering from burn-out than other workers. Whilst, as anticipated, it was found that ST workers had similar levels of traumatic stress to those found in firefighters, the levels of anxiety and depression were similar to those found in non-trauma-related jobs. The results relating to burn-out were also rather unexpected and, despite around one-fifth of ST workers experiencing emotional exhaustion and low personal achievement, only 6% had elevated levels of depersonalization, which suggests that the ST workers are able to maintain their emotional connection with primary trauma victims. On the other hand, the scores for dissociation showed that dissociation was being used significantly more by males than by females in order to deal with distressing material. This finding raised an issue regarding the cognitive structures underpinning what, on the surface, may appear very similar constructs. Is it possible that depersonalization is a sign that a worker is failing to cope with his/her work, whilst dissociation is being used as a coping technique? It was interesting to note that, in the six factors emerging from the exploratory factor analysis, dissociation did not appear to be associated with any of the other components, including depersonalization. The finding that primary physical and emotional awareness were associated with secondary trauma was also interesting. It had been noticed during the assessments that the workers who scored most highly on these dimensions were able to describe in detail the changes that took place in their bodies when they were dealing with distressing material. Inspection of the data also showed a high correlation between neuroticism and the two primary awareness symptoms ($p < 001$), suggesting that there may be a link between neuroticism, hypervigilance and reactivity to the psychophysical signs of distress. The factor analysis also confirmed the findings of Adams *et al.* (2006) by showing secondary traumatic stress and burn-out to be separate factors; however, the personal achievement element of burn-out was not correlated with the symptoms of emotional exhaustion and depersonalization, moving to be part of a personal well-being factor which included mental fitness, assertiveness, social support and involvement.

The assessment of the ST workers has provided an opportunity to consider the impact of working with traumatizing material; however, there is a need for further exploration to examine some of the issues which arise. For example, what is the benefit of recognizing early physical or emotional responses to traumatic material? Does dissociation prevent investigators and analysts from noticing subtle trauma-related evidence? Is there a way to identify the most appropriate coping skills for individual workers? Is it possible to develop an organisational culture which promotes post-trauma growth?

References

Adams, R.E., Boscarino, J.A., Figley, C.R. (2006) Compassion fatigue and psychological distress among social workers: a validation study. *American Journal of Orthopsychiatry* **76**(1), 103–108.

Alexander, C. (1999) Police psychological burnout and trauma. In Violanti, J.M., Paton, D. (eds), *Police Trauma*. Springfield, IL: Charles C. Thomas.

Alexander, D.A., Klein, S. (2001) Ambulance personnel and critical incidents – impact of accident and emergency work on mental health and emotional wellbeing. *British Journal of Psychiatry* **178**, 76–81.

Breslau, N., Peterson, E.L., Schultz, L.R. (2008) A second look at prior trauma and the posttraumatic stress disorder effects of subsequent trauma. *Archives of General Psychiatry* **65**(4), 431–437.

Burns, C.M., Morley, J., Bradshaw, R., Domene, J. (2008) The emotional impact on and coping strategies employed by police teams investigating internet child exploitation. *Traumatology* **14**, 20–31.

Cornille, T.A., Meyers, T.W. (1999) Secondary traumatic stress among child protection service workers: prevalence, severity and predictive factors. *Traumatology* **5**(1), 15–31.

Damasio, A. (2003) *Looking for Spinoza – Joy, Sorrow and the Feeling Brain.* London: Heinemann.

Eysenck, H.J., Eysenck, S.B.G. (1987) *Manual of Eysenck Personality Questionnaire.* Sevenoaks, UK: Hodder and Stoughton.

Ferguson, E., Cox, T. (1993) Exploratory factor analysis: a user's guide. *International Journal of Selection and Assessment* **1**(2), 84–94.

Figley, C.R. (1995) *Compassion Fatigue: Coping with Secondary Traumatic Stress Disorder in Those Who Treat the Traumatised.* New York: Brunner Routledge.

Folkman S., Lazarus, R.S. (1980) An analysis of coping in a middle-aged community sample. *Journal of Health and Social Behaviour* **21**, 219–239.

Gann, M., Corpe, U., Wilson, I. (1990) The application of a short anxiety and depression questionnaire to oil industry staff. *Journal of the Society of Occupational Health* **40**, 138–142.

Goldberg, D., Bridges, K., Duncan-Jones, P., Grayson, D. (1988) *British Medical Journal* **297**, 897–899.

Hanson, R.K., Roberts, J.K. (2006) Use of exploratory factor analysis in published research – common errors and some comment on improved practice. *Educational and Psychological Measurement* **66**(3), 393–416.

Jackson, S.E., Turner, J.A., Brief, A.P. (1987) Correlates of burnout among public service lawyers. *Journal of Occupational Behaviour* **8**, 339–349.

Ludick, M., Alexander, D., Carmichael, T. (2007) Vicarious traumatisation: secondary traumatic stress levels in claims workers in the short-term insurance industry in South Africa. *Problems and Perspectives in Management* **5**(3), 99–109.

Maslach, C., Jackson, S.E. (1981) The measurement of experienced burnout. *Journal of Occupational Behaviour* **2**(99), 99–113.

Mitchell, M., Stevenson, K., Poole, D. (2000) *Managing Post-incident Reactions in the Police Service.* Sudbury, UK: HSE Books.

NHS (2008) Know your limits: http://units.nhs.uk/index.php [accessed 12 July 2009].

North, C.S., Tivis, L., McMillen, J.C., Pfefferbaum, B., Cox, J., Spitznagel, E.L. *et al.* (2002) Coping, functioning, and adjustment of rescue workers after the Oklahoma City bombing. *Journal of Traumatic Stress* **15**(3), 171–175.

Parslow, R.A., Jorm, A.F., Christensen, H., Rogers, B., Strazdins, L., D'Souza, R.M. (2004) The association between work stress and mental health: a comparison of organizationally employed and self-employed workers. *Work and Stress* **18**(3), 231–244.

Paton, D., Violanti, J.M., Smith, L.M. (2003) Posttraumatic psychological stress: individual, group and organizational perspectives on resilience and growth. In Paton, D., Violanti, J.M., Smith, L.M. (eds), *Promoting Capabilities to Manage Posttraumatic Stress – Perspectives on Resilience.* Springfield, IL: Charles C. Thomas.

Rotter, J. (1966) Generalized expectancies for internal versus external control of reinforcements. *Psychological Monographs* **80** (609).

Saakvitne, K.W., Pearlman, L.A. (1996) *Transforming the Pain – A Workbook on Vicarious Traumatisation.* New York: W.W. Norton.

Shalev, A.Y., Yehuda, R. (1998) Longitudinal development of traumatic stress disorders. In Yehuda, R. (ed.), *Psychological Trauma.* Washington, DC: American Psychological Association.

Steed, L., Bicknell, J. (2001) Trauma and the therapist: the experience of therapists working with perpetrators of sexual abuse. *Australian Journal of Disaster Studies* 2002(1): http//www.massey.ac.nz./~Trauma/issues/ 2001–1/steed [accessed 20 October 2009].

Steiner, C., Perry, P. (1999) *Achieving Emotional Literacy.* London: Bloomsbury.

Sterud, T., Ekeberg, O., Hem, E. (2006) Health status in the ambulance services: a systematic review. *BioMed Central Health Services Research* **6**(82): http//www.biomedcentral.com/1472–6963/6/82 [accessed 20 October 2009].

Tabachnick, B.G., Fidell, L.S. (1996) *Using Multivariate Statistics.* New York: Harper Collins.

Tedeschi, R.G., Calhoun, L.G. (1996) The Posttrauma Growth Inventory: measuring the positive legacy of trauma. *Journal of Traumatic Stress* **9**, 455–471.

Tehrani, N., Walpole, O., Berriman, J., Reilly, J. (2001) A special courage: Dealing with the Paddington rail crash – *Occupational Medicine* **5**(2), 93–99.

Tehrani, N. (2004) *Workplace Trauma – Concepts, Assessment and Interventions.* London: Brunner Routledge.

Tehrani, N. (2008) Trauma support for emergency services. *Crisis Response* **4**(3), 42–43.

Tehrani, N., Cox, S.J., Cox, T. (2002) Assessing the impact of stressful incidents in organizations: the development of an extended impact of events scale. *Counselling Psychology Quarterly* **15**(2), 191–200.

Tehrani, N., MacIntyre, B., Maddock, S., Shaw, R., Illingworth, R. (2007) Rehabilitation: maintaining a healthy workforce. In Houdmont, J., McIntyre, S. (eds), *Occupational Health Psychology – European Perspectives on Research, Education and Practice.* Castlo da Maia: ISMAI.

Vrklevski, L.P., Franklin, J. (2008) Vicarious trauma: the impact on solicitors of exposure to traumatic material. *Traumatology* **14**, 106–118.

Wilson, J., Lindy, J. (1994) *Countertransference in the Treatment of PTSD*. New York: Guilford.

Wilson, J.P., Thomas, R.B. (2004) *Empathy in the Treatment of Trauma and PTSD*. London: Routledge.

Yessen, J. (1995) Preventing secondary traumatic stress disorder. In Figley, C.R. (ed.), *Compassion Fatigue: Secondary Traumatic Stress Disorder from Treating the Traumatized*. New York: Brunner Mazel.

Part II

Traumatized organisations and business continuity

Chapter 8

The impact of trauma within organisations

Susan Klein and David Alexander

Introduction

Viewed from the perspective of the individual employee, work-related crises can have serious consequences. Work plays a major role in our lives. Not only is it an essential source of income, but work shapes our personal development and identity. Also, Tapsell and Tunstall (2008) remind us that, in relation to their place of employment, people display a sense of place which is infused with personal meaning and belonging.

There are three good reasons why employers should seek to mitigate the adverse effects of traumatic events in the workplace. First, there is the obvious humanitarian reason, reflecting a concern for fellow human beings. Second, a workforce that feels secure and well catered for is likely to be more productive. Third, there are inescapable legal requirements. Employers have a duty of care, which is enshrined in both common and statute law. This responsibility can be discharged through the provision of appropriate training, risk assessment, safety procedures, audit and monitoring and suitable post-incident systems of welfare and support. The costs of such preparation can easily be justified against the potential costs an injured or distressed employee may exact through a successful compensation claim, and through the premature loss of expensively trained personnel.

A traumatic experience is one that overwhelms or threatens to overwhelm the capacity of an individual, organisation or community to cope. Common features include: threat to life and/or limb; exposure to horrifying sights and other sensory stimuli; various kinds of profound loss, including fatalities; systemic disruption to communication, transport and public utilities; and social dislocation.

Major disasters, triggered by natural and/or human causes, are becoming more common, and their effects are more extensive. Sundnes and Birnbaum (2003) calculated that, between 1951 and 2000, there had been 7312 catastrophes, resulting in over nine million fatalities and occasioning $961 895 000-worth of damage. Moreover, their legacy in terms of human suffering has been incalculable. Trauma comes in many guises. Some events are largely restricted in their effects on the individual, whereas others impact whole communities and even countries. Some events are man-made, including criminal acts and terrorism, as well as technological accidents; others are natural, such as floods and earthquakes. This latter distinction between natural and man-made is not, however, on careful examination, quite so sharp. For example, generally speaking, earthquakes do not kill people; poorly designed and constructed buildings do. Also, if phenomena such as tsunamis and flooding are attributable to global warming, which in turn relates to man's behaviour, then the extent to which these events are wholly natural is questionable. Cultural influences may also determine the subjective meaning of a trauma. The authors noted that, after the Pakistan earthquake of 2005, many of the victims were informed by the imams that the so-called 'natural event' was indeed man-made, due to the failure of the locals to adhere sufficiently to the Muslim code of that region.

Events such as transportation accidents are described as 'big bang' disasters, which allow little time for preparation due to their suddenness and unexpectedness. Other events, such as pandemics, are referred to as 'rising tide' events because of their slower evolution and progressive effects. Whilst the effects of these two broad categories overlap, there are some differences between them. The effects of flooding can be long-term, due to sewage contamination and the displacement of persons. There may also be considerable anger due to (alleged) inadequate preventative measures by the authorities (Tapsell and Tunstall, 2008).

A pandemic will impose special demands on NHS staff and will require best practice guidance, according to the Department of Health (2009a). There will be a need to sustain the resilience of staff, as they will have to deal with extreme stressors, relating not only to their patients but also to their own health and that of their families. Other rising tide events, which caused massive economic as well as personal physical and emotional ill-health, were the outbreaks of bovine spongiform encephalopathy (Peck, 2005).

These typologies do not do justice to the variety of adverse experiences to which an employee might be subject as a consequence of one single event. For example, Alexander (1991) described the range of experiences endured by the men who survived the *Piper Alpha* oil platform disaster in 1988. These experiences included: fire; explosion; toxic fumes; exposure to death and mutilation; threat to life and limb; helplessness (due to the loss of firefighting and communication systems); a lack of rescue craft and helicopters; and inadequate evacuation procedures and medical facilities. In relation, therefore, to any work-related trauma, careful analysis is required to identify the full scale of the employee's experience. This assessment should include how the organisation and its members react to the event. The second author noted how one of his patients, who had suffered the traumatic amputation of his fingers, was subjected to further trauma when one of his colleagues proceeded to hose away the blood and the remnants of his fingers down a sluice.

In the workplace, trauma may not just refer to adverse events unexpectedly visited upon an unsuspecting employee. Some workers have a responsibility to deal with the traumatic events endured by others. This is true, for example, of rescue and emergency services, healthcare services, the military and those who provide humanitarian aid. The impact of their work will be principally addressed in other chapters of this book.

Aims

This chapter will address:

• Normal reactions to trauma.
• The prevalence of post-traumatic psychopathology.
• At-risk factors of adverse reactions to trauma.
• Children and young persons.
• The effects of terrorism (including chemical, biological, radiological and nuclear agents).
• The role of the media.
• Crisis preparation and interventions.

Normal reactions to trauma

Janoff-Bulman (1992) conceptualized trauma as a challenge to three basic precepts of living:

1   The world is essentially a good place.
2   Individuals are worthy and valuable.
3   Life events are meaningful and purposeful.

A catastrophic event compromises our faith in the validity of these assumptions and this effect, in turn, has a pervasive and pernicious impact on many aspects of our lives and functioning. The miscellany of normal reactions to trauma has been widely documented elsewhere (e.g. Alexander, 2005). Figure 8.1 classifies these under four subheadings: emotional, cognitive, social and physical.

Employers and employees should also be aware of how groups and communities react after traumatic incidents. It is worth considering employees of an organisation as representing a community, in view of the shared values, ideals and the dynamics which prevail among them. Tyhurst (1951) identified three typical phases of community responses to trauma. The first phase, the *impact* phase, is initiated by the onset of the trauma and remits when that stressor is removed or significantly diminished. About 15% of those involved during this phase will be able to think rationally and constructively. On the other hand, about three-quarters of those exposed are likely

Emotional	**Physical**
➤ Shock, numbness, denial ➤ Fear, anxiety ➤ Survivor guilt (at surviving an event in which others perished) ➤ Performance guilt (the belief that one did not do well enough to help others) ➤ Helplessness and hopelessness ➤ Anger (directed in many directions, including at helpers)	➤ Hyperarousal (e.g. exaggerated startle response) ➤ Insomnia ➤ Inability to relax ➤ Loss of appetite ➤ Physical complaints (often vague and diffuse) ➤ Lack of energy and drive
Cognitive	**Social**
➤ Dissociation ➤ Confusion ➤ Impaired memory and concentration ➤ Reduced self-esteem ➤ Hypervigilance (exaggerated sense of risk) ➤ False attributions (e.g. blaming all subsequent failures in life on the trauma) ➤ Flashbacks and unbidden memories of the trauma	➤ Withdrawal (even from sources of support) ➤ Irritability ➤ Loss of trust in others ➤ Avoidance of reminders of the trauma

Figure 8.1 Normal reactions to trauma.

to be stunned and numbed. The remainder are likely to be paralysed by fear, anxiety and confusion. The *recoil* phase is defined as beginning when the group escapes from the trauma, at which time they are likely to want to engage with others and to talk about what they have been through. The final phase, the *post-trauma* phase, is characterized by the awareness among the community of what they have endured and lost and are likely to have to face in the future. This phase can also be associated with disillusionment and disappointment, due to failed promises of help, and by other stressors, including continued intrusions from the media and by extended legal procedures.

Some readers may be surprised that no mention has been made of panic. Despite the popular images portrayed by the media of panicking crowds, this is not a common reaction (Durodié and Wessely, 2002). Self-control, altruism and adaptive behaviour are more typical than is panic. Subsequent events, such as the London terrorist bombings (Rubin *et al.*, 2008) and the attacks on the World Trade Center (Dwyer and Flynn, 2005), confirm their view.

Panic is a self-interested response and is most likely to occur when individuals feel completely trapped, when there is no firm leadership and when help is on a first come–first served basis. This does raise the question of how groups might respond to a terrorist attack using chemical, biological, radiological or nuclear (CBRN) agents. One important corollary of the fact that panic is not a common reaction is that employers and authorities can entrust the general population with accurate and prompt information about the trauma.

The ripple effect

A trauma can create effects well beyond those on the primary victim. It is possible to identify at least six different groups of victims (Taylor and Frazer, 1982). Their classification of victims is provided below:

- *Primary victims* – those at the very heart of the trauma.
- *Secondary victims*, e.g. family and friends of the primary victim.
- *Third-level victims*, e.g. emergency, rescue and other responders.
- *Fourth-level victims*, e.g. members of the workforce or community who offer to help.
- *Fifth-level victims*, e.g. those indirectly involved.
- *Sixth-level victims*, e.g. those who might have been directly involved but for some reason were not.

A recent incident in Aberdeen demonstrated the scale of this effect. One morning, a young worker was dragged through some machinery. Others desperately tried to release him and to stop the equipment. They failed, however, to do so, and they subsequently experienced performance guilt. Others who rushed to the scene were met with body parts distributed through the machinery. The manager, summoned to the incident, experienced helplessness and horror. Similarly, a young police officer who was the first responder was markedly distressed. The young worker had been a temporary colleague standing in for a colleague on leave. The latter felt bad and experienced survivor's guilt. In addition to those who were affected at the scene, there was also the suffering and distress of the bereaved wife and two children.

Bereavement

Survivors of trauma have to cope not only with the direct effects of the catastrophic event but also the effects of any traumatic loss, including that of a colleague or loved one. Whilst most individuals cope successfully with grief without professional help, a number of individuals do require special assistance because their reactions are particularly severe, prolonged or delayed. Prognostic factors for these pathological grief reactions have been well defined by Parkes (1985), and are listed in Figure 8.2.

Grief reactions can adversely affect most domains of life, including the ability to work. Work performance may be compromised by impaired memory and concentration, avoidance of the site of the work-related trauma, and low mood and tearfulness. After about 6 months, most normal reactions have remitted considerably but, particularly in the case of traumatic death, it can take 4 or more years before a reasonable level of adjustment is achieved. Employers should be alert to the anniversary reaction, which happens about a

Type of death	Type of relationship	Type of bereaved person
Sudden, unexpected	Volatile (i.e. 'love/hate')	Insecure, anxious
Mutilation	Highly dependent	Psychiatric history
No body available		Lack of experience of loss
'Mysterious'		Unresolved previous losses
		Lack of support
		Current life problems

Figure 8.2 Poor prognostic indicators following loss by death.

year post-trauma and often triggers a resurgence of acute grief reactions. In terms of how employers should react to the bereaved, it is advisable to: avoid clichés and platitudes (e.g. 'he's had a good innings'); tolerate their apparent lack of appreciation and courtesy; listen (rather than talk at); and provide reassurance that the reactions are normal. If the employer has to give important information to the bereaved employee, the information should be brief and simple, in order that it can be remembered by someone who is probably suffering from impaired memory and concentration. It may be helpful also to write down essential information and provide an appropriate contact number. In a multicultural society, moreover, cultural and religious differences with regard to attitudes to death, grieving practices and burial rituals must be taken into account by employers.

Post-traumatic psychopathology

Although most individuals come through traumatic events without developing a post-traumatic psychiatric disorder, there is a significant number whose reactions merit professional help.

This section will consider the following International Classification of Diseases (ICD-10; WHO, 1992) psychiatric conditions: an acute stress reaction; post-traumatic stress disorder; adjustment disorders; and enduring personality change after a catastrophic experience. Epidemiological data are available in Perkönnig et al. (2000) and Fairbank et al. (2000). Caution should be exercised in comparing the results from different epidemiological studies because investigators may have used different diagnostic criteria, samples and time frames (Klein and Alexander, 2009).

Acute stress reaction (ASR)

This is short-lived disorder following exceptional mental and/or physical stress. It should endure no more than a few hours or days on removal from the stressful situation. The condition is associated with shock, a constricted field of consciousness and attention, and a fluctuating miscellany of symptoms, including depression, anxiety, withdrawal, agitation and autonomic hyperreactivity.

Post-traumatic stress disorder (PTSD)

When first introduced into the *APA Diagnostic and Statistical Manual* (DSM-III) in 1980, this diagnosis introduced a degree of order over a burgeoning list of trauma-related diagnoses; it legitimized suffering by attributing the reactions to the external event rather than by blaming a weak individual, and stimulated valuable research. However, there are problems with the diagnosis.

According to the ICD-10, to merit this diagnosis the individual has to have been subjected to a stressful event or situation (either short- or long-lasting) of an exceptionally catastrophic nature, which is likely to cause pervasive distress in almost anyone. Unfortunately, this so-called stressor criterion is not the same as that which is required in the diagnosis of PTSD according to the DSM-IV. As a consequence, and confusingly, there is only about a 30% concordance between the two taxonomies. Patients can legitimately have PTSD according to the ICD-10 but not according to the DSM-IV (the diagnostic criteria of the DSM-IV are more stringent). However, at least with both taxonomies there is an agreement that the symptoms must have endured for about a month before a definitive diagnosis can be made. This is because the core symptoms of PTSD (according to the DSM-IV and the ICD-10) are quite normal in the short-term, namely, re-experiencing phenomena (such as flashbacks), avoidant behaviour and hyperarousal (usually accompanied by hypervigilance). The guidelines of the National Institute for Clinical Excellence (NICE, 2005) refer to a month as a period of watchful waiting, in an effort to ensure that normal reactions are not inappropriately medicalized and that professional interventions are not initiated such that they might compromise the normal healing and recovery processes of the individual and the community.

Flashbacks are vivid and dramatic replays of the trauma and occasion the same kind of distress experienced at the time of the trauma. They are most often visual, but they may also be auditory, olfactory or even kinaesthetic. Avoidant behaviour manifests itself in many ways, including by avoiding the scene of the trauma and anybody associated with it, and even by not talking and/or reading about the event. Hyperarousal means that the person overreacts to sudden and unexpected noises and other stimuli. It is commonly associated with hypervigilance, which is an exaggerated sense of being at risk of further trauma.

PTSD varies in prevalence after different kinds of trauma, but it is important to note that it is less likely to occur as a single diagnosis. Depression is likely to accompany PTSD in about 50% of cases; anxiety (generalized and phobic) is very commonly associated with PTSD, and alcohol and/or substance misuse is co-morbid with PTSD in about 50% of males and in about 30% of females with PTSD (Klein and Alexander, 2009). It is very important that there is not an undue focus on PTSD, such that other important and treatable conditions are under-diagnosed and therefore not treated.

PTSD is generally more severe after man-made trauma, terrorist incidents in particular. It also has the propensity to become chronic after major catastrophe. A 10 year follow-up of the survivors of the *Piper Alpha* oil platform disaster established that 21% still had the symptoms of PTSD (Hull *et al.*, 2002). It should also be noted that chronic pain, circulatory and musculoskeletal symptoms are also likely to be reported by PTSD patients.

Adjustment disorders (AD)

As defined in the ICD-10, these are:

States of subjective distress and emotional disturbance, usually interfering with social functioning and performance, and arising in the period of adaptation to a significant life change or to the consequence of a stressful life event.

Anxiety and depression are the two most dominant emotional themes. ADs should remit within about 6 months, or 2 years in the case of a depressive one.

Enduring personality change after a catastrophic experience (EPC)

This is a severe, chronic disorder which follows a very traumatic experience, including being taken hostage, being tortured and being a prisoner of war. The features are:

- A hostile and distrustful attitude.
- Social withdrawal.
- Feelings of helplessness and hopelessness.
- A chronic sense of being on edge.
- Estrangement.

At-risk factors

Since not all individuals develop a diagnosable post-traumatic condition, the question arises as to why some individuals do and others do not go on to suffer a particular condition. This question cannot be answered with reference only to a simple, reductionist model based on the severity and/or nature of the trauma. Even more sophisticated models, involving cognitive/informational, biological or conditional factors do not generate an adequate answer. Brewin *et al.* (2000) have conducted a meta-analysis to identify the weighted contribution of pre-traumatic, peri-traumatic and post-traumatic factors to the diagnosis of PTSD. Generally, post-traumatic factors, such as a lack of support, tend to be more powerful in their predictive value, but none has an impressive predictive validity.

Unfortunately, there is no single screening measure of sufficient specificity and sensitivity to enable us to screen out employees who may be vulnerable to adverse reactions to trauma, although Brewin and his colleagues have used, with some success, a screen-and-treat model following the London bombings (Brewin *et al.*, 2008).

Some general guidance with regard to at-risk factors for PTSD are as follows:

- Genetic predisposition.
- Personal/familial history of mental illness (including substance misuse).
- Female gender (although the results are not always consistent).
- Childhood sexual abuse.
- Younger age.
- Lower socio-economic and educational level.
- Previous trauma (including bereavement).
- Severity of trauma and proximity to it.
- Concurrent life stresses.

The last item may have a complex relationship with the most recent trauma. For some individuals it may have an inoculating effect; for others there may be a cumulative effect. Perhaps the key issue is whether or not the individual believes that he/she has coped successfully with the earlier event(s). In their study of paramedics in Scotland, Alexander and Klein (2001) noted that there was not a simple linear positive correlation between dealing with previous traumatic work-related incidents and perceived competence in dealing with them. Indeed, for about 10% of individuals, whilst there was initially improvement with increased experience, further exposure led to a decline in their competence and confidence.

Raphael (2008) has proposed a systemic approach with regard to which factors are likely to be protective and which are likely to be injurious to the individual's mental health in relation to trauma:

Protective factors:

- Compassionate and effective leadership.
- Formal planning and preparation for an emergency response.
- An informed and flexible approach to external factors involved in the emergency and its aftermath.

Injurious factors:

- A lack of clear command and decision-making.
- Bullying and negative management strategies.
- Blame and scapegoating.
- A lack of appreciation of workers, except in commercial terms.

Children and young persons

Teachers and others who are involved with children and young persons in the workplace should be familiar with how individuals in these age groups react to trauma. As Williams *et al.* (2008) report, children are both resilient and vulnerable. Their recovery trajectory will reflect their stage of development, availability of support, the scale of disruption around them, including deaths of family, friends and teachers, whether or not they are displaced from their schools, homes and communities, and pre-existing family psychopathology.

Children and young persons are not just 'little adults', and whilst they display some similar post-traumatic reactions as adults, they are not identical. For example, children show less numbing and may act out their distress through play. The younger ones show more overt aggression, destructiveness and repetitive play. Pre-school children may regress to earlier stages of development, and will often respond in accordance with their parents' responses. Some children may withhold their own emotional expressions to protect their parents. On the other hand, school-age children may withdraw from teachers and parents and display a preoccupation with death. Self-limiting physical complaints, such as head and stomach aches and dizziness, may be reported. A disconcerting observation is that of a significantly increased prevalence of alcohol and substance misuse after trauma by young persons with PTSD (Reed *et al.*, 2007).

Occasionally, children and young persons may be exposed to extreme violence, as occurred at the Dunblane school in Scotland and at the Virginia Polytechnic Institute and State University and the Columbine High School in the USA. In such cases, teachers have a need to deal with individuals' sense of violation of safety. Experts such as Raphael (2008) recommend a rapid return to the institution after any trauma, as this has a normalizing effect and enables survivors to be with their peers.

The personal observations of the first author, after the Sri Lankan tsunami, suggest that schools should not be used as temporary mortuaries after major calamity, and that the issue of new school uniforms helps to raise morale.

Terrorism

Unfortunately, there is no single satisfactory definition of terrorism. However, most emphasize the unlawful use of violence against civilian populations to instil terror in an effort to achieve some political and/or religious goal. The creation of terror is of course *sine qua non*, as terrorism is psychological warfare.

More specifically, the aims of terrorists are to:

- Create mass anxiety, fear and panic.
- Create helplessness and hopelessness.
- Destroy assumptions about personal safety.
- Disrupt various elements of the infrastructure of the community or workplace.
- Demonstrate the incompetence of the authorities to protect its citizens.
- Encourage the authorities to overreact through, for example, repressive legislation and excessive security.

Although terrorists rarely achieve their longer-term goals, employers need to be prepared, but not at the cost of creating unnecessary alarm and creating a fortress mentality. Similarly, preparatory measures must not be at the expense of all other legitimate priorities and responsibilities to the workforce. Other dilemmas facing employers are how to create vigilance without siring xenophobia and paranoia, and how to maintain a high level of security without compromising civil and personal liberties.

Certain trades, industries and businesses are particularly vulnerable to the effects of terrorism, as was shown by the large percentage of Americans who refused to travel abroad after the destruction of the World Trade Center and by the massive loss to the tourist industry after the bombings at hotels in Bali and Pakistan.

It has also been shown above that terrorist acts tend to generate higher levels of psychopathology than other trauma. Also, there may be increased consumption of cigarettes and alcohol, as there was after the Oklahoma bombing.

Chemical, biological, radiological and nuclear (CBRN) threats

According to the authorities, it is a matter of when and not if with regard to terrorists using one of these agents. Probably the least likely agent to be used is nuclear, but the other agents are reasonably accessible and have certain advantages. Alexander and Klein (2006) have outlined their key advantages. Most agents cannot be detected by the human senses, creating vestigial fears of the unknown and unpredictable. Also, there would be an initial uncertainty as to which specific agent or agents had been deployed. Lastly, there would be no clearly defined local point from which it could be assumed that the situation would improve. From an employer's point of view, some steps taken by the authorities post-incident could serve as major impediments to the workforce. Employers and their employees would have to contend with contaminated buildings being cleaned, barrier environments and quarantine. Contaminated individuals may develop a sense of being stigmatized. Decontamination may be associated with a lack of attention to privacy and modesty, as was reported after the sarin attack on the Tokyo underground by the Aum Shinrikyo cult.

Children would be particularly vulnerable to some agents because of their higher respiratory rate and greater skin:surface mass ratio (Alexander and Klein, 2006).

Although no Western country has been subjected to a CBRN attack, we can learn from industrial accidents, such as the meltdown of the Chernobyl nuclear plant, the radiological contamination incident in Goiânia, Brazil, and the anthrax scares which followed the attacks on the World Trade Center in 2001. From all of these incidents, as well as the aforementioned sarin attack by the Japanese cult, it is known that for every contaminated person there will be many who fear that they have been contaminated and will seek medical attention. In the case of the last incident, the ratio of affected to not affected (but feared they were) was 1:450. After the Brazilian event, 125 800 persons were screened but only 249 were found to be contaminated. Despite the fact that they were not contaminated, thousands presented with vomiting, diarrhoea and rashes – all signs consistent with acute radiation sickness.

Bartholomew and Wessely (2002) have written extensively about mass psychogenic illness (MPI), in which individuals genuinely believe they have been stricken with some condition, manifest many of its signs and seek medical help. Employers and the authorities will have to cater for this widely reported phenomenon. It will be unhelpful to dismiss their concerns as merely those of the 'worried well'. Engel et al. (2002) have also advised against dismissing these concerns, as this is likely only to raise suspicions about a conspiracy or about an uncaring employer. Such dismissal might also encourage the employees to redouble their efforts to persuade others of the genuineness of their symptoms (Hadler, 1996).

Media

The media can also influence how individuals and organisations react to traumatic events. They can perpetuate some of the unhelpful myths about disasters, including that looting and panic are common after disasters and that disasters affect everybody equally. The media can also encourage unhelpful rumours. After the crash in 1992 of an Israeli cargo plane into the suburbs of Amsterdam, normal responses to trauma yielded to rumours about radioactive materials on board the plane – a rumour which generated a public health crisis. The media also tend prematurely to attribute blame and to find scapegoats. After the Swedish discotheque fire in Göteborg, the emergency services were unjustly vilified. Similarly, Gheytanchi et al. (2007) reported how rumours were spread about violent gangs having shot several people after Hurricane Katrina. As a consequence, rescue and emergency operations were discontinued. The reality was that individuals had discharged firearms, but only to attract the attention of these very services.

Employers should consider carefully how they might avoid such outcomes by harnessing the media. They are experts at their business. Fortunately, increasingly, the media are better informed and act more constructively, partly due to the efforts of the Dart Foundation for Journalists. The media can conduct helpful campaigns to disseminate accurate information about an incident, its effects, and where and when individuals can seek help.

Preparation and interventions

Preparation

Tehrani (2001) has developed an extensive trauma management programme but, as the London Chamber of Commerce and Industry (2003) confirmed, many organisations have no plans for responding to serious traumatic incidents. Such plans are, however, essential for the legal, economic and humanitarian reasons described at the start of this chapter. Rao (2006) described the serious consequences of there being no major incident plan available to cope with the Bhopal gas leak in India.

The Department of Health (2009b) guidance document describes how trauma management necessitates key personnel to be appointed to manage an event at a strategic, tactical and operational level. Such personnel must be familiar, in general terms, with the normal and psychopathological reactions to trauma and with those indicators which suggest that professional help may be required. Some of these indicators are represented below:

- Excessive denial.
- Excessive use of alcohol, cigarettes and/or food.
- Excessive irritability.
- Over- or under-work.
- Unusually poor work performance.
- Unusual carelessness.
- Unusually socially withdrawn.
- Unexpected physical symptoms.

In many commercial and industrial organisations there is a network of agencies which would be involved were there to be an incident. For example, the authors were recently required to advise on the management of the psychosocial response to a helicopter crash which resulted in a number of fatalities. Although this incident was of limited proportions, compared to a major offshore catastrophe, it engaged a considerable number of agencies and individuals, all of which had to be coordinated into an effective response. They included two helicopter firms, the Oil Chaplaincy, personnel of an oil company, divers, rescue personnel, coastguards, social workers, the police, local council personnel and pathologists, as well as the many bereaved families and colleagues. The Department of Health guidance recommends that there has to be a Lead Agency, an agreed common strategy, regular interagency meetings, and a clear definition of responsibilities to avoid unnecessary duplication or gaps in care and welfare provision (Department of Health, 2009b, pp. 53–54).

The agreed strategy should reflect a philosophy of care, which includes the following principles (Department of Health, 2009b):

• Services should be tailored to meet varying needs.
• Longer-term needs must be anticipated.
• Initial acute reactions tend to peak and decline over the first month.
• Subsequent unexpected events may compromise adjustment.
• Those with genuine post-traumatic psychopathology may delay reporting their condition.
• At-risk factors should guide interventions and psychosocial responses.
• Anniversary reactions should be anticipated.

Preparation requires training, and organisations need to regard this as an investment. Such costs can be weighed against the cost of losing staff through compensable injury. Training also requires realistic exercises in which the major incident plans are rigorously tested. Exercises also develop confidence in translating plans into action (Department of Health, 2009b).

Interventions

Guided by the Galenic principle of 'First, do no harm', some general points will also be made about different kinds of non-specialist interventions, which will be discussed in further detail in other chapters. In addition, a few comments about responding to workplace trauma will be made.

General

Whilst it is important that employers create a climate of care in which their employees will feel free to acknowledge emotional needs and difficulties, employers should not be too paternalistic after trauma. The main aim is to restore the individual to a level of functioning and to enhance his/her natural resilience. A sensitive approach can be helpful, one which encourages (rather than forces) workers to return to work, identifies realistic deadlines and pace of work, and ensures time off for events such as funerals.

There is no substantive evidence that trained counsellors or mental health professionals have an active role at the earliest stages of a traumatic incident. Evidence from the lay public and the emergency services indicates that people will normally turn to family, friends and colleagues. There is also a legitimate concern that premature intervention by professionals may discourage effective self-help or compromise the natural healing capabilities of individuals and groups.

It is common, particularly after catastrophic events, that VIPs (such as politicians and the most senior executives of a firm) wish to visit the site of the incident and to meet survivors, rescuers, etc. Such visits and expressions of concern can be healing, but they may also be viewed as intrusive if conducted too early, and they may give rise to suspicions about ulterior motives. Similarly, taking photographs of the disaster site should only be done with discretion and, preferably, with permission. Such sites may have a special significance to grieving colleagues.

How one communicates with survivors can also be crucial. The second author, after the *Piper Alpha* oil platform disaster, wrote to all survivors inviting them to a reunion. Very few replied. A follow-up telephone call confirmed that they tended to ignore official letters, whereas the invite by telephone ensured that almost every survivor attended the event.

Leaders of the incident response must acknowledge their own needs, particularly if the response is prolonged, otherwise they too can become victims. They should also be able to acknowledge their own sense of loss, after the trauma, whilst demonstrating that they are still functional: this provides a very good model.

A suitably realistic and compassionate approach by managers would include:

- Monitoring work performance and welfare for several months post-trauma.
- Providing accurate and sensitively presented information.
- Providing 'psycho-education', e.g. about normal and pathological reactions.
- Providing information about where to obtain help (e.g. from helplines such as the Sudden Trauma Information Service Helpline [STISH], www.stish.org).

Specific interventions

- *Peer support*. Employers are fortunate, as they have within their organisations an invaluable source of assistance for trauma-affected colleagues, that is their peers. Peer support is not new; it was introduced formally into the Los Angeles police department in 1981 and has been used in the military for many years (sometimes referred to as the 'buddy system'). With suitable training and investment from the institution, it can provide much-needed help when delivered by individuals who are credible and non-threatening. Providing such support may also enhance job satisfaction.
- *Critical incident stress debriefing (CISD)*. Introduced in the late 1980s, CISD developed into a very popular approach which had the aims of reducing distress and preventing the development of post-traumatic psychopathology (Everly and Mitchell, 1997). Subsequent research data have dampened the initial enthusiasm (NICE, 2005), although the quality of the challenging data has been questioned (e.g. Regel, 2007). The debate has not been closed, although most authorities would probably agree that one-off and mandatory sessions are likely to be either ineffective or, worse, harmful (particularly since they may cause retraumatization through premature and/or overexposure to reminders of the traumatic event). This does not mean that informal chat among colleagues should be discouraged – quite the opposite. Also, it does not mean that there should be no operational debriefs from which lessons can be learned. These should be encouraged: trauma is the history of lessons not learned!
- *Trauma risk management (TRiM)*. This is not a treatment but a peer-based method of assessing colleagues 3 and 28 days post-trauma to identify those who may require professional help. It was pioneered by the Royal Marines (Greenberg *et al.*, 2008) but

has now been used in other settings, including the emergency services. It has the advantage of being conducted by trained peer personnel and of not requiring any detailed exploration of the index trauma. It awaits, however, rigorous evaluation but has high face validity.

- *Psychological first aid (PFA)*. One of its pioneers (Raphael, 1986) emphasizes that this is not a single intervention but a broad package of measures. It aims to reduce physical and psychological suffering, ensure security and safety, develop the healing potential of the individuals, groups and communities and identify those most in need of further help (e.g. triage).

The four interventions above do require some degree of training, particularly with regard to knowledge about normal and pathological reactions to trauma, at-risk factors for pathological ones and the normal trajectories of adjustment. Mental health professionals may help in their learning and training but it would be wise for them not to lead the programme, as this may medicalize normal reactions. The final point to be noted about PFA is that it addresses physical needs first, in line with Maslow's hierarchy of needs.

Conclusions

- Work plays an important role in our lives.
- Work-related trauma can have far-reaching and devastating consequences.
- Most psychological and psychosocial reactions should be regarded as normal in the first instance.
- The workplace can represent a source of help and healing.
- Employers should develop a trauma management plan, which should be:

  - Well tried and tested.
  - Sufficiently resourced for training and implementation.
  - Communicated throughout the workplace.
  - Based on the best empirical evidence and advice available.
  - Wedded to a 'climate of care' in order that staff will come forward when in need.

- At-risk factors should be used to identify those who may require help.

- Outreach and wide-scale communication should be used to identify 'hidden' victims and to encourage those who are reluctant to come forward.
- Resilience is the norm, even in the wake of the most disturbing events, such as terrorist ones.

References

APA (1980) *Diagnostic and Statistical Manual of Mental Disorders, 3rd edn.* Washington: APA.

Alexander, D.A, (1991) Psychiatric intervention after the *Piper Alpha* disaster. *Journal of the Royal Society of Medicine* **84**, 8–11.

Alexander, D.A. (2005) Early mental health intervention after disasters. *Advances in Psychiatric Treatment* **11**, 12–18.

Alexander, D.A., Klein, S. (2001) Ambulance personnel and critical incidents. *British Journal of Psychiatry* **178**, 76–81.

Alexander, D.A., Klein. S. (2006) The challenge of preparation for a chemical, biological, radiological or nuclear terrorist attack. *Journal of Postgraduate Medicine* **52**, 126–131.

Bartholomew, R., Wessely, S. (2002) Protean nature of mass sociogenic illness. From possessed nuns to clinical and biological terrorism fears. *British Journal of Psychiatry* **180**, 300–306.

Brewin, C.R., Andrews, B., Valentine, J.D. (2000) Meta-analysis of risk factors for posttraumatic stress disorder in trauma-exposed adults. *Journal of Consulting and Clinical Psychology* **68**, 748–766.

Brewin, C.R., Scragg, P., Robertson, M. *et al.* (2008) Promoting mental health following the London bombings: a screen and treat approach. *Journal of Traumatic Stress* **21**, 3–8.

Department of Health (2009a) Pandemic Influenza. Psychosocial care for NHS staff during an influenza pandemic: www.dh.gov.uk/en/PublicationsandstatisticsPublicationsPolicyandGuidance/DH_103168 [accessed 30 October 2009].

Department of Health (2009b) NHS Emergency Planning Guidance, Planning for the psychosocial and mental health of people affected by major incidents and disasters: interim national strategic guidance www.dh.gov.uk/prod_consum_dh/groups/dh_digitalassets/documents/digitalasset/dh_103563.pdf [accessed 22 May 2010].

Durodié, B., Wessely, S. (2002) Resilience or panic? The public and terrorist attack. *Lancet* **360**, 9349, 1901–1902.

Dwyer, J., Flynn, K. (2005) 102 Minutes. *The Untold Story of the Fight to Survive Inside the Twin Towers.* London: Arrow Books.

Engel, C.C., Adkins, J.A., Cowan, D.N. (2002) Caring for medically unexplained physical symptoms after toxic environmental exposures:

effects of contested causation. *Environmental Health Perspectives* **110**, 641–647.

Everly, G.S., Mitchell, J.T. (1997) *Critical Incident Stress Management (CISM): A New Era and Standard of Care in Crisis Management.* Ellicot City, MD: Chevron.

Fairbank, J.A., Elbert, L., Costello, E.J. (2000) Epidemiology of traumatic events and post-traumatic stress disorder. In Nutt, D., Davidson, J.R.T., Zohar, J. (eds), *Post-traumatic Stress Disorder. Diagnosis, Management and Treatment.* London: Dunitz; 17–27.

Gheytanchi, A., Joseph, L., Gierlach, E. *et al.* (2007) The dirty dozen. Twelve failures of the hurricane Katrina response and how psychology can help. *American Psychologist* **62**, 118–130.

Greenberg, N., Langston, V., Jones, N. (2008) Trauma risk management (TriM) in the UK armed forces. *Journal of the Royal Army Medical Corps* **154**, 124–127.

Hadler, N.M. (1996) Evidence for work-related musculoskeletal disorders. *Journal of Occupational and Environmental Medicine* **38**, 1083–1084.

Hull, A.M., Alexander, D.A., Klein, S. (2002) Survivors of the *Piper Alpha* oil platform disaster: long-term follow-up study. *British Journal of Psychiatry* **181**, 433–438.

Janoff-Bulman, R. (1992) *Shattered Assumption: Towards a New Psychology of Trauma.* New York: Free Press.

Klein, S., Alexander, D.A. (2009) Epidemiology and presentation of post-traumatic disorders. *Psychiatry* **8**, 282–287.

London Chamber of Commerce and Industry (2003) *Disaster Recovery: Business Tips for Survival.* London: London Chamber of Commerce and Industry.

NICE (2005) *Post-traumatic Stress Disorder (PTSD): The Management of PTSD in Adults and Children in Primary and Secondary Care.* London: National Collaborating Centre for Mental Health.

Parkes, C.M. (1985) Bereavement. *British Journal of Psychiatry* **146**, 11–17.

Peck, D.C. (2005) Foot and mouth outbreak: lessons for mental health services. *Advances in Psychiatric Treatment* **11**, 270–276.

Perkönnig, A., Kessler, R.C. Storz, S. *et al.* (2000) Traumatic events and post-traumatic stress disorder in the community: prevalence, risk factors and comorbidity. *Acta Psychiatrica Scandanavica* **101**, 46–59.

Rao, K. (2006) Lessons learnt in mental health and psychosocial care in India after disasters. *International Review of Psychiatry* **18**, 547–552.

Raphael, B. (1986) *When Disaster Strikes: How Individuals and Communities Cope with Catastrophe.* New York: Basic Books.

Raphael, B. (2008) Systems, science, and populations. In Blumenfield, M., Ursano, R.J. (eds), *Intervention and Resilience after Mass Trauma.* Cambridge: Cambridge University Press; 1–47.

Reed, P.L., Anthony, J.C., Breslau, N. (2007) Incidence of drug problems in young adults exposed to trauma and posttraumatic stress disorder: do early life experiences and predispositions matter? *Arch Gen Psychiatry* **64**(12), 1435–1442.

Regel, S. (2007) Post-trauma support in the workplace: the current status and practice of critical incident stress management (CISM) and psychological debriefing (PD) within organizations in the UK. *Occupational Medicine* **57**, 411–416.

Rubin, G.J., Brewin, C.R., Greenberg, N. *et al.* (2005) Psychological and behavioural aspects of terrorism. *PTSD Research Quarterly* **13**, 1–18.

Sundnes, K.O., Birnbaum, M.L. (2003) Health and disaster management: guidelines for evaluation and research in the utstein style. *Prehospital Disaster Medicine* **17**(suppl 3), 1–177.

Tapsell, S.M., Tunstall, S.M. (2008) 'I wish I'd never heard of Banbury': the relationship between 'place' and health impacts from flooding. *Health and Place* **14**, 133–154.

Taylor, A.J.W., Frazer, A.G. (1982) The stress of post disaster body handling and victim identification work. *Journal of Human Stress* **8**, 4–12.

Tehrani, N. (2001) A special courage: dealing with the Paddington rail crash. *Occupational Medicine* **51**, 93–99.

Tyhurst, J.S. (1951) Individual reactions to community disaster: the natural history of psychiatric phenomena. *American Journal of Psychiatry* **107**, 764–769.

WHO (1992) *The Tenth Revision of the International Classification of Diseases and Related Health Problems* (ICD1–10). Geneva: WHO.

Williams, R., Alexander, D.A., Bolsover, D., Bakke, F.K. (2008) Children, resilience and disasters: recent evidence that should influence a model of psychosocial care. *Current Opinions in Psychiatry* **21**(4), 338–344.

Chapter 9

Trauma-organised systems and parallel process

Sandra L. Bloom

Trauma-organised systems

This chapter takes a seemingly obvious but fundamentally radical position that organisations – including human service organisation – are, like individuals, living systems (Senge *et al.*, 2004). Being alive, they are vulnerable to stress, particularly chronic and repetitive stress. Chronic stress stealthily robs an organisation of basic inter-personal safety and trust and thereby robs an organisation of health. Organisations, like individuals, can be traumatized, and the result of traumatic experience can be as devastating for organisations as it is for individuals. As a result, many human service delivery networks are functioning as 'trauma-organised systems' (Bentovim, 1992).

The impact of chronic stress and adversity on organisations has thus far been minimized and denied, except in the most dramatic of circumstances. As a result, managers and leaders remain largely unaware of the multiple ways in which organisational adaptation to chronic stress creates a state of dysfunction, which in some cases virtually prohibits the proper delivery of services to the individual clients who are the source of the organisation's original mission, while damaging many members of the organisation's workforce. Just as the encroachment of trauma into the life of an individual client is an insidious process that turns the past into a nightmare, the present into a repetitive cycle of re-enactment and the future into a terminal illness; in a parallel way, chronic strain insidiously has an impact on an organisation. As seemingly logical reactions to difficult situations pile upon each other, no-one is able to truly perceive the funda-mentally skewed and post-traumatic basic assumptions upon which that logic is built. As an earthquake can cause the foundations of a building to become unstable, even while the building still stands apparently intact, so, too, does chronic repetitive stress destabilize the cognitive and affective foundations of shared meaning that is necessary for a group to function and stay whole.

Parallel process

The concept of parallel process, taken out of the individual context and applied to organisations, is a useful way of offering a coherent framework that can enable organisational leaders and staff to develop a way of thinking 'outside the box' about what *has* happened and *is* happening to their service delivery systems, based on an understanding of the ways in which trauma and chronic adversity affect human function.

> *When two or more systems – whether these consist of individuals, groups, or organisations – have significant relationships with one another, they tend to develop similar affects, cognition, and behaviours, which are defined as parallel processes. . . . Parallel processes can be set in motion in many ways, and once initiated leave no one immune from their influence* (Smith *et al.*, 1989, p.13).

Clients bring their past history of traumatic experience into the social service sectors, consciously aware of certain specific goals but unconsciously struggling to recover from the pain and losses of the past. They are greeted by individual service providers, subject to their own personal life experiences, who are more or less deeply embedded in entire systems that are under significant stress. Given what we know about exposure to childhood adversity and other forms of traumatic experience, the majority of service providers have experiences in their background that may be quite similar to the life histories of their clients, and that similarity may be more or less recognized and worked through (Felitti *et al.*, 1998).

The result of these complex interactions between traumatized clients, stressed staff, pressured organisations and a social and economic environment that is frequently hostile to the aims of recovery is often the opposite of what was intended. Staff in many treatment programmes suffer physical and psychological injuries at alarming rates and thus become demoralized and hostile. Their counter-aggressive responses to the aggression in their clients help to create punitive environments. Leaders become variously perplexed, overwhelmed, ineffective, authoritarian or avoidant as they struggle to satisfy the demands of their superiors, to control their subordinates and to protect their clients. When professional staff and non-professionally trained staff gather together in an attempt to formulate an approach to complex problems, they are not on the same page. They share no common theoretical framework that informs problem solving. Without a shared way of understanding the problem, what passes as treatment may be little more than labelling, the prescription of medication, and behavioural management. When troubled clients fail to respond to these measures, they are labelled again, given more diagnoses and termed 'resistant to treatment'.

In this way, our systems inadvertently but frequently recapitulate the very experiences that have proved to be so toxic for the people we are supposed to help. Just as the lives of people exposed to repetitive and chronic trauma, abuse and maltreatment become organised around the traumatic experience, so too can entire systems become organised around the recurrent and severe stress of trying to cope with a flawed mental model based on individual pathology, which is the present underpinning of our helping systems. When this happens, it sets up an interactive dynamic that creates what are sometimes uncannily parallel processes.

Trauma theory brings context back to human services while integrating the importance of the biological discoveries of the last several decades. There are currently significant efforts directed at helping systems to become trauma-informed. The goal of this chapter is a practical one: to provide the beginnings of a coherent framework for organisational staff and leaders to more effectively provide trauma-informed care for their clients by becoming *trauma-sensitive* themselves. This means becoming sensitive to the ways in which clients, staff, managers, groups, policy makers, regulators and systems are impacted by individual and collective exposure to overwhelming stress and adversity.

When tragedy strikes: the impact of chronic stress and collective trauma

When tragedy strikes, the whole organisation becomes traumatized, a collective experience that disaster researcher Kai Erikson termed 'collective trauma':

> . . . *a blow to the basic tissues of social life that damages the*

bonds attaching people together and impairs the prevailing sense of communality (Erikson, 1994, p. 233).

Because we are group animals, we identify with the institutions to which we are affiliated. Patient deaths and injuries – from natural causes, accidents and, most particularly, suicide, and deaths while in restraints or the death of a child under the surveillance of child protection workers, staff deaths or injuries, loss of leaders, lawsuits, downsizing – all may overwhelm overall organisational function as well as every individual connected to the organisation. Just as individuals respond to acute stress and chronic stress in variable ways, so too can organisations experience the effects of both acute and chronic stressors. The effects of stress in organisations and within whole systems are cumulative. A series of small, unrelated, stress-inducing incidents can add up to a mountain of stress in the eyes of people who work in, and receive services within, these settings.

Lack of basic safety

Workplaces that are experienced as fundamentally unsafe – physically and emotionally dangerous, untrustworthy environments – are experienced collectively as dangerous as well. When this occurs, the basic trust that supports complex problem solving and high productivity is eroded. The list of behaviours that can trigger mistrust in staff is a long one and includes both verbal and non-verbal behaviour: silence, glaring eye contact, abruptness, snubbing, insults, public humiliation, blaming, discrediting, aggressive and controlling behaviour, overtly threatening behaviour, yelling and shouting, public humiliation, angry outbursts, secretive decision making, indirect communication, lack of responsiveness to input, mixed messages, aloofness, unethical conduct – all can be experienced as abusive managerial or supervisory behaviour (Ryan and Oestreich, 1998). According to Bill Wilkerson, CEO of Global Business and Economic Roundtable on Addiction and Mental Health, mistrust, unfairness and vicious office politics are among the top 10 workplace stressors (Collie, 2004).

Loss of emotional management

One group of investigators has argued that:

... emotions are among the primary determinants of behaviour at work ... and profoundly influence both the social climate and the productivity of companies and organisations (Pekrun and Frese, 1992, p. 154).

Under normal conditions, an organisation manages and contains the emotional contagion that is an inevitable part of human group functioning through normal problem-solving, decision-making and conflict-resolution methods and group norms that must exist for any organisation to operate effectively. These are the norms that enable the group to tolerate the normal amount of anxiety that exists among people working on a task, tolerate uncertainty long enough for creative problem solutions to emerge, promote balanced and integrated decision making so that all essential points of view are synthesized, contain and resolve the inevitable conflicts that arise between members of a group, and complete its tasks (Bloom, 2004a).

In organisations under chronic, relentless stress, however, this healthier level of function is likely to be sacrificed in service of facing repetitive emergency situations, and entire organisations may begin to look like highly stressed individuals. Traumatized people often develop chronic hyperarousal as the central nervous system adapts to the constancy of threat. Similarly, organisations may become chronically hyperaroused, so that everything becomes a crisis. When this happens, the capacity to triage what is important and must be immediately attended to, and what can be postponed, is lost. Stress levels universally increase for everyone and, as one manager has said, 'It's like managing with your hair on fire'. Under conditions of chronic crisis, emotional distress escalates, tempers become short, decision making becomes impaired and driven by impulse, while pressures to conform reduce individual and group effectiveness (Ryan and Oestreich, 1998).

Dissociation and organisational amnesia

Just like individuals, if they are to learn, organisations must have memory. Some modern philosophers believe that all memories are formed and organised within a collective context (Halbwachs, 1992). Organisational memory refers to stored information from an organisation's history that can be brought to bear on present decisions. Corporate knowledge, like individual knowledge, exists in two basic forms: explicit knowledge, which is easily codified and shared asynchronously; and tacit knowledge, which is experiential, intuitive and communicated most effectively in face-to-face encounters. Explicit knowledge can be articulated with formal language. It is that which can be recorded and stored in the more concrete organisational storage bins: records, policies and procedure manuals, training curricula, orientation programmes, organisational structure and lines of authority, and other educational and written materials (Weick, 1979).

Tacit knowledge is that knowledge which is used to interpret the information – in clinical circles more commonly referred to as 'clinical wisdom'. It is knowledge that is more difficult to articulate with language and lies in the values, beliefs and perspectives of the system (Lahaie, 2005; Othman and Hashim, 2004). Tacit knowledge resides within the individual memories of every person who is or has ever been a part of the organisation, is cumulative, slow to diffuse, is rooted in the human beings who comprise the organisation, and creates organisational culture. Every person who leaves an organisation takes a part of the organisational memory out the door with them. As a result, over time and with sufficient loss, the organisation may develop organisational amnesia that affects learning and adaptation (Kransdorff, 1998). Corporate amnesia becomes a tangible problem to be reckoned with when there is a loss of collective experience and accumulated skills through the trauma of excessive downsizing and layoffs (Newsbriefs, 2000).

The result of organisational amnesia may be a deafening silence about vital but troubling information, not dissimilar to the deafening silence that surrounds family secrets such as incest or domestic violence. There is reason to believe that maintaining silence about disturbing collective events may have the counter-effect of making the memory even more potent in its continuing influence on the individuals within the organisation as well as the organisation as a whole, much as silent traumatic memories continue to haunt traumatized individuals and families (Pennebaker *et al.*, 1997).

Organisational miscommunication

Under increasing levels of organisational stress, the vital communication that is the lifeblood of an organisation starts to break down. As stress increases, perception narrows, more contextual information is lost and circumstances deteriorate to more extreme levels before they are noticed, all of which leads to more puzzlement, less meaning and more perceived complexity. Communication is necessary to detect error and crises tend to create vertical communication structures when, in fact, lateral structures are often more appropriate for detection and diagnosis of problems. Research has shown that organisations are exceedingly complex systems that can easily drift toward disaster, unless they maintain resources that enable them to learn from unusual events in their routine functioning. When communication breaks down, this learning does not occur (Marcus and Nichols, 1999).

Organisations that already have poor communication structures are more likely to handle crises poorly (Kanter and Stein, 1992). Instead of increasing interpersonal communications, people in crisis are likely to resort to the excessive use of one-way forms of communication. Under stress, the supervisory structure tends to focus on the delivery of top-down information flow, largely characterized by new control measures about what staff and clients can and cannot do. Feedback loops erode under such circumstances and morale starts to decline as the measures that are communicated do not alleviate the stress or successfully resolve the crisis. Complex collective responses are all more vulnerable to this kind of disruption than are older, simpler, more over-learned, cultural and individual responses.

Increased authoritarianism

When danger is real and present, effective leaders take charge and give commands that are obeyed by obedient followers, thus harnessing and directing the combined power of many individuals in service of group survival. When a crisis occurs, centralization of control is significantly increased, with leaders tightening reins, concentrating power at the top and minimizing participatory decision making (Kanter and Stein, 1992). Even where there are strong beliefs in the democratic way of life, there is always a tendency in institutions, and in the larger containing society, to regress to simple, hierarchical models of authority as a way of preserving a sense of security and stability. This is not just a phenomenon of leadership – in times of great uncertainty, everyone in the institution colludes to collectively bring into being authoritarian organisations, as a time-honoured method for providing at least the illusion of greater certainty, and therefore a diminution of anxiety (Lawrence, 1995).

However, when a state of crisis is prolonged, repetitive or chronic, there is a price to be paid. The tendency to develop increasingly authoritarian structures over time is particularly troublesome for complex organisations. Chronic crisis results in organisational climates that promote authoritarian behaviour, and this behaviour serves to reinforce existing hierarchies and create new ones. Communication exchanges change and become more formalized and top-down. Command hierarchies become less flexible, power becomes more centralized, people below stop communicating openly and, as a result, important information is lost from the system (Weick, 2001).

The centralization of authority means that those at the top of the hierarchy will be far more influential than those at the bottom, and yet better solutions to the existing problems may actually lie in the hands of those with less authority. Authoritarian leadership is likely to encourage the same leadership style throughout the organisation. The loss of democratic processes results in oversimplified decision making and the loss of empowerment at each organisational level reduces morale and increases interpersonal conflict.

As a result, the organisational norms for all staff are likely to endorse punitive behaviour, empathic failure and traditional methods for managing difficult situations. It is hard to imagine a situation more detrimental to long-lasting, positive change in the lives of people with complex problems. As for the staff, when authoritarian behaviour comes to dominate a situation, the result can also be devastating. Unchecked authoritarians can become bullies at any organisational level, but when they are given power they can become petty tyrants.

Silencing of dissent and organisational alexithymia

The greater the authoritarian pressures in an organisation, and the greater the chronic stress, the greater is the likelihood that strenuous attempts will be made to silence dissent. Empirical data show that *organisational silence* emerges out of workers' fear to speak up about issues or problems they encounter at work (Morrison and Milliken, 2000). These underground topics become the undiscussables in an organisation, covering a wide range of areas, including decision-making, procedures, managerial incompetence, pay inequity, organisational inefficiencies and poor organisational performance (Ryan and Oestreich, 1998).

Dissent is even less welcome in environments characterized by chronic stress when dissent is seen as a threat to unified action. As a result, the quality of problem analysis and decision making deteriorates further. If this cycle is not stopped and the organisation allowed opportunity to recuperate, the result may be an organisation that becomes as rigid, repetitious and ultimately destructive as do so many chronically stressed individuals (Bloom, 2004b). Organisational alexithymia – the inability to give words to feelings – becomes a significant barrier to constructive change as the number of undiscussable topics accumulates. The silencing of dissent is dangerous to organisational and individual well-being, because dissent serves as corrective feedback within an organisation that can avert disaster if attended to in time.

Decision making and conflict management

As systemic stress increases and authority becomes more centralized, organisational decision-making processes are likely to deteriorate, becoming less complex, more driven by impulse, with a narrowing of focus and attention only to immediate threat. Long-term consequences of decisions may not be considered and alternatives remain unexplored (Janis, 1982). As work-related stressors increase, employees develop negative perceptions of their co-workers and organisational leaders and this may precipitate serious decreases in job performance. Conflict over the content of task-related issues can be very useful, but emotion inevitably accompanies conflict and the heat of a conflict over issues can spill over into interpersonal conflict rather easily. Without good conflict management skills in the group, task-related conflict can lead to even more misunderstanding, miscommunication, and increased team dysfunction, instead of providing the kind of enriching discourse that can lead to creative problem solving. The bottom line is that if people in a group do not like and respect each other and spend their time in personal conflict, the group as a whole will perform badly. Chronic stress puts an added burden on old conflicts, which are likely to emerge with a vengeance and propagate new conflicts.

Hierarchical structures concentrate power and, in these circumstances, power can easily come to be used abusively and in a way that perpetuates rather than attenuates the concentration of power. Transparency disappears and secrecy increases under this influence. Communication networks become compromised as those in power become more punishing, and the likelihood of error is increased as a result. In such a situation, conflicts tend to remain unresolved, tension and resentment mount under the surface of everyday group functioning. Interpersonal conflicts that were suppressed during the initial crisis return, often with a vengeance, but conflict resolution mechanisms, if ever in place, deteriorate under stress.

Disempowerment and learned helplessness

Under these conditions, helplessness, passivity, and passive–aggressive behaviours on the part of the subordinates in the hierarchy increase, while leaders become increasingly controlling and punitive. In this way the organisation becomes ever more radically split, with different parts of the organisation assuming the role of managing and/or expressing different emotions that are then subsequently suppressed (Bloom, 2004a). Such conditions as these make an organisation ripe for collective disturbance that may go unresolved and unrecognized, while policy changes are made that ensure that the underlying conflicts will remain out of conscious group awareness.

Learned helplessness at work has been defined as a debilitating cognitive state in which individuals often possess the skills and abilities necessary to perform their jobs, but exhibit suboptimal or poor performance because they attribute prior failures to causes which they cannot change, even though success may be possible in the current environment (Campbell and Martinko, 1998). In a controlling, non-participatory environment exercising top-down management, every subsequent lower level of employee is likely to become progressively disempowered. After years, decades and even generations of controlling management styles, reversing this sense of disempowerment can be extremely difficult, particularly under conditions of chronic, unrelenting organisational stress. Helpless to protect themselves, feeling embattled, hopeless and helpless, the staff and management often engage in risky risk avoidance in which risk management policies prevent healthy change and adaptation.

Increased aggression

The most feared form of workplace aggression is physical violence, but every episode of violence has a history. Violent physical or sexual assault in the workplace always emerges within a context and can usually be traced to various kinds of less appreciated forms of violence that may occur routinely within an organisation. Dirty looks, defacing property, stealing, hiding needed resources, interrupting others, obscene gestures, cursing, yelling, threats, insults, sarcasm, the silent treatment, damning with faint praise, arbitrary and capricious decisions, ignoring input, unfair performance evaluations, showing up late for meetings, causing others to delay actions, spreading rumours, back-stabbing, belittling, failing to transmit information, failing to deny false rumours, failing to warn of potential danger – all of these actions on the part of management, staff and clients are forms of aggression which can terminate in the emergence of physical violence (Spector, 1997).

Stressful times are difficult for employees and as interpersonal conflict increases, it is likely that workers will express their anger, frustration and resentment in a variety of ways that have a negative effect on work performance. Frequently, bureaucracy is substituted for participatory agreement on necessary changes, and the more an organisation grows in size and complexity, the more likely this is to happen (Huberman, 1964). Research has demonstrated that the lower performance gets, the more punitive leaders become, and that very possibly just when leaders need to be instituting positive reinforcing behaviours to promote positive change, they instead become increasingly punitive (Sims, 1980).

A sure sign of an increase in aggression in the workplace is an escalation of vicious gossip and unsubstantiated rumour. Research shows that 70% of all organisational communication comes through this system of informal communication, and several national surveys have found that employees used the grapevine as a communication source more than any other vehicle (Crampton *et al.*, 1998). Not only that, but the grapevine has been shown to communicate information far more rapidly than formal systems of communication. Rumours fill in the gap where facts are absent and the grapevine may become poisoned by unsubstantiated rumour and gossip. All of this lends itself to the promotion of a toxic environment.

Unresolved grief, re-enactment and organisational decline

Losses to the organisation are likely to be experienced individually as well as collectively (Carr, 2001). For the same reason, failures of the organisation to live up to whatever internalized ideal the individual has for the way that organisation should function are likely to be experienced individually and collectively as a betrayal of trust, a loss of certainty and security, a disheartening collapse of meaning and purpose. Sudden firings or other departures of key personnel, the sudden death of a leader or otherwise influential employee, may be experienced as organisationally traumatic. The effects of downsizing, mergers, hostile takeovers, cuts in programme funding, changes in roles, increased and burdensome demands of insurance companies – all may be experienced as examples of more widespread chronic disasters (Erikson, 1994).

As workers in this field have determined:

> ... the relationship between employee and organisation are: deep-seated, largely unconscious, intimately connected to the development of identity, and have emotional content (Carr, 2001, p. 429).

Because of this connectedness between individual and collective identity, and because all change involves loss, organisational change and grieving tend to go hand-in-hand (Carr, 2001). It is clear that the ways in which grief, loss and termination are handled have a significant impact on employee attitudes. Unresolved grief can result in an idealization of what has been lost that interferes with adaptation to a new reality. The failure to grieve for the loss of a leader may make it difficult or impossible for a new leader to be accepted by the group. In fact, one author has noted that:

> Nostalgia is not a way of coming to terms with the past (as mourning or grief are) but an attempt to come to terms with the present (Gabriel, 1993, p. 132).

Traumatized individuals are frequently subject to traumatic re-enactment, a compulsive reliving of a traumatic past that is not recognized as repetitive and yet which frequently leads to re-victimization experiences. Re-enactment is a sign of grief that is not resolved. Instead the trauma and the losses associated with it are experienced over and over, relentlessly. An organisation that cannot change, that cannot work through loss and move on, is likely to develop patterns of re-enactment, repeating past failed strategies without recognizing that these strategies may no longer be effective. This can easily lead to organisational patterns that become overtly abusive.

The rigid repetition of the past and the inability to adapt to change may lead to organisational decline and, possibly, dissolution. Increases in conflict, secrecy, scapegoating, self-protective behaviours, loss of leader credibility, rigidity, turnover, decreases in morale, diminished innovation, lowered participation, non-prioritized cuts and reduced long-term planning are common problems associated with periods of decline (Cameron *et al.*, 1987). All of these behaviours can be seen as inhibitors of organisational learning and adaptation.

Conclusion

Organisational change is always challenging and all too frequently fails (Pascale *et al.*, 2000). But constant and rapid adaptation to a rapidly changing environment has become a basic necessity for organisational survival. In treating individual survivors of traumatic life events and sustained adversity, it has become clear that having a different way to assess and formulate past and current dilemmas is frequently the beginning of a healing and even transformative process (Bloom, 1997). This chapter entertains the possibility that, if members of organisations can similarly adopt a trauma-informed mental model that enables them to collectively assess and constructively respond to recurrent stress in a different way, transformative organisational change may be possible.

References

Bentovim, A. (1992) *Trauma-organized Systems: Physical and Sexual Abuse in Families*. London: Karnac Books.

Bloom, S.L. (1997) *Creating Sanctuary: Toward the Evolution of Sane Societies*. New York: Routledge.

Bloom, S.L. (2004a) Neither liberty nor safety: the impact of fear on individuals, institutions, and societies, Part II. *Psychotherapy and Politics International* **2**, 212–228.

Bloom, S.L. (2004b) Neither liberty nor safety: the impact of trauma on individuals, institutions, and societies. Part I. *Psychotherapy and Politics International* **2**, 78–98.

Cameron, K.S., Whetten, D.A., Kim, M.U. (1987) Organizational dysfunctions of decline. *Academy of Management Journal* **30**, 126.

Campbell, C.R., Martinko, M.J. (1998) An integrative attributional perspective of empowerment and learned helplessness: a multimethod field study. *Journal of Management* **24**, 173–200.

Carr, A. (2001) Understanding emotion and emotionality in a process of change. *Journal of Organizational Change Management* **14**, 421–434.

Collie, D. (2004) Workplace stress: expensive stuff: http://www.emaxhealth. com/38/473.html [accessed 22 October 2009].

Crampton, S.M., Hodge, J.W., Mishra, J.M. (1998) The informal communication network: factors influencing grapevine activity. *Public Personnel Management* **27**, 569.

Erikson, K. (1994) *A New Species of Trouble: The Human Experience of Modern Disasters.* New York: W.W. Norton.

Felitti, V.J., Anda, R.F., Nordenberg, D., Williamson, D.F., Spitz, A.M., Edwards, V. *et al.* (1998) Relationship of childhood abuse and household dysfunction to many of the leading causes of death in adults. The adverse childhood experiences (ACE) study. *American Journal of Preventative Medicine* **14**, 245–258.

Gabriel, Y. (1993) Organizational nostalgia – reflections on 'The Golden Age'. In Fineman, S. (ed.), *Emotion in Organizations.* Thousand Oaks, CA,: Sage.

Halbwachs, M. (1992) *On Collective Memory.* Chicago, IL: University of Chicago Press.

Huberman, J. (1964) Discipline without punishment. *Harvard Business Review* **42**, 62–68.

Janis, I.L. (1982) Decision making under stress. In Goldberger, L., Breznitz, S. (eds), *Handbook of Stress: Theoretical and Clinical Aspects.* New York: Free Press.

Kanter, R.M., Stein, B.A. (1992) *The Challenge of Organizational Change: How Companies Experience It and Leaders Guide It.* New York: Free Press.

Kransdorff, A. (1998) *Corporate Amnesia: Keeping Know-how in the Company.* Woburn, MA: Butterworth-Heineman.

Lahaie, D. (2005) The impact of corporate memory loss: what happens when a senior executive leaves? *Leadership in Health Services* **18**, xxxv–xlvii.

Lawrence, W.G. (1995) The presence of totalitarian states-of-mind in institutions. Paper read at the Inaugural Conference on 'Group Relations' of the Institute of Human Relations, Sofia, Bulgaria, 1995: http://humannature.com/free-associations/lawren.html [accessed 23 November 2006].

Marcus, A.A., Nichols, M.L. (1999) On the edge: heeding the warnings of unusual events. *Organization Science: A Journal of the Institute of Management Sciences* **10**, 482.

Morrison, E.W., Milliken, F.J. (2000) Organizational silence: a barrier to change and development in a pluralistic world. *Academy of Management Review* **25**, 706.

Newsbriefs (2000) More knowledge; song strikes chord. *Computing Canada* **12 May**.

Othman, R., Hashim, N.A. (2004) Typologizing organizational amnesia. *The Learning Organization* **11**, 273.

Pascale, R.T., Millimanm, M., Gioja, L. (2000) *Surfing the Edge of Chaos: The Laws of Nature and the New Laws of Business*. New York: Crown Business.

Pekrun, R., Frese, M. (1992) Emotions in work and achievement. *International Review of Industrial and Organizational Psychology* 7, 153–200.

Pennebaker, J.W., Paez, D., Rime, B. (eds) (1997) *Collective Memory of Political Events*. Mahwah, NJ: Lawrence Erlbaum.

Ryan, K., Oestreich, D. (1998) *Driving Fear out of the Workplace: Creating the High Trust, High Performance Organization*. San Francisco, CA: Jossey Bass.

Senge, P., Scharmer, C.O., Jaworski, J., Flowers, B.S. (2004) *Presence: Human Purpose and the Field of the Future*. Cambridge, MA: Society for Organizational Learning.

Sims, H.P. Jr (1980) Further thoughts on punishment in organizations. Academy of Management. *Academy of Management Review* 5, 133.

Smith, K.K., Simmons, V.M., Thames, T.B. (1989) 'Fix the women': an intervention into an organizational conflict based on parallel process thinking. *Journal of Applied Behavioral Science* 25, 11–29.

Spector, P.E. (1997) The role of frustration in antisocial behavior at work. In Giacalone, R.A., Greenberg, J. (eds), *Antisocial Behavior in Organizations*. Thousand Oaks, CA: Sage.

Weick, K.E. (1979) *The Social Psychology of Organizing*. Reading, MA: Addison-Wesley.

Weick, K.E. (2001) *Making Sense of the Organization*. Malden, MA: Blackwell.

Chapter 10

The influence of organisational culture in dealing with workplace conflict

An ethical and cultural perspective

Sarah Vaughan

Introduction

Innovation, increased trade and the dissemination of ideas and values in a globalized world have created a very challenging, complex and interconnected business environment, which impacts all areas of organisational performance. Organisations must not only face the challenges of operating worldwide, but they are also required to adopt alternative managerial approaches to the consequences of global operations within the workplace: an increase in the cultural diversity of the workforce, broader job descriptions, increased flexibility, structural changes of work, constantly changing work schedules, longer working hours, coupled with the competitive demands of increased productivity or performance. The unfamiliar array of values, attitudes, perceptions, languages and cultures at a personal and organisational level in a globalized environment provides potential for challenge, dispute and conflict in the workplace. How conflict emerges, escalates and is resolved is shaped by culture, both at the organisational level (internal factors) and by the national culture in which business operates (external factors).

Whilst conflict is natural and useful for solving problems and developing relationships (Amason, 1996), it can be disruptive and can lead to inappropriate and harmful workplace behaviours when unresolved or mismanaged (Edmondson *et al.*, 2001). Persistent and escalatory exposure to such behaviours, which include physical or verbal aggression, bullying or victimization, is traumatic in nature and has serious physical and psychological consequences both for the targeted employee and the organisation as a whole (Tehrani, 2004).

Just as trauma leaves a person changed, both psychologically and physiologically (Van der Kolk and Van der Hart, 1991), it also changes an organisation and can have a cumulative effect in organisations that have experienced cases of workplace conflict and violence.

This chapter will explore, by focusing on the case of one organisation, the characteristics of the French national and business culture as antecedent to the perceptions of conflict and their interplay with organisational culture and ethics in dealing with workplace conflict, violence and trauma.

Culture

Culture (Figure 10.1) refers to the shared knowledge and meanings systems (D'Andrade, 1984) – values, beliefs, expectations and goals – by members of a particular group of people and that distinguishes them from members of other groups. Hofstede (1984, p. 51) referred to culture as 'the collective programming of the mind', passed down from generation to generation through parenting, schooling, professional and general societal organisations. It comprises social norms – appropriate or inappropriate attitudes and behaviours – which impact activities and thus organisational control and coordination. Schein (1985) developed a three-level model of culture, from the most to the least apparent – behaviours and artefacts, beliefs and values, and underlying assumptions and values.

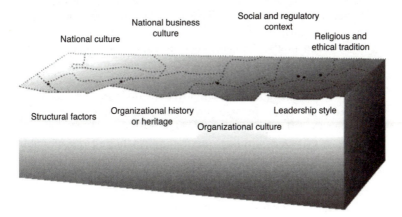

Figure 10.1 Cultural factors that influence how organisations deal with workplace conflict and crisis.

National culture shapes behaviours and structures the perceptions and implicit theories of management. It is thought to influence between 25% and 50% of the variation in employee and managerial attitudes (Gannon, 1994), since individuals who share motives, values and beliefs are likely to interpret and evaluate situational events and management practices in a similar way. Whilst it is not easy to disentangle national culture from organisational and professional culture, cultural factors that are generated and evolve within an organisation must be distinguished from those that derive from France's distinct historical, philosophical and religious legacy.

The external environment: France's national culture

Whilst found at many different levels – social, professional, regional or national – cultural differences are particularly potent at the national level because of generations of socialization into the national community. The cultural 'programming' therefore helps to determine the national predispositions and evaluate the conduciveness and tolerance in each culture to conflict and inappropriate behaviours taking place.

Hofstede (1980, 1993) identifies how management theories and practices are constrained by national cultures and their respective dimensions:

- *Power distance (PDI)*. This dimension indicates the extent to which a society expects and accepts a high degree of inequality in institutions and organisations. In a country with a larger than mean power distance, such as France (68 points on the PDI, 24% higher than the world average), organisations are characterized by formal centralized hierarchies, top-down management styles and low employee involvement in decision-making processes. In high power-distance countries, managers rely on formal rules and procedures (Smith *et al.*, 1995), compliance is expected without questioning, including questionable business practice (Cohen *et al.*, 1996). Lower power-distance cultures are more likely to favour the emergence of social and environmental initiatives, which result in organisational contexts that are safer for truth-telling and whistle-blowing (Ringov and Zollo, 2007).
- *Uncertainty avoidance (UAI)*. Uncertainty-avoiding societies are

rule- and routine-orientated, have a low tolerance of risk and generally find it difficult to adapt to new social and environmental demands and practices. France's UAI score is 86, 34% higher than the world UAI average. It is a culture that strongly resists changes to its traditional beliefs and institutions. In organisational terms, high UAI countries tend to resort to bureaucratic practices to alleviate the unpredictability of future events, and are less innovative because championing roles that overcome organisational inertia to innovations are less likely to be accepted (Shane, 1993, 1995).

- *Individualism (IDV)*. This dimension relates to the extent to which personal goals, preferences and performance take precedence over collective ones. In terms of organisational life, individualistic cultures respect and value personal characteristics and achievement and are predominantly task-focused. Individuals prefer work settings in which they can make their own decisions, challenge the norm and be evaluated on individual rather than collective performance. Cultures high in collectivism will privilege group harmony, loyalty and personal relationships. France has a high IDV score of 71, 65% more than the world average, which may cause group members to seek differences amongst themselves to enhance their own self-image (Kim and Markus, 1999). Research on the individualism–collectivism dimension has revealed its importance in conflict resolution styles. High IDV cultures accept disagreements and conflicts as natural and inevitable, and will be assertive and direct in their approach to conflict. Low IDV cultures, on the other hand, dislike social disorganisation or disagreements and will tend to avoid conflict (Ting-Toomey, 1985).

- *Masculinity (MAS)*. Masculine societies value assertiveness, career advancement, competitiveness and materialism, as opposed to the 'feminine' values of relationships, sensitivity and the quality of life. Organisations in feminine societies will place a strong emphasis on social relations, inclusion, cooperation and solidarity. In masculine societies, organisations will be more task-oriented, are more likely to be male dominated (especially in management) and the motivation more materialistic. As masculine societies are more likely to define occupations by gender, Baumeister and Tice (2004) suggest that masculinity inhibits helping behaviours. France has a relative low masculinity score of 43, which is 14% below the world average, implying a focus on equality and solidarity (*Liberté, Egalité et Fraternité*) and dominant values of preservation and care. Interestingly, the French word *patron*, beyond meaning 'boss', also includes some elements of caring about subordinates.

Language and context

Hall (1977) made the distinction between high- or low-context cultures and how explicit or implicit the language of the culture is. France is a high-context culture, meaning a high discrepancy between what is said and what is meant, leaving place for a shared familiarity of allusions, historical or cultural references. Such a culture demands sensitivity and perceptiveness in distinguishing the two meanings. It also requires different listening skills to grasp the contextual meaning, which include focusing on the way of relating, sometimes at the expense of content. The organisational implications are to be found in these intrinsically 'grey areas' of French communication style, which are open to misunderstanding and disagreement. The French language 'can be imprecise in the most precise way' (Baudry, 2000, p. 32) and management may seek to strategically preserve this ambiguity, either until goals, values and tasks are clearly defined, or simply to avoid confrontation.

Morality, ethics and notions of accountability

France has a Roman Catholic heritage: 85% of the French declare themselves to be Catholic, even if less than 15% declare themselves as practising (Gannon *et al.*, 1994). Catholicism, with its strong emphasis on duty and its authoritarian structure, has shaped French conservatism and rigidity. Misgivings about whistle-blowing, for example, date back to the eighteenth century, when the Catholic Church collaborated with the French government in demanding that parishioners inform the legal courts on what they knew about cases (through '*monitoires*'). The more recent Second World War and the Occupation of France have equally contributed to the negative perceptions and resistance to whistle-blowing.

The French intellectual tradition requires ethics to be positioned with reference to philosophical and moral thought (Pesqueux and Quintallet, 1994). The Age of Enlightenment brought a radical break from the theocentric vision of morality towards intrinsic freedom and autonomy as the basic rights of all individuals. Moral obligations – behaviours and underlying principles – no longer came from transcendental religions, but from tangible social situations. Secular morality was transferred to the individual. Curiously, however, accountability has no counterpart in French. Periphrases have to be used to express its meaning, despite the emergence of the recent word '*redevabilité*' which, in usage, is applied to the group or third party. Lack of personal or individual accountability is part of the French system.

French management culture

French society has the unique characteristic of being ruled by a powerful and homogeneous management elite which connotes an identity, *les cadres*, who have at least 5 years of university education at the *Grandes Ecoles*. Over 60% of France's CEOs are fostered by these highly elite and selective schools operating, and 90% of the assets traded on the French stock markets in the 1990s were managed by graduates from only two such schools (Bertrand *et al.*, 2004). Whilst meritocratic in nature, they represent the structure and functioning of the uppermost tier of France's system of higher education, and are primarily the preserve of students issuing from, or destined for, the economically rich fractions of the French *haute bourgeoisie* (Wacquant, 1997). French management culture is consequently perceived as an intellectually (rather than interpersonally) demanding profession, and one which provides social recognition and position, as opposed to exclusively financial gains (Naulleau and Harper, 1993).

Access to the *Grandes Ecoles* is via a selective and highly competitive preparatory school system, which has been much criticized for the psychological, emotional, intellectual and social pressure it exerts on students. Bullying and harassment by teachers are behaviours which are regularly denounced, and it is feared that these classes may well provide a model for future toxic management behaviours, in that they create a culture in which the person is systematically criticized and belittled.

France's social traditions with regard to workplace conflict and safety

There have been several landmark events in France in recent years which particularly frame the French socio-economic and regulatory context with regard to psychosocial risks and trauma in the workplace:

- The increased consideration given to mental health dimensions in the Ministry of Labour surveys (DARES) and in studies by work doctors (*enquêtes SUMER*).
- A government white paper (CNMATS, 1999) recognizing psychological trauma as a result of workplace violence.
- The Law for Social Modernisation (No. 2002–73, 2002) introduced new articles in French Employment Law recognizing workplace bullying (L122–49 to L122–54) and extending the notion of duty of care to psychological safety (L230–2-1).
- The Institut National de Recherche et de Sécurité publication on workplace health and safety.
- The electoral agenda of President Sarkozy which included psychosocial risks and workplace violence. The Health and Work Minister, Xavier Bertrand, constituted a steering committee in October 2007 and their recommendations (Nasse and Légeron report) for prevention and intervention strategies were made to the government in March 2008:

    - The audit of the educational provision of health and safety issues in the management curriculum within the French *Grandes Ecoles* system in May 2008 (William Dab report). The steering committee made recommendations for content (learning goals and competencies) and pedagogic methodology (technical versus a moral/ethical standpoint).
    - The French social partners concluded a national multi-industry agreement on stress at work in early July 2008, which seeks to implement the 2004 European framework agreement on work-related stress.

Despite this regulatory framework, there are a number of flaws in the subsequent applications, due to ambiguity on the one hand (workplace bullying, for example, remains a vague concept in French Law, as the law refers to the effects of bullying without explaining its causes) and the notion of flexible law on the other. In a cross-country comparison conducted by the Organisation for Economic Cooperation and Development, France has the highest level of administrative regulation of 20 developed countries, ahead of the USA, Denmark, Australia, Canada and the UK (OECD, 1999). As Montesquieu elegantly wrote, 'Useless laws weaken necessary ones'. *De facto* tolerance of misdemeanour creates a flexible definition, thus placing the power to determine 'acceptable' and 'unacceptable' behaviours outside the legislative constraints with positions of hierarchy and authority (Baudry, 2000, p. 116).

Company A – the internal environment

Industry culture

Company A is in the higher education sector in France. The industry in France has undergone significant changes over the past 10 years, due to:

* *Nature of market.* Organisational behaviour in the education sector is different, as the source of competitive advantage is intellectual, based on individual academic excellence, and whereby institutions compete for rank and academic status.
* *Regulation.* A number of reforms and regulatory texts (mostly due to international accreditation standards) have accelerated major cultural changes in the internal management processes of educational institutions in France. Institutions are required to integrate a permanent research faculty into their management structure, modifying the leadership that institutions must provide. There are frequent misunderstandings with faculty occupying line-management positions, derived from certain assumptions about their role or identity. Such misunderstandings play a significant role in the emergence and escalation of conflict.
* *Internationalization.* The education sector is a highly competitive environment and there is increased pressure amongst institutions to perform and survive globally.

Structural factors

The organisation has undergone rapid growth over the past 7 years, during which the programme portfolio, student and faculty numbers have doubled. The overall workforce in Company A now totals 183 (66 women), with an average age of 41, equally distributed amongst management (including faculty) and administrative positions; 91% of employees are French nationals.

More men hold middle and top management positions, whilst women occupy primarily administrative positions. The relative absence of women in leadership positions contributes to a patriarchal and masculine management style and discourse. This permeates formal communication (with an emphasis and focus on competition, entrepreneurialism and aggression) and informal interpersonal relationships, for example, the differentiated use, according to gender, of the personal pronoun *tu* or *vous* at executive level, which creates separate signs and communities, not only in terms of relative power but also on dimensions such as involvement, openness, cohesion and alliance. Gender-biased jokes prevail and frame decision-making processes (recruitment practices, for example).

Turnover is high amongst faculty but this is consistent with the institution's strategy of recruiting young research professors, for whom the institution is a stepping stone at the beginning of their careers. All departing professors are surveyed to identify their motivations for leaving: the frequently cited answers include the availability of job opportunities at other institutions, a perception that their research activity is not recognized or respected by top management, and a lack of motivation to take on management positions which might affect their research performance. For recruitment to new positions, all faculty positions advertised are filled for the given academic year but the hybrid faculty/management positions remain vacant for significantly longer periods of time. Turnover in administrative staff is low, due to the economic environment of the location, but annual appraisals evidence some dissatisfaction with working conditions – little control over tasks, low participation in the decision-making process and a perception of a general lack of recognition by top management.

Absenteeism is relatively low (an average of 1.17 days of sick leave) in all the employee categories.

Organisational culture

Organisational culture, similarly to national culture, includes dimensions such as power and authority relationships, uncertainty avoidance and risk, communication and consultation (Tayeb, 1994) but which are unique to each organisation. Based on a process of participative observation and evidence gathered from external auditors (notably certification and accreditation bodies), Company A can be characterized in the following way:

- *Entrepreneurial.* Company A is one of the youngest institutions on its market, in a culture which venerates history and tradition. It has undergone rapid growth and has proved agile in diversifying its programme portfolio faster than its competitors. It is considered innovative and entrepreneurial by others in the industry and this spirit is recognized by its stakeholders and translated in the activities of key employees. Tensions and sources of conflict are inherent in such an environment: daily conflicts of tasks, priorities and preferences, role ambiguity and subjective perceptions of individual performance and rewards. These organisational characteristics generate high stress levels within the organisation and result in verbal and non-verbal behaviours which may be considered or experienced as abusive.
- *Efficiency-focused.* Productivity is the key focus, as are cost-effective development strategies. The company stresses goals (in terms of budget and time constraints) and emphasizes the importance of getting things done and maintaining a pace faster than that of its competitors. The educational environment is a culture of speech and discourse: argumentation and debate is long, vocabulary and role models are tough. Little time, in contrast, is accorded to the project implementation phase and it is difficult to record and respect decisions, actions and projected completion dates. Pressure and stress escalates as completion dates and deadlines loom.
- *Quality-orientated.* The organisation is ISO 9001-certified, which requires it to develop and implement a set of routines and procedures for programme design, delivery, service and support. Research has shown that cultures which support quality implementation emphasize standardization and conformity to rules. For Company A the standards have not become institutionalized practice, resulting in a constant chain of corrective actions (rather than efficient preventative measures), which require immediate attention. As a consequence, stress and tension escalate as emergency decisions bottleneck at management level.
- *Values-orientated.* A statement of Values and Ethics was adopted in the organisation in 2002, subsequent to extensive stakeholder consultation (faculty, administrators, students, corporate partners). A shared understanding of the values – respect, tolerance and trust; commitment and responsibility; honesty and integrity; teamwork and solidarity – and behavioural expectations for students (both on and off campus) are articulated in a Student

Charter. It is a key element of the student regulatory framework. However, this is not the case for faculty and staff, where the understanding of the values has not been formulated in clear standards of behaviour and practice. Becker and Fritzsche (1987) evidence that for the French there is a belief that the ethical code is in itself sufficient: they conclude that this is optimistic, if not to say idealistic. Without a shared meaning of the values for faculty and staff and no explicit expectations in terms of behaviour, it is left to each individual employee to attach meaning and judgement to their own and others' behaviours. Patterns of understanding emerge among the different subgroups to which the employee belongs, determined by individual or personal factors (skills, knowledge and personality) and professional factors (status, position) but also framed by situational or organisational precedents. In the cases of workplace violence and conflict that Company A has experienced, the lack of explicit and normative behaviours resulted in group pressure to comply with the interpretations of others.

- *Communication.* Language in Company A is a binary 'them and us' (students/administration, faculty/staff, top management/employees), and one which conveys power (the elite, directive). Such language constructs an environment where labelling is tolerated and introduces principles of marginalization of people who do not meet the normative standards set by the majority.

Leadership and management style

Cultural values and practices, as well as organisational structure, affect what leaders do (House *et al.*, 1997). The French tradition is patriarchal and paternalistic and implies alternate periods of tyranny and absence (Baudry, 2000). In Company A the management style oscillates between delegation and authoritarianism:

- *Laissez-faire leadership* – meaning literally 'let others do' or 'hands off', in which the Director gives his management team freedom to determine goals, make decisions, and resolve problems on their own. Whilst effective with the more senior and experienced managers, the more inexperienced managers feel insecure with such delegation and resort to inaction. Laissez-faire leadership can be perverse and destructive, since it fails to discourage inappropriate behaviours and may even be perceived as tolerant of negative behaviours (Salin, 2003).

• *Centralized decision-making.* When deadlines and targets are not met, top-down control is exerted and decision-making becomes hierarchical, individualized (opaque) and centralized. As a consequence, individual managers become disempowered and the different management committees, which serve upward and downward information flows and participative decision-making, subsequently become ineffective. As a result, employees feel unable to voice issues and problems and tend to withhold their opinions with regard to managerial practice and procedures, organisational inefficiency and inequitable promotion and rewards systems. The sense of injustice escalates when management practice does not occur in a transparent and appropriate manner (Maslach *et al.*, 2001).

For Company A, the sudden changes result in individual and organisational frustration, incompetence and inefficiency. Conflict and violence emerge as an expression of the negative effects of the reversal in styles.

Organisational history of conflict and trauma

In the context of organisational change, Company A experienced two cases of workplace bullying within a 3 year period, 2005–2008.

Case 1: An international research assistant was subjected to extreme mistreatment at the hands of his research supervisor and head of department. The pervasive behaviours – including blackmailing behaviour, withholding official documents and delaying employment and visa procedures, setting impossible tasks and deadlines, and using the assistant's work as his own – continued over a period of 1 year. The research assistant's health began to suffer and several members of faculty, who were aware of the situation, provided personal and individual support to the victim. None of the faculty alerted management or used the formal communication channels within the organisation to alert or generate an investigation (Health and Safety Committee, trade union representatives, grievance procedures). It was only an emergency intervention by management (after a faculty member spoke up) that prevented the victim from taking his life. The victim did not pursue formal grievance procedures.

From an organisational perspective, the case highlights the degree of organisational silence: individual faculty members, despite an awareness of the situation, did not seek to collectively speak up or risk rocking the boat. In subsequent interviews, reasons for not speaking up included fear of negative repercussions or of not being believed, a feeling that it was not their responsibility to do so and, for some, an implicit belief that speaking up would not make a difference. This is consistent with research findings, that employees must believe that speaking up will be both effective and not too personally costly (Ashford *et al.*, 1998). There is also evidence of a lack of organisational learning: as the victim did not pursue official grievance procedures and the faculty member involved was dismissed from the organisation on grounds unrelated to the case, the case was not made public or used to raise levels of awareness on the issue. The case was considered to be an isolated case and attributed to some extent to the personality of the perpetrator, and hence the organisational values, policies and practices which had facilitated the bullying behaviours in the first place were not questioned.

Case 2: A senior member of the management team became the target of extreme negative behaviour from a new direct report, subsequent to the reorganisation of one of the departments. Behaviours included undermining the manager in meetings, questioning decisions previously agreed upon, withholding or delaying the communication of vital information, spreading gossip and rumours and making false allegations and pernicious personal attacks. The manager experienced devastating consequences of traumatic stress (physical and emotional repercussions), due to the degree and intensity of the repeated personal attacks – affecting identity, values and self-concept – over a period of 18 months. The manager was absent from work for 14 months.

Organisational attempts to deal with this bullying situation were unsuccessful. Formal grievance procedures were started and legal action requesting termination was taken. The manager

> returned to work after the period of sick leave to a new position within the institution on a part-time basis. Both the bully and the target are still in the organisation.

From an organisational perspective, the case illustrates the difficulty in overcoming organisational silence and denial associated with upward bullying, alien to the French hierarchical mindset: of the cases of proven bullying published on the French Ministry of Justice website, 91% of the perpetrators were in a hierarchically superior position (Bonafons *et al.*, 2008). In this case, as in the first, there was difficulty in gathering testimonials, reticence to whistleblow and a tendency to mistake the bullying behaviours for personal animosity and clash of cultures. There was also the long-term destructive effects of workplace violence at an organisational level: costs were personal (for witnesses or staff who worked on the case), social (erosion and disintegration of the organisational climate), legal and reputational (deterioration of the image of the organisation). The organisation had difficulty in rehabilitating victims when the sources and factors which triggered the bullying (individual and organisational) remained present within the workplace, and there was a resistance within the organisational structure and organisational culture to learn from the case and design living policies with regard to workplace violence. Whilst management condemns bullying, it fosters it in its management choices and style (Cru, 2001).

Conclusion/implications

The case of Company A illustrates the interplay of national and organisational cultures and their role as facilitators and contributors to the dynamics of workplace violence and conflict. It raises concerns about the individual and organisational reactions in the aftermath of the crisis and demonstrates how new patterns of behaviour emerge. When conflict remains unresolved, or when organisations fail to question their processes and practices, distorted and dysfunctional behaviours appear, both individually and institutionally. The workplace becomes a polluted environment which, rather than discouraging inappropriate behaviours, tolerates or encourages dysfunctional employees. As a system, the traumatized organisation may respond to cases of workplace violence and conflict by tougher, more inflexible and even hostile management practices which are as abrasive and destructive as the behaviours they initially sought to eradicate.

The national cultural perspective seeks to provide insight into the variables and drivers which facilitate or obstruct the design and implementation of prevention and/or intervention strategies. The power distance of a culture, and consequently the level and nature of control, will help to determine with whom, and at what level, risk factors will be examined and supportive policy decisions made. The degree of collaborative and community focus will provide insight into how deeply entrenched the values of well-being are, impacting not only the nature of potential strategies but also how their effectiveness can be measured. Hofstede's dimensions, if considered synergistically, may provide an understanding to fashion policy and organisation-wide action to reduce or resolve incidences of workplace violence and conflict.

The correlation with organisational culture is strong. However, organisational culture, because rooted in practice, changes and evolves at a more rapid pace and, together with leadership, will provide the overriding factor in advocating, motivating and controlling a process to facilitate and develop a workplace culture of respect, and encourage an environment where the organisation is better prepared to recognize and deal with the causes of violence and trauma.

References

Amason, A.C. (1996) Distinguishing the effects of functional and dysfunctional conflict on strategic decision making: resolving a paradox for top management teams. *Academy of Management Journal* **39**, 123–148.

Ashford, S. J., Rothbard, N.P., Piderit, S.K., Dutton, J.E. (1998) Out on a limb: the role of context and impression management in selling gender-equity issues. *Administrative Science Quarterly* **43**, 23–57.

Baudry, P. (2000) *French and Americans, the Other Shore*, Morhange, J.-L. (trans.). Berkeley, CA: Les Frenchies Inc.

Baumeister, R.F., Tice, D.M. (2004) Masculinity inhibits helping in emergencies: personality does predict the bystander effect. *Journal of Personality and Social Psychology* **49**(2), 420–428.

Becker, H., Fritzsche, D.J. (1987) Business ethics: a cross-cultural comparison of managers' attitudes. *Journal of Business Ethics* **6**, 289–295.

Bertrand, M., Kramarz, F., Schoar, A., Thesmar, D. (2004) Politically connected CEOs and corporate outcomes: evidence from France: http//www.mit.edu/~aschoar/politics_fulldraft4.pdf [accessed 31 July 2009].

Bonafons, C., Jehel, L., Hirigoyen, M.F., Coroller-Beque, T.A. (2008)

Encephal. *Revue de Psychiatrie Clinique Biologique et Thérapeutique* **34**(4), 419–426.

Cohen, J.R., Pant, L.W., Sharp, D.J. (1996) A methodological note on cross-cultural accounting ethics research. *International Journal of Accounting* **31**(1), 55–66.

Cru, D. (2001) Le mal-être au travail, comment intervenir? *Travail, Genre et Sociétés* **5**, 57–73.

D'Andrade, R.G. (1984) Cultural meaning systems. In Shweder, R.A., LeVine, R. (eds), *Culture Theory: Essays on Mind, Self, and Emotion.* Cambridge, UK: Cambridge University Press; 88–119.

Edmondson, A.C., Roberto, M., Watkins, M. (2001) Negotiating asymmetry: a model of top management team effectiveness. Presented at Academy of Management Meetings, Washington, DC, August 2001.

Gannon, M.J. (1994) *Understanding Global Cultures: Metaphorical Journeys through 17 Countries.* Thousand Oaks, CA: Sage.

Hall, E.T. (1977) *Beyond Culture.* New York: Anchor Press/Doubleday.

Hofstede, G. (1980) *Culture's Consequences: International Differences in Work-related Values.* Beverly Hills, CA: Sage.

Hofstede, G. (1984) The cultural relativity of the quality of life concept. *Academy of Management Review* **9**(3), 389–398.

Hofstede, G. (1993) Cultural constraints in management theories. *Academy of Management Executive* **7**(1), 81–94.

House, R.J., Wright, N.S., Aditya, R.N. (1997) Cross-cultural research on organizational leadership: a critical analysis and a proposed theory. In Early, P.C., Erez, M. (eds), *New Perspectives in International Organizational Psychology.* San Francisco, CA: New Lixington Press; 535–625.

Kim, H., Markus, H.R. (1999) Deviance or uniqueness, harmony or conformity? A cultural analysis. *Journal of Personality and Social Psychology* **77**(4), 785–800.

Maslach, C., Schaufeli, W.B., Leiter, M.P. (2001) Job burnout. *Annual Review of Psychology* **52**, 397–422.

Naulleau, G., Harper, J. (1993) A comparison of British and French management cultures: some implications for management development practices in each country. *Management Education and Development* **24**(1), 14–25.

OECD 1999. VII. Cross country patterns of product market regulation: http://www.oecd.org/dataoecd/52/4/2088199.pdf [accessed 21 July 2009].

Pesqueux, Y., Quintallet, J. (1994) *l'Ecole des Managers de Demain.* Paris: Collection Gestion Economica.

Ringov, D., Zollo, M. (2007) Corporate responsibility from a socio-institutional perspective. The impact of national culture on corporate social performance. *Corporate Governance Journal* **7**(4), 476–485.

Salin, D. (2003) Ways of explaining workplace bullying: a review of enabling, motivating and precipitating. *Human Relations* **56**(10), 1213–1232.

Schein, E.H. (1985) *Organizational Culture and Leadership.* San Francisco, CA: Jossey Bass.

Shane, S. (1993) Cultural influences on national rates of innovation. *Journal of Business Venturing* **8**(1), 59–73.

Shane, S. (1995) Uncertainty avoidance and the preference for innovation championing roles. *Journal of International Business Studies* **26**(1), 47–68.

Smith, P.B., Peterson, M.F. *et al.* (1995) Role conflict, ambiguity, and overload: a 21-nation study. *Academy of Management Journal* **38**(2), 429–452.

Tayeb, M. (1994) Organizations and national culture: methodology considered. *Organization Studies* **15**, 429.

Tehrani, N. (2004) Bullying: a source of chronic post traumatic stress? *British Journal of Guidance and Counselling* **32**(3), 357–366.

Ting-Toomey, S. (1985) Toward a theory of conflict and culture. In Gudykunst, W., Stewart, L., Ting-Toomey, S. (eds), *Communication, Culture, and Organizational Processes*. Beverly Hills, CA: Sage; 71–86.

Van der Kolk, B., Van der Hart, O. (1991) The intrusive past: the flexibility of memory and the engraving of trauma. *American Imago* **48**, 423–454.

Wacquant, L. (1997) Reading Bourdieu's Foreword to the English-language translation of Pierre Bourdieu. *La Noblesse d'État. Grandes Écoles et Esprit de Corps* (Paris: Editions de Minuit, 1989). *The State Nobility*. Cambridge: Polity Press.

Chapter 11

Risk, business continuity and the parts people play

Julia Graham and Tim Chadwick

Introduction: the risk landscape and the management of risk

As the commercial, legal, regulatory, political, financial, social, technological and security environment becomes more complex, global, interconnected, challenging and 'risky' than ever before, the effective management of risk is clearly key to an organisation achieving its objectives and, in certain cases, its survival. Risk is often viewed purely in the negative, and about prevention; however, the discipline of risk management is concerned with both the 'upside' of risk and maximizing opportunities and the 'downside' of risk and addressing problems. As Steve Fowler, CEO of the Institute of Risk Management (IRM), cites:

> Risk management provides us with a framework for dealing with and reacting to uncertainty (Fowler, 2006).

The more an organisation understands all the risks it faces, the more calculated risks it can take, which can result in a healthier, more agile, more productive and more profitable company. As outlined in BS31100:

> Through a dynamic risk management process and an understanding of the context in which the organisation exists, risks can be effectively identified, analysed, evaluated, treated, monitored and reviewed (BSI, 2008).

The route to effective risk management is good quality management information, viewing the risk landscape as a whole and not in silos, and consequently understanding how all of the working parts operate. Today's modern risk manager consequently manages risk across the organisation, using the tools and techniques of what is becoming accepted as enterprise risk management (ERM). Research undertaken by the UK Association of Insurance and Risk Management (AIRMIC) and consultants DNV concluded that ERM key success factors involve a risk response that is PACED:

- Proportionate to the level of risk faced by the organisation and its risk profile.
- Aligned with other activities in the organisation.
- Comprehensive involving all parts of the organisation.
- Embedded with core processes.
- Dynamic and responsive to the changing risk landscape.

In 2008 the UK Health and Safety Executive published a report which highlighted the key success factors for effective health and safety management as leadership, involvement, learning, accountability and communication – which are very similar to those of ERM.

The reader might conclude from this introduction that much of what follows and which is heralded as good risk management practice is equally good management practice and makes good business sense.

When risks become incidents

Today's organisations face a myriad of different kinds of risks that can impact on their ability to meet their objectives, such as financial risks, strategic risks, operational risks, credit risks, market risks, etc. One of the key organisational controls and response mechanisms to risks such as technology failure, civil disturbance and protest, acts of terrorism, utilities failure, loss of buildings and denial of access, failure of an outsourced supplier, severe weather, kidnap, the effects of pandemics and internal and external adverse events that can all result in serious damage to or loss of assets, injury or death is business continuity management (BCM).

While all the risks cited as examples have a direct and/or indirect impact on people, a number of them have a clear potential trauma component, should they materialize and become significant incidents.

How an organisation responds to significant incidents can have a major bearing on the organisation's employees, management, brand, reputation, share price, clients and suppliers. Good management of incidents can have a disproportionate benefit and value to organisations, such as enhanced brand and reputation, increased morale and employee goodwill and enhanced shareholder confidence and value. In stark contrast, poor management of an incident can have serious consequences, from which some organisations will never recover and may even fail. 'Business-as-usual' processes and resources are ill-equipped to deal with the scope, demands, intensity and pace of significant incidents; an effective organisational response requires pre-thought, senior level sponsorship, leadership, planning, the identification and sourcing of key resources and solutions, communication, training and exercising. While insurance can cover many aspects of the financial loss associated with incidents, it cannot and does not replace or deliver the organisation's response to an incident – this can only come from the organisation. The response to an incident isn't something that can be 'made up' in short order when the unthinkable happens. This is where BCM comes into play.

This chapter provides a business continuity and incident management practitioner perspective, and focuses on:

- Defining what BCM is and, specifically, the role that incident management plays in helping organisations effectively manage incidents.
- Outlining the key things organisations need to have in terms of incident management to ensure they are prepared and can respond in a timely and effective way.
- Demonstrating through a number of short case studies how incident management was used to manage real organisational incidents, and the specific people and trauma issues and interventions that were deployed.

Business continuity management

Business continuity management is a growing and evolving management discipline, which is increasingly becoming recognized as good management practice. The British Standard for Business Continuity Management, BS25999 (BSI, 2007), defines business continuity as the 'strategic and tactical capability to plan for and respond to incidents and business disruptions in order to continue business operations at an acceptable pre-defined level'. While the ultimate purpose of business continuity is to ensure that the organisation's critical activities can be continued or recovered in the event of an incident, the outcome of business continuity is also the protection of:

- The interests of the organisation's people and other key stakeholders.
- Information.
- Reputation and brand.
- Value creating activities.

While organisations implement business continuity to reflect the nature, scale and complexity of their operations and their culture, there is a well-recognized and fundamental distinction between two types of plans and teams:

- Incident management (sometimes referred to as crisis management).
- Business continuity.

The precise scope of incident management plans and teams may differ from organisation to organisation, but typically an incident management team has responsibility for:

- Assessing the nature and impacts of the incident.
- Taking immediate control of the incident.
- Containing the incident.
- Managing and co-coordinating the organisation's overall response to the incident until its conclusion.
- Communicating with stakeholders.

In contrast, business continuity plans and teams typically have responsibility for managing the more operational response in relation to employees, customers, suppliers, etc., the recovery and reinstatement of critical processes, and the restoration of lost work-in-progress following an incident. Both types of plans and teams work 'hand-in-hand' to deliver an effective recovery. In this chapter we will focus on the incident management team, plan, processes and deployment, and provide some examples of the people considerations including trauma management issues.

Hoping for the best, preparing for the worst – building a successful incident management response

Man has developed complicated models to manage complicated risks, but these appear to have a habit of failing. How can it be that risks clearly identified as hovering on the horizon have been at worst ignored and at best managed with an apparent level of breathtaking incompetence (World Economic Forum, 2009)?

Man is naturally a creature of the short term, taking comfort from the fact that we are managing what threatens our immediate objectives. It is harder to manage the monster coming over the hill, especially if these risks are viewed in isolation from the other risks they interconnect with, and especially if governments, government agencies and organisations manage them in isolation.

We naturally have short-term horizons – and the upfront costs of risk mitigation can look disproportionately large relative to the expected benefits. Coupled with short-termism, this can lead to the 'not in my term of office' approach. Organisations need to move away from the mind set of 'it cannot happen to us' to the mind set of 'what if it occurs?'. Thinking needs to be longer term and more joined up.

Incident management teams, plans and processes and capability cannot be magically conjured up when an incident has already taken place; it takes forethought, ownership and planning. Management of an organisation are responsible for owning incident management and for exercising leadership in establishing the environment within which informed decisions can be taken by informed and properly skilled and equipped teams.

To be effective, an organisation's incident management approach and teams need to interface with the overall culture of the organisation, and should not be created in isolation. Failure to recognize the importance of integration can result in an incident management team that is isolated from an organisation and lacks knowledge, networks, wider resources, goodwill and empowerment at a time when this is most crucial.

The team – created from a blueprint or by design?

There is no formula or blueprint that guarantees the perfect incident management team. However, experience points towards there being a number of key success factors that underpin high performing incident management teams.

Team functionality, roles and responsibilities

The make-up of an incident management team should reflect the scale, nature, culture and complexity of an organisation, and the broad range of risks and incidents that it could face. The team membership should be sufficiently broad, functionally covering a number of disciplines, e.g. HR, communications, technology, facilities management, legal, key business sectors, etc., to enable the leader of the team to pick the specific members and functions, skills and competencies needed to match the particular shape of an incident when it occurs. An incident management team's membership may be supplemented with external individuals and resources, should these not exist internally. A good example of this is having a predetermined external trauma specialist and counselling expert as members of the team, with associated helplines or other resources, which can be called upon in the event of incident that has a trauma component to it.

All team members should have clearly defined incident management roles and responsibilities and understand how they fit into the wider team, coupled with the decision-making authority that they will have in an incident. Briefing team members and checking their understanding is important; and this should also be tested when the team is exercised, given its criticality.

Identifying and selecting team members

Managing an incident well requires team members who can work effectively under significant duress, deal with uncertainties and conflicting information and priorities, remain clear-headed and focused, and take and implement decisions at pace. There are many key challenges in identifying and selecting team members. Since day-to-day working life rarely tests individuals in the way an incident does, insights into how an individual will respond to the pressure of an incident may be limited. However, analysing how individuals cope with tight deadlines, for example in a project environment, and how people react to challenge, tensions and conflict in a business-as-usual context, either on an individual basis or within a group, can often reveal some key indicators on the potential suitability of an individual for future service within the incident management team. Organisations also need to recognize that, sometimes, those best equipped to be effective in an incident are not necessarily always the most obvious or senior individuals in organisations. This can create some interesting discussions where diplomacy is required to ensure the support of key stakeholders for the team and those that make up the team, so that when the team is invoked, their incident management responsibilities and authorities are not undermined.

Potential team members need to understand what is likely to be asked of them in the event of an incident, and to have both the ability and appetite to be part of an incident management team. If either of these two elements is missing, the team is destined to under-perform (Kaye and Graham, 2006). It may suffer from decision-making paralysis and inaction, and individuals may be damaged psychologically by the experience of an incident because they are ill-equipped to cope in an incident environment. Team members can become acutely affected incident victims. There is consequently a duty on an organisation to consider carefully who it should select to serve on its incident management team, and to ensure that individuals are not unduly pressured to accept these responsibilities and are empowered to decline and say 'no' should there be sufficient and sensible reasons to do so. An unwilling team member may not only become a victim but a liability to those other team members at a critical time.

Exercising has a key role to play in helping to validate that a team has the right membership and individuals involved. However, even if an organisation has taken all practical steps to ensure that the most appropriate individuals are part of the incident management team, it should be recognized that people can behave differently when faced with the challenge of an incident; any victim or emergency responder after an incident will be in an altered state of consciousness. The degree of that alteration is the variable (Hawkins-Mitchell, 2004). There will therefore always be a degree of uncertainty around how individual members and the team will perform in a live incident, and this must be understood and taken into consideration by the team leader (and his/her alternate).

The plan and exercising

The dynamics for a successful crisis management plan include:

- Being integrated and organisation-wide.
- Being easily accessible and quick to implement.
- Ability to deal with multiple developments and inter-dependencies.
- Clear definitions of what an incident is and processes for notification, escalation and invocation.
- Equipping the team members with clear roles, responsibilities and relevant expert resources.
- Enabling the team to be contacted 24/7 and providing the team with physical and virtual locations to meet.
- Identifying key actions with timescales.
- A communications infrastructure.
- Being flexible to changes in circumstances.

The better the plan, the better the team that uses that plan and the better the team can manage through the abnormal circumstance they are likely to face during and following a crisis. Plans should be reviewed periodically or as part of a significant organisational change to ensure they remain current and fit for purpose.

The team and the plan should be regularly exercised against a number of scenarios, to help stress-test the plan and its processes, validate contact information and member accessibility, and build confidence, understanding and capability among the team, in preparation for when an incident occurs.

Leadership is key

Strong 'incident-capable' leadership within an incident scenario is key. Incident-capable leadership may be significantly different to the style of leadership that fits with an organisation's day-to-day culture. Managing incidents effectively often requires a leader to be able to quickly process and make sense of large amounts of disparate, imperfect, incomplete and often conflicting information, assess a situation and developments using the talents he/she has around him/her, and use judgement and information to make significant decisions decisively under duress, at a pace substantially quicker than in a business-as-usual environment. Where an organisation's dominant leadership style is highly participative and decision making is very collaborative and consensus-driven, it will typically take too long to make decisions and make it very difficult to exert a level of control over the incident. This can present some organisations with real challenges when it comes to identifying an incident-capable leader, and gaining agreement that a leadership style different to the organisation's norm is both desired and acceptable in an incident environment.

The naturalistic decision-making (NDM) framework emerged as a means of studying how people actually make decisions and perform cognitively complex functions in demanding situations. These include situations marked by time pressure, uncertainty, vague goals, high stakes, team and organisational constraints, changing conditions and varying amounts of experience.

The NDM framework focuses on cognitive functions such as decision making, sense making, situational awareness, and planning. Many researchers agree that good teams monitor their performance and self-correct; offer feedback; maintain awareness of roles and functions and take action consistent with that knowledge; adapt to changes in the task or the team; communicate effectively; anticipate each others needs and coordinate their actions (Zsambok and Klein, 1997).

Rhona Flin (1996) describes the role of the individual leading the on-scene response, the person responsible for interpreting the situation, adapting plans and managing the response process. Flin highlights the fact that the professionalism and effectiveness of most emergency and disaster response activities belies the complexity of the command role and the substantial and complex demands that this role makes on those who fulfil it. Personal, psychological and group factors interact with incident characteristics to determine response effectiveness and well-being. Flin further argues that, irrespective of the quality of plans and procedures, the psychological parameters introduced by the presence of the incident manager can affect the quality of their implementation and the extent to which events are contained or escalate. The nature, number and diversity of the demands triggered by a disaster calls for the cooperative input of several individuals. Moreover, the complexity and ambiguity inherent within the response process often requires that incident managers call upon their colleagues to obtain appropriate information, make decisions and decide on a course of action to deal with the demands encountered to a far greater extent than would be required when responding to more routine events.

Incident management team people issues

There are a number of people issues that can directly impact on an incident management team's performance during an incident. What follows are three key examples of issues to be particularly aware of.

Safety of incident management team members' family, friends and relatives

Do you know for sure how you would react if faced by an incident that touched you, your family, friends or colleagues? Do you know how you would react if a pandemic did reach material levels of infection, or a dirty bomb exploded in your community? The answer is, probably not. Incident management plans must accommodate how people might behave in an unpredictable way with unpredictable consequences. Research has concluded that people will generally do as instructed if they have confidence that their loved ones are safe and that instructions have been tested and proven – and that any safe havens are indeed just that – prepared and well organised.

An organisation cannot expect its people – including the incident management team – to operate effectively if the people concerned are worrying about others.

Incident management team fatigue

When incidents occur, they usually have the characteristics of being extremely intense, focused and adrenaline propelled experiences. Incident management teams need to dedicate significant amounts of time to exerting control over an incident and delivering a myriad of actions to ensure that the incident is contained and effectively managed. A combination of adrenaline and long hours often results in sleep loss, both in terms of quantity and quality. Research (Culpin and Whelan, 2009) suggests that even relatively minor reductions in sleep can have significant effects, for example a reduction of 1.5 hours' sleep for one night alone can result in a reduction in daytime alertness of 32%. Poor and insufficient sleep as a direct consequence of being involved in managing an incident can cause fatigue, attention difficulties, headaches, memory problems, concentration problems and mood changes. It is important to monitor the health and fatigue levels within incident management team members, and to ensure that members have predefined capable and available alternates who can replace them before their well-being and performance significantly decreases.

It's good to talk

Given the nature, seriousness and sometimes distressing aspects of incidents, although the incident management team is focused on helping others, the incident management team members should also not be forgotten, since they themselves may have indirectly or directly experienced a level of trauma associated with the incident. It is important that incident management team members are properly debriefed following an incident, and that a watching brief is maintained on those members who may be vulnerable to post-traumatic stress. These dynamics can change or evolve over a period of time, and it should not be assumed that the absence of immediate evidence of trauma can be taken as evidence of no longer-term effects. Those within close proximity to such individuals, e.g. line management, need to be adequately briefed on potential tell-tale signs of post-traumatic stress and advised on what they should do if they observe or believe indicators exist, using external expert guidance and support as appropriate.

How did it go?

All organisations should squeeze every learning point out of every incident which they define as material. Many incident managers and business continuity managers travel through their careers without encountering a material incident. When they do happen, organisations must learn and, where appropriate, adopt changes and improve their response. Key success factors can be quantitative (the value of assets recovered, the level of downtime and loss of revenue) or qualitative (perceived harm to the brand or reputation of an organisation). Where do people fit in here? The answer is everywhere. As with any rehearsal, the urgency of the real thing will be missing. Mapping out what actually happened should fuel future responses. How did people respond, did the teams operate as expected, did people react as planned, did customers support or desert you and why, and if the same or a similar event happened again, how would you have reacted differently – how does the approach and content of plans and teams need to change?

Case studies: trauma management and people issues as an integral component of incident management – from theory to practice

Case study 1. We're in the hands of experts – it's all a load of fuss

Businesses remain committed to demonstrating support to their people and to environmental issues. Supporting expeditions which provide a high profile and visible opportunity to do this can be used to capture a wide interest by the direct participation of a few. A cautionary warning is, however, that if you put your organisation and some of its people into a spotlight and things go wrong, an ensuing crisis is of as high a profile if not higher profile, than any success . . . bad news can be good news to parts of the media.

An expedition of young people from several parts of the world set sail with high expectations of the clean up work that they would undertake in the Antarctic and the great profile that this would achieve in tugging at the consciousness of the readers of the newspaper that would track their adventure.

The company that supported the adventure had designed and communicated an incident and business continuity plan and although this had been considered by some to be an over-engineered reaction, its existence was to prove vital.

As the young explorers under the guidance of their expedition host set sail in a yacht from South America, one of the explorers was taken ill and over a period of just a few days became increasingly unwell. As the seriousness of the situation became apparent the person in charge on the yacht raised an alarm. When the first call came into the company, those who took that call feared the worst. Miles from land, miles from medical experts, if the illness on board was serious, their prognosis of the situation was grim. They immediately invoked the incident management plan and took control but it was too late – the young explorer by then had already died.

It became evident very early on that the other young people on board had not appreciated for some while the death of their colleague, continuing to attempt resuscitation.

The incident management plan had a pre-appointed psychologist, travel repatriation specialist and lawyer – as well as individuals from each business represented on board. On the advice of these professionals, two plans swung into action:

- Focusing on the deceased, their family and colleagues
- Focusing on the people who had survived, their families, colleagues and their collective well-being

Plan 1 involved, with the police, communicating the terrible news to the family of the deceased and complying with their request to see their child returned home as soon as possible, which involved repatriation of the body avoiding red tape in an unfamiliar part of the world with an offer of support and advice.

Plan 2 involved making sure that the young people and their crew were taken care of, counselled and protected from media interest.

Delivering Plan 1 took the courage of local managers, careful offers of counselling to family and colleagues and a sympathetic arm of condolence to be extended in an unobtrusive way by the company. Media interest was high as the expedition had been tracked by a newspaper from the home country of the deceased and the company involved was very visible and the names and locations of those taking part became public knowledge. Actions were taken and communications issued with the permission of family and involvement of colleagues and co-ordinated by a central team.

Delivering Plan 2 involved the creation of a small team who travelled to South America who set up a base and environment in which to receive the survivors. As with Plan 1, actions were taken and communications issued with the permission of family and involvement of colleagues and coordinated by the same central team. The survivors were kept together and counselled as a team who knew how it had been and understood how others in the team felt. After just over a week this team was broken up and individuals travelled back, each with a familiar escort, to their home country.

Lessons to take away:

- Be sure that the profile of an event if things go wrong is worth taking the risk.
- Conduct a risk assessment and have plans in place that match the assessment.
- Do not rely on those who arrange events to do your job and to manage your risk.
- Use experts and know who these are and how to reach them before an event needs to use them.
- Listen and respond to what your expert advisors say.
- Appreciate that post-trauma reactions can be immediate and longer-term.
- Acknowledge that more than one plan may be needed if there is more than one situation to recover.
- Co-ordination is key.
- Communication should be honest, appropriate and coordinated.
- Accept that there is no blueprint for recovery and that plans and teams must be flexible to meet needs as they arise – and change.
- Don't forget the recovery teams – they may have shouldered much of the pressure and stress of the event and may need caring for too.

Case study 2. Managing resilience and response to a pandemic – it's hysterical

The risk of a pandemic has never strayed far off the risk radar and awareness has been raised from time to time by outbreaks of severe acute respiratory syndrome (SARS) – 'avian flu' and 'swine flu'.

People, organisations and governments have reacted differently to this risk, but there is a common theme regarding the specialist incident and business continuity required. An incident involving a health scare can create mass hysteria and irrational reaction, especially when so many people are affected or think that they might be. The World Health Organization (WHO) provides a mechanism using pandemic phases which, if used as triggers for action, can cause disproportionate reaction. These phases can be tracked by following WHO web alerts but can also provide a way of building up hysteria globally from a source which carries credibility and respectability. Phases can blind the incident manager and business continuity planner as they become transfixed by the need to act, regardless of whether the triggers really do indicate the need to escalate. And of course if an organisation does not react, then their people may react anyway. Trying to manage and control hysteria is no easy business.

What makes this so challenging is that this subject is complex, outcomes are unpredictable and uncertain, and taking control can be almost impossible as people take control of the response themselves. Coupled with different cultural reactions, often based on the experience of previous and similar diseases, such as SARS, the business continuity planner must take account of global and local perspectives – political, social, economic, cultural and sector-specific.

How do you plan, react and communicate in such circumstances? The first action, as with any other scenario, is to gather and monitor the facts, analyse and share them. Where is the risk, how is it perceived and what is the organisation doing to manage this? A global organisation took the following strategy:

- Tell people what you know; be open, honest and proportionate.
- Be fair but firm in communication; don't encourage people to follow their own course of action.
- Take care not to unintentionally amend contracts of employment in the way that you issue advice; questions and answers are a good way of addressing issues.
- Take and communicate independent expert advice; it's easy for an organisation to unintentionally provide medical opinions.
- Respect and reflect local differences. Some governments require employers to provide face masks, other cultures demand them, and some cultures consider them a waste of time and a personal intrusion. Some governments will run temperature checks at the point of entry to their country, others will not. No solution is wrong – but the business continuity manager has to understand and react to these.
- If you have interventions, such as the issue of drugs such

as Tamiflu, these have a shelf-life, need medically supervised distribution and ultimately you have no control over who takes the drugs in question – for example, employees may pass drugs to their family, rather than take them themselves.

According to Chris Woodcock (2005), managing director at the UK-based pan-European crisis and risk management consultancy, Razor, there are steps required in preparing for a pandemic or the threat of one:

- *Enlightenment.* Making people able to understand the risks and benefits (and their interactions).
- *Behavioural changes.* Making people aware of potential risks and benefits helps them to make the right choices.
- *Trust building.* Assisting health education bodies to generate and sustain trust.
- *Conflict resolution.* Assisting health education bodies to involve major stakeholders and affected parties to take part in the risk–benefit evaluation.

Chris goes on to explore the stepping stones towards developing a communications plan. Communicators need to specify in advance:

- Purpose of communication (orientation, behavioural advice, involvement).
- Aspects of risk–benefit debate (risk challenges, benefit problems).
- Types of audiences to be approached.
- Available risk communication resources and channels.
- Follow-up after the risk communication programme is completed.
- Design for evaluation.

Trust and credibility cannot be produced or manufactured but only earned in terms of performance and effective communication. Pandemics are hard to predict, manage and communicate. People will react and overreact differently. Reactions can be stimulated by past experiences and cultural and government drivers. But fear is real and organisations should face and not dismiss this. Open communication building trust and using expert advice can allay concerns. Think and research widely.

Organisations in the southern hemisphere entered their winter in 2009 before the northern hemisphere and provided some useful pointers – as did the governments of Australia and New Zealand, who reacted with proportionality.

References

BSI (2007) Business continuity code of practice; Part 1, BS25999, British Standards Institution: http://shop.bsigroup.com/ProductDetail/?pid=000000000030169700 [accessed 2 November 2009].

BSI (2008) Risk management code of practice, BS31100, British Standards Institution: http://shop.bsigroup.com/en/ProductDetail/?pid=000000000030191339 [accessed 2 November 2009].

Culpin, V., Whelan, A. (2009) The wake-up call for sleepy managers. *Ashridge Journal* **Spring**.

Flin, R. (1996) *Sitting in the Hot Seat: Leaders and Teams for Critical Incident Management*. Chichester, UK: Wiley.

Fowler, S. (2006) Foreword – everybody's business: an introduction to the risk management universe. In Hillson, D. (ed.), *The Risk Management Universe – A Guided Tour*. London: British Standards Institution.

Hawkins-Mitchell, V. (2004) *Emotional Terrors in the Workplace: Protecting Your Business's Bottom Line*. Brookfield, CT: Rothstein Associates.

Kaye, D., Graham, J. (2006) *A Risk Management Approach to Business Continuity*. Brookfield, CT: Rothstein Associates.

Woodcock, C. (2005) Pandemic or pandemonium? Drawing on crisis management best practice to prepare for the worst: http://www. continuitycentral.com/feature0277.htm [accessed 6 November 2009].

World Economic Forum (2009) Global risks 2009: http://www.weforum.org/pdf/globalrisk/globalrisks09/contributors.htm [accessed 2 November 2009].

Zsambok, C.E., Klein, G. (1997) *Naturalistic Decision Making*. Mahwah, NJ: Lawrence Erlbaum.

Part III

Organisational
interventions

Supporting the police following the 7/7 London terrorist bombs – an organisational approach

Noreen Tehrani, Christie Rainbird and Bernadette Dunne

Introduction

On 7 July 2005, suicide bombers attacked London's transport system during the morning rush hour. At 8:50 a.m. three bombs exploded within seconds of each other. The first bomb exploded on a Circle Line train between Liverpool Street and Aldgate, the second on the westbound Circle Line at Edgware Road, and the third on the southbound Piccadilly Line train between Kings Cross and Russell Square. Almost an hour later, a fourth bomb exploded on a bus in Tavistock Square. The bombings occurred at a time that the UK was hosting the first full day of the G8 summit at Gleneagles in Scotland, and London was celebrating winning the bid to host the 2012 Summer Olympics. The bombs killed 52 commuters and four suicide bombers and at least 700 people were injured, many seriously. The terrorist attacks caused a severe disruption to London's transport and communications systems and stretched the resources of all the emergency services. British Transport Police Officers were amongst the first on the scene; most were involved as rescuers but some experienced the bomb blasts as primary victims. Body recovery commenced when all the live casualties had been rescued and continued for 2 weeks. The British Transport Police Service (BTP) is the UK's national police force for railways, providing a policing service for rail operators, their staff and passengers. The BTP service is funded by the train operations companies to reduce crime and disruption on the railways. In 2005 the service employed 2774 police officers and 1204 police staff, and during the previous year the service had handled over 250 fatalities and 100 serious injuries on railway property. Most frontline BTP police officers, therefore, would expect to deal with several suicides and other deaths during a year (British Transport Police, 2006).

Major incidents and the police

There is an increasing interest in the effect that disasters can have upon emergency workers (Paton and Violanti, 2006; Volanti *et al.*, 2006; Greene, 2001). However, police officers tend to have longer-term involvement with disaster victims than the other services in terms of their roles of body removal, identification and investigation. Despite their exposure to trauma, the prevalence of PTSD in police officers undertaking rescue/recovery duties at the World Trade Center disaster was half that observed in other involved groups (Perrin *et al.*, 2007) and the number of police officers with PTSD was 6.2%, significantly lower than in other groups of workers. This finding is consistent with a study undertaken on the police who were involved in body recovery following the *Piper Alpha* disaster (Alexander and Wells, 1991), in which it was found that police officers emerged from their experiences unscathed and in some cases had gained from their experience. A longitudinal study of police involved with the Paddington rail crash showed that 3% of police officers experienced a late-onset PTSD (Luce *et al.*, 2003).

Trauma management in BTP

Prior to 2005, BTP had employed an individual-focused counselling approach to dealing with the impact of major rail crashes on their employees. Counsellors would be engaged to provide counselling and support typically at the scene of the disaster. In the autumn of 2004, the Commander of the London North Area of BTP commissioned a pilot study to introduce a more organisational approach to the provision of trauma support. The trauma management programme was adapted from a generic approach which had been shown to be effective in a number of organisations (Tehrani, 2004) and is described in Chapter 14. At the time of the London bombings, a number of training courses had already taken place and 23 BTP officers in supervisory and management roles had been trained in crisis management, demobilization and defusing. A draft trauma policy had also been prepared by Occupational Health, which was to introduce the BTP Trauma Support Programme that had been designed to support officers engaged in the normal day-to-day incidents that occurred on the railways, as well as the other policing activities that involved the officers in dealing with violent and disturbing incidents.

Dealing with the disaster (day 1)

Within the first few hours following the bombings, several hundred officers and staff were being deployed in dealing with this major incident. Officers entered the underground tunnels to rescue the injured and confused passengers and later to recover the bodies of the dead. The number of BTP employees involved in dealing with the 7/7 bombings made it impossible to employ the approach that had been designed for a smaller-scale incident, where a relatively few officers would be deployed. On the day of the bombings, the BTP senior management team met and took the decision to activate the major incident trauma support programme, which was coordinated by the Occupational Health Department. The day of the bombings was difficult and demanding for all concerned, with the situation being made more difficult because of the serious disruption of the transport and telecommunications systems. The bombing of the bus in Tavistock Square, close to the then headquarters of BTP, resulted in many of the injured passengers and distressed bystanders being taken into the BTP building, where they were offered first aid, help and support from the officers and staff working there.

Risk assessment and initial support (days 2–10)

Over the next 10 days, 321 BTP employees became involved in one or more aspects of dealing with the bombings. The main task assumed by Occupational Health during the first few days was to ensure that officers' basic health and well-being needs were met. The Occupational Health team established a number of clinics on different sites in London. Using advice provided by the Health Protection Agency, the Fire Service and other safety consultants, and following a risk assessment, the initial activities were focused on the direct impact of the bombs on officers. Respiratory/cardiovascular and hearing tests, together with testing for smoke and dust inhalation and contact with toxic biological substances, was put in place for officers who had been directly involved in the rescue and recovery of passengers. Officers were also given an opportunity to talk about their involvement in the rescue activities and recovery of passengers, and were reminded of the importance of taking time to rest and recover from their experiences.

During the first 10 days, preparations were made to identify a suitable location for a Trauma Support Centre, where officers and staff could be screened and provided with information and support. Despite having to travel into London, which was difficult for some, it was found that choosing a hotel in central London would be preferable for access and convenience, rather than trying to organise a location outside London. It was also decided to adopt a screen-and-treat approach to the trauma support, which required the development of a physical and psychological screening protocol for the initial trauma assessment. During the first few days, Occupational Health worked on the development of a number of information and guidance sheets for BTP employees, their families and friends. As the internal counselling resources were limited, it was decided to augment the in-house resources with additional trauma counsellors and debriefers; it was essential that the counsellors were experienced in working with emergency services dealing with disasters. The role of the counsellors and debriefers at the initial assessment was to be available to talk with those employees who were found to be suffering from high levels of anxiety, depression or traumatic stress. One of the most important tasks during the first few days was to identify the officers and staff who had been exposed to the bombings: (a) as a passenger on one of the trains or the bus; (b) as a rescuer or first aider in a private capacity; or (c) had been deployed in the rescue and recovery process.

Initial assessment (IA: within 14 days of the bombing)

The Trauma Support Centre consisted of a large reception area and a number of smaller consultation rooms. Light snacks, water, fruit juice and hot drinks were available throughout the day. Employees attending the Trauma Support Centre were welcomed by one of the two administrators who maintained the database of employees who had been reported as having been exposed to some aspect of the bombings. The administrators were an essential part of the team, as they organised the appointments, handed out the assessment questionnaires and made sure that the employees were comfortable.

Whilst every effort was made by management to provide a complete list of people requiring an assessment, it became clear over the following days and weeks that many more people had been involved than had been initially anticipated. Attending officers and staff would frequently identify other colleagues who they felt should have been invited for the assessment. By the end of the initial assessment, 266 employees had attended. The initial assessment included a physical check-up, assessment of their level of trauma exposure and the completion of two clinical questionnaires, the Hospital Anxiety and Depression Scale (Snaith and Zigmond, 1994) and the Impact of Events Scale (Extended) (Tehrani et al., 2002). The questionnaires were scored by the administrators. Each employee was seen individually by an Occupational Health nurse, who checked their physical well-being and the results of their completed questionnaires. 105 employees who had been found to have high levels of symptoms were offered an opportunity to have individual sessions, using a model of debriefing which allowed the employee to describe his/her actual experiences but avoiding the need to reactivate his/her emotional responses (Tehrani, 2004). The Trauma Support Centre provided an environment in which the BTP employees had time to quietly reflect on what had happened during the previous fortnight.

Follow-up and referral to trauma clinic (FU: 6–8 weeks)

Between 6 and 8 weeks after the bombings employees with high initial scores were followed up. Following an agreement between BTP and the London Development Centre for Mental Health, BTP officers and staff were given an opportunity to access a free traumatic stress clinic for screening and treatment (Brewin et al., 2008). The BTP Occupational Health practitioners administered the Trauma Screening Questionnaire (Brewin et al., 2002) and initially identified nine employees who appeared to be appropriate for referral to the trauma clinic. These employees were referred to the trauma clinic in September 2005, by which time the clinic had begun to deliver services.

Mid-term assessment (MTA: 6–8 months)

Six months after the bombings, all the officers and staff who had attended the initial assessment were contacted and asked to complete the HADS and the IES-E for a second time. Where officers were found to have high scores, additional support was offered by Occupational Health and, where appropriate or requested by the employee, a referral was made to the Trauma Support Clinic.

Third assessment and survey (TA: 11 months)

In May 2006 officers and staff were sent a survey which also included the IES-E; it was decided to undertake the survey 1 month prior to the anniversary, to avoid the results being affected by emotional impact or the media coverage and, in addition, the identifying of vulnerable employees who might need additional support during the anniversary. The survey gathered a range of information including: demographics, levels of involvement, personal experiences and feelings, previous traumatic exposures, subsequent traumatic exposures, sickness absence, help and support received. 96 BTP employees who completed the third assessment and survey, 57 of whom had not been involved, had an initial or follow-up assessment.

Anniversary support

In the week before the anniversary, employees with high trauma scores were contacted and offered the support of their OH advisor. A briefing note was also prepared for managers, which provided information on the symptoms of post-traumatic stress and guidance on the best way to support their teams. Members of the Occupational Health team were present at stations and at other memorial gatherings. A number of officers and members of the staff found that the anniversary gathering reactivated their traumatic memories and responses and were provided with personal support from the Occupational Health nurses and trained BTP officers.

Final assessment (FA)

For those BTP employees who did not complete the survey in May 2006, a further attempt was made to gather information; however, it was thought appropriate to leave a gap of 6 months to allow the impact of the anniversary to dissipate. Unfortunately, by this time some of the BTP employees had left the service or did not wish to take part in any further assessments. However, an additional 58 employees did complete the IES-E between November and December 2006.

Traumatic stress clinic (TSC) referrals

Twenty-six officers and staff were referred to the TSC by Occupational Health and six self-referred, with 19 of the referrals taking place within the first 6 months. Three of the employees chose not to take up the referral; of those who attended, five were found to have an adjustment disorder, one a dysthymic disorder, one a major depressive disorder, 12 were diagnosed with PTSD and the remainder were assessed as not having a significant psychiatric condition. Seven required no treatment, 13 were discharged and, 2 years after the bombings, five were still receiving treatment.

Results

At the initial assessment, mean scores of 264 BTP employees were: anxiety, 2.91 (SD = 3.293); depression, 1.39 (SD = 2.090); avoidance, 4.85 (SD = 6.225); arousal, 3.35 (SD = 5.046); and re-experience, 5.34 (SD = 7.198). The numbers of employees experiencing moderate or severe level of symptoms on HADS were: anxiety, 6 (2%); depression, 0 (0%); IES-E avoidance, 26 (10%); arousal, 10 (4%); and re-experience, 14 (5%). At the mid-term assessment (6–8 months), the mean scores had fallen: t-test (95% CI): anxiety, $t = 14.165$, df 265, $p < 0.001$; depression, $t = 10.657$, df 265, $p < 0.001$; avoidance, $t = 12.776$, df 265, $p < 0.001$; arousal, $t = 11.034$, df 265, $p < 0.001$; and re-experience, $t = 12.394$, df 265, $p < 0.001$. At the mid-term assessment, all the BTP employees tested scored below the IES-E cut-off levels of 50 and were found to be in the normal range for HADS. At the third assessment, one employee had IES-E scores above the cut-off level. At the final assessment, four employees had IES-E scores above the cut-off level; however, it was found that all the employees with high scores at the final assessment also had high scores at the initial assessment and were being treated by the traumatic stress clinic.

Survey findings

The survey that was carried out 11 months after the bombings found that most of the BTP employees (92%) involved in dealing with the aftermath of the bombings were police officers. There was a wide range in the length of service, with 44% having less than 5 years' service and 61% less than 15 years' service. 85% were male and 28% had managerial responsibility. There were no significant differences between the IES-E scores of BTP employees based on age, sex or length of service. Of the 96 BTP employees who completed the survey there was a high level of involvement in dealing with the bombings, with 7% having witnessed the bombs exploding on a train or bus, 79% having worked at the scene of the bombings, 49% having feared for their safety, 50% serving as rescuers, 17% supporting the bereaved, 21% administering first aid, 54% witnessing people with severe injuries, 25% attending to the dying, 28% involved in body removal, 16% running the mortuary, 11% involved in body identification, and 3% who knew at least one of the victims. The strength of association between these experiences and the IES-E scores at the initial assessment (IA), mid-term assessment (MA) and the third assessment (TA) was tested using a Pearson correlation (Table 12.1).

Exposure to suicides and bomb threats on the railways

Whilst it is a normal part of the role for some BTP officers to recover body parts following an accident or suicide on the railway, of the 90 BTP employees who responded to this question in the survey, 66.7% had never had to deal with body recovery tasks, 24 had handled less than six bodies, five officers had handled between six and 20 bodies and one officer had handled 70 bodies. In the 11 months following the London bombings, 55% of officers undertook no body handling; 39 officers handled less than six bodies and three officers between six and 12 bodies. Prior to the London bombings, 74% of officers had never dealt with a bomb threat and the remaining officers had dealt with between one and five bomb threats. During the 18 months following the London bombings, 78% of officers did not have to deal with a bomb threat and 22% had handled between one and 10 bomb threats each. No significant correlation was found between the number of deaths or bomb threats handled and the level of trauma symptoms.

Levels of satisfaction with support

The survey assessed the level of satisfaction the BTP employees experienced with the support they had been provided. The most frequently accessed source of support was from Occupational Health, which is not surprising, as the Occupational Health assessment was made available during working hours to all officers and staff affected by the bombings. Debriefing was also provided through Occupational Health to officers and staff who were found to have high levels of anxiety, depression or trauma symptoms. Support from colleagues, families and friends was used by many of the BTP employees. A few employees attended counselling sessions, visited their GP or were referred to the trauma clinic. Table 12.2 gives the levels of satisfaction with the support provided, as recorded on a three-point scale (no help – quite helpful – very helpful).

Table 12.1 Activities associated with higher levels of traumatic stress at the IA, MTA and TA

Assessment	Time at the scene	Fear for own safety	Worked as rescuer	Supported bereaved	Provided first aid	Witnessed seriously injured	Attended to dying	Body removal	Running mortuary
IES-E scores at IA	0.455** 0.001 (n = 53)	0.339** 0.009 (n = 58)	0.408** 0.001 (n = 59)	0.288* 0.028 (n = 58)	0.541** 0.000 (n = 57)	0.371** 0.004 (n = 59)	0.334* 0.010 (n = 58)	-0.023 0.831 (n = 58)	-0.277* 0.039 (n = 56)
IES-E scores at MTA	0.440** 0.001 (n = 54)	0.335* 0.010 (n = 59)	0.317** 0.013 (n = 60)	0.241 0.066 (n = 59)	0.426** 0.001 (n = 58)	0.309* 0.016 (n = 60)	0.262* 0.045 (n = 59)	-0.023 0.862 (n = 57)	-0.223 0.095 (n = 57)
IES-E scores at TA	0.226* 0.017 (n = 94)	0.464** 0.000 (n = 111)	0.257** 0.006 (n = 112)	0.112 0.240 (n = 111)	0.277** 0.003 (n = 111)	0.228** 0.016 (n = 112)	0.210* 0.026 (n = 112)	0.272** 0.004 (n = 109)	-0.068 0.486 (n = 108)

$* p < .05$
$** p < .01$

Table 12.2 Levels of satisfaction with support provided

Support response	OH assessment	Debriefing	Counselling	GP	Family/friends	Colleagues	Trauma clinic
	(n = 123)	(n = 100)	(n = 16)	(n = 19)	(n = 91)	(n = 76)	(n = 19)
No help	19 (15%)	11 (11%)	7 (43%)	5 (26%)	7 (8%)	2 (3%)	7 (37%)
Quite helpful	70 (57%)	43 (43%)	8 (50%)	6 (32%)	31 (34%)	25 (34%)	2 (10%)
Very helpful	34 (28%)	46 (46%)	1 (6%)	8 (42%)	53 (58%)	49 (66%)	10 (53%)

The most supportive groups identified in the survey were colleagues, family and friends and the trauma clinic. The groups identified as being least helpful were counsellors, the trauma clinic (see Discussion) and GPs. The Occupational Health assessments were recorded as either quite helpful or extremely helpful by 85% of the employees, and 89% of employees found the first-line debriefing provided by Occupational Health helpful.

Discussion

Undertaking research in organisations in the midst of a disaster is fraught with difficulties. The primary tasks for BTP in the days following the 7 July terrorist attacks were to rescue the injured, recover the bodies, deal with the possibility of more bombs, protect the public from danger and gather forensic information to help in the identification of the bombers and their associates. Despite these significant policing pressures, BTP management remained aware of its responsibility to provide the resources necessary to protect the health and well-being of its employees and to record and monitor the effectiveness of its trauma support programme. The role and skills of BTP's Occupational Health Service in presenting the benefits of a screen-and-treat trauma programme to senior management was an important element in the adoption of the trauma support programme. The results of the initial assessment indicated that the majority of BTP employees handled the rescue and recovery work without any significant psychological disturbance. However, a small number of officers experienced increased levels of distress associated with the tasks they had undertaken, rather than fulfilling a particular role, duty or managerial responsibility. Six months after the bombings, most of the officers had returned to normal levels of psychological functioning. Although at the final assessment there was a small increase in the level of trauma symptoms, for all but a small number of employees who were receiving therapy at the trauma clinic, these were at a non-clinical level. Following the Paddington rail crash, a similar survey of police officers was undertaken, which found that, 6 months after the rail crash, 13% of the officers were suffering stress and 6% PTSD (Ingham et al., 2001). This study also identified a number of risk factors associated with increased levels of PTSD, which included: (a) working longer than 12 hours at the scene; (b) being involved in supporting the injured; or (c) having ongoing contact with distressed members of the public. The

BTP study also identified some risk factors which supported the Paddington crash findings, in that the length of time working at the scene, being fearful for one's own safety, providing first aid, witnessing people who had been seriously injured and attending to the needs of the dying were associated with raised levels of PTSD.

BTP employees tended to find informal support from their family, friends and colleagues to be very helpful; the importance of good relationships was also found in police officers engaged in body handling following the *Piper Alpha* disaster (Alexander and Wells, 1991), where the use of humour and talking to colleagues was found either helpful or very helpful by over 90% of officers (Chapter 2). The support provided by Occupational Health in terms of assessment, information and debriefing was found to be helpful by BTP employees; however, the satisfaction results for the trauma clinic were less clear, with almost equal numbers of employees finding the support provided by this specialist psychological service to be either very helpful or of no help. It is interesting to note that only 12 (4.5%) of the BTP employees involved in dealing with the bombings received a formal diagnosis of PTSD at the trauma clinic and that five BTP employees were still in therapy 2 years after the bombings.

Front-line workers in the emergency services face difficult and distressing situations on a daily basis; however, meeting the demands of a disaster requires the trauma support programme to be adapted, following a risk assessment to ensure that an appropriate level of support can be delivered. Although the elements of the programme adopted remained the same as that provided for day-to-day traumatic events, the way the support was delivered needed to be adapted, with more of the responsibility for coordinating and delivering the programme being undertaken by Occupational Health, rather than by line management.

The evaluation of the support provided to BTP employees can be criticized on the grounds that the research design did not meet the criteria required for random controlled trials; however, for ethical reasons a random assignment of employees to no-treatment or waiting list control groups would have been unacceptable. These results have shown that, when dealing with a disaster, emergency services need to be aware of the risks and, wherever possible, reduce these risks by managing the level of exposure of individual officers, and where individual officers or staff are exposed to the badly injured, dying victims or bereaved family members, additional support and monitoring is provided.

Acknowledgements

The authors would like to thank Willie McCafferty, Area Commander, London North, British Transport Police, who supported this research.

References

Alexander, D.A., Wells, A. (1991) Reactions of police officers to body-handling after a major disaster: a before and after comparison. *British Journal of Psychiatry* **159**, 527–555.

Brewin, C.R., Rose, S., Andrews, B., Green, J., Tata, P., McEverdy, C. (2002) A brief screening instrument for posttraumatic stress disorder. *British Journal of Psychiatry* **181**, 158–162.

Brewin, C., Scraggs, P., Robertson, M., Thompson, M., D'Ardenne, P., Ehlers, A. (2008) Promoting mental health following the London bombings: a screen and treat approach. *Journal of Traumatic Stress* **21**(1), 3–8.

British Transport Police (2006) 2005–2006 statistical bulletin: www.btp.police.uk/documents/statsbulletin2.pdf

Collins, S., Long, A. (2003) Working with the psychological effects of trauma: consequences for mental health care workers – a literature review. *Journal of Psychiatric and Mental Health Nursing* **10**(4), 417–424.

Dunn, A. (2001) Trauma aftercare: a four stage model. In Spiers, T. (ed.), *Trauma – A Practitioner's Guide to Counselling*. Hove, UK: Brunner-Routledge.

Figley, C.R. (1999) Police compassion fatigue – theory, research, assessment, treatment and prevention. In Violanti, J., Douglas Paton, D. (eds), *Police Trauma*. Springfield, CT: Charles C. Thomas.

Greene, C.L. (2001) Human remains and psychological impact on police officers: excerpts from psychiatric observations. *Australian Journal of Disaster and Trauma Studies*: http://www.massey.ac.nz/~trauma/issues/2001-2/greene.htm [accessed 28 August 2008].

Ingham, B., Luce, A., Cording, H., Firth-Cozens, J. (2001) The well-being of Metropolitan Police service staff involved in the Paddington incident – 1 year survey. Unpublished report, University of Northumbria, Newcastle upon Tyne, UK.

Luce, A., Cording, H., Firth-Cozens, J. (2003) The well-being of Metropolitan Police service staff involved in the Paddington incident – follow-up survey. Unpublished report, University of Northumbria, Newcastle upon Tyne, UK.

Paton, D., Violanti, J. (2006) Policing in the context of terrorism: managing the traumatic stress risk. *Traumatology* **12**(3), 236–247.

Perrin, M.A., DiGrande, L., Wheelter, K., Thorpe, L., Farfel, M., Brackbill, R. (2007) Differences in PTSD prevalence and associated risk factors among World Trade Centre Disaster rescue and recovery workers. *American Journal of Psychiatry* **164**(9), 1385–1394.

Snaith, R.P., Zigmond, S.S. (1994) The Hospital Anxiety and Depression Scale Manual. Windsor: NFER Nelson.

Tehrani, N. (2004) *Workplace Trauma. Concepts, Assessment and Intervention*. Hove, UK: Brunner-Routledge.

Tehrani, N., Cox, T., Cox, S. (2002) Assessing the impact of traumatic incident: the development of an extended impact of events scale. *Counselling Psychology Quarterly* **9**, 25–36.

Volanti, J.M., Castellano, C., O'Rourke, J., Paton, D. (2006) Proximity to the 9/11 attack and suicide ideation in police officers. *Traumatology* **12**(3), 248–254.

Chapter 13

Models of crisis management

Sonia Handa, Lillian Krantz, Eileen Delaney and Brett Litz

Introduction

Workplace trauma is unique but ubiquitous. Different forms of trauma, ranging from bullying and harassment to natural disasters and acts of terrorism, contribute to the increasing number of traumatic exposures in today's workplace that can affect the performance and productivity of employees and clients at all levels. Organisations have a vested interest in mitigating the impact of workplace trauma, a responsibility to identify those in need of care and to make state-of-the-art secondary prevention treatment readily available. Consequently, the demand for crisis management is a major public health issue worldwide.

Adults spend one-third of their lives at their place of work (Everly and Feldman, 1985), making the work context a significant and efficient venue for health promotion, accident and interpersonal conflict prevention and, if need be, crisis management. In responding to workplace traumas, organisations have the responsibility to use evidence-based interventions to assist workers who may be at risk of mental health problems stemming from exposure to workplace trauma. If intervention strategies are employed that have no scientific evidence to support their use, resources will be wasted and, worse, employees will be given false hope that they will be helped in substantive ways. To date, it is unclear whether standard practices are informed by science. This is unfortunate because some forms of early crisis intervention have been shown to reduce the adverse impact of exposure to traumatic events and to assist individuals in regaining functional abilities (Litz and Bryant, 2009). However, the majority of this research has not been conducted in the workplace and only a limited number of studies have examined the impact of typical forms of workplace care. In this chapter, we explore different forms of primary and secondary prevention methods commonly used in crisis management and provide a critical evaluation of these methods. The goal is to provide a summary of the state of the field to inform workplace practice.

Primary prevention strategies

Every workplace is subject to a number of foreseeable risks, which may be inherent to the work environment itself or due to an outside source. In response, organisations can attempt to implement primary prevention programmes which aim to minimize the negative effects of trauma by intervening before an event takes place. These programmes endow individuals with skills and information to enhance their readiness, or 'psychological preparedness', which can potentially act as a buffer against the development of post-traumatic stress disorder (PTSD) and other biological, social, psychological and spiritual problems that might arise from traumatic exposure (Feldner et al., 2007). Typical interventions provide employees and management with preparatory information about the nature and types of potential traumas they can experience at their workplace, the skills and behaviours that minimize risk, and how to respond if an event should occur.

Currently, primary prevention programmes are most common in contexts and occupations that inherently involve exposure to potentially traumatizing events, such as the military, fire and police departments, and emergency medical settings (Feldner et al., 2007). Primary prevention initiatives vary considerably and can include programmes in the form of classroom-style lectures, such as: pre-deployment briefings that set accurate expectations of combat for military service members (WRAIR, 2007); behavioural and coping skills training, such as risk mitigation and response strategies used by healthcare workers to help identify and contain violent patients (Edelman, 1978); or peer outreach programmes, such as the Police Organization Providing Peer Assistance programme, that aim to mitigate concerns and anxiety felt by fellow officers (Bender, 2006). Unfortunately there is little if any research that shows these practices to be useful or effective in preventing significant stress reactions, thus sustaining normal functioning. It is even less clear what type of prevention would be useful in lower-risk settings or non-emergency settings. In accordance with the US Occupational Safety and Health Act (1979), efforts to provide primary prevention in corporate settings are frequently coordinated through employee assistant programmes (EAPs), human resources (HR), occupational health and even security. For example, human resources might design employee benefit programmes, EAPs might offer coping skills training and counselling services, and security might design and facilitate emergency evacuation procedures (CSTS, 2006).

Studies examining EAPs have both underscored their value for workplace counselling and highlighted the lack of coordinated research in this domain (McLeod, 2008). Furthermore, a review of the evidence for workplace counselling, commissioned by the British Association for Counselling and Psychotherapy, indicated that it had questionable validity and therefore had limited value in guiding effective practice. Therefore, it appears that more research and development is needed to ensure that EAPs are providing sufficient care to their workers.

Primary prevention programmes, whether they are found in emergency or non-emergency settings, aim to provide their employees with guidance and information on how to manage post-trauma reactions (should a severely stressful event happen). However, more research, in the form of randomized controlled trials (RCTs), is needed to inform best practice in both settings. Gaining consensus on best practice is particularly important, given that, in the age of terror and with the possibility of natural and industrial disasters affecting large numbers of workers, many organisations have learned the lessons of 9/11 and are beginning to develop and implement training programmes and procedures to help workers should the worst occur (Benedek *et al.*, 2006). Ideally, organisations need to have a plan to assess employees' level of exposure to various aspects of a trauma and have readily available and easily mobilized support and care resources. However, in the workplace, there are complicated power relationships and employers cannot be heavy-handed about what they offer and the manner in which they offer it. This is an especially delicate matter when groups of similarly exposed colleagues might have occasion to talk about a traumatic event in the workplace. In general, organisations need to balance the need to organise a response and have resources available with the need for privacy and confidentiality.

Secondary prevention strategies

Secondary prevention refers to actions taken in the acute aftermath of a trauma, with the aim of easing distress and preventing chronic difficulties. There are a number of existing programmes and interventions of this nature; however, most are not evidence-based and there is contention about best practices. Intervention strategies differ in the amount of training and resources required to deliver them. They also differ in regards to timing of delivery, ranging from the immediate aftermath of a traumatic event (targeting all individuals) to later interventions provided at least 2 weeks after the event (targeting only those who are symptomatic and impaired). The optimal period for intervention, however, remains unclear. In the immediate aftermath of a workplace trauma, the majority of employees will experience an initial period of psychological distress, but most will successfully mobilize their natural coping resources to resume normal functioning without intervention (Litz *et al.*, 2002). Intervening prematurely and with individuals who are likely to recover on their own may interfere with natural recovery, but waiting too long may lead to the entrenchment of symptoms and exacerbation of distress in those who are unable to cope on their own. We now detail the interventions and their costs and benefits.

Critical incident stress debriefing and critical incident stress management

Prior to 2002, critical incident stress debriefing (CISD) was the modal intervention strategy employed internationally to individuals immediately after experiencing severe, direct or indirect, trauma (Litz, 2008, p. 504). Since then, however, its use has been called into question because an increasing number of studies have failed to find evidence for its ability to prevent the development of PTSD. CISD, first introduced by Mitchell (1983), pioneered the development and implementation of several similar interventions, known collectively as psychological debriefing (PD) (Bisson, 2008). Although the content, process and goals of PD approaches vary, there are many commonalities among each approach, with CISD being the most recognized and used worldwide (Mitchell and Everly, 1996). Despite the lack of evidence of its efficacy, CISD remains a recommended policy among a diverse set of organisations, such as emergency service personnel, EAPs, schools, disaster relief agencies and military organisations, in large part due to the face validity of the intervention and the fact that CISD is typically well appreciated by workers and work cultures because it normalizes reactions and is not a formal clinical treatment.

As a crisis intervention, CISD is designed for individuals to share their common normal response to extreme and abnormal circumstances, with the ultimate goal of reducing acute stress and risk for PTSD (Mitchell, 1983). The intervention is set up as a guided group discussion, which provides an opportunity for emotional ventilation, normalization of symptoms, and reorganisation of thoughts into a cohesive, rational narrative (Bisson, 2008). This process is believed to help accelerate recovery and to help identify struggling participants who need additional care. The debriefing session, lasting between 3 and 4 hours, is administered in seven stages, often within days of the trauma, by at least one facilitator who is part of the work culture (Mitchell and Everly, 1996). The facilitator's role is to encourage disclosure and processing of the traumatic event as well as educate participants about the nature of stress reactions and effective coping.

Despite the popularity of CISD, the appropriate population for CISD and its overall effectiveness is not only unclear in theory and in practice but also by empirical research standards. In theory, debriefing is intended as a secondary intervention for indirect victims, particularly emergency personnel who are well versed in the area of stress management (Litz et al., 2002). However, Mitchell and Everly's (1996) CISD approach claims that those who have experienced extreme trauma (primary victims) could also benefit from CISD, with the one caveat that they may also need to seek additional care. CISD is contradictory because it mandates intervention for all personnel involved in a trauma scene, even though it espouses that early responses are normal and most people recover from exposure to trauma. Although CISD assumes that everyone exposed to a potentially traumatic event is at risk of developing pathology and can benefit from an opportunity to share their experience and learn about trauma and adaptive coping, it also may not be appropriate for all. In particular, some empirical research demonstrates that CISD may be intrusive and disruptive to the normal stress response of some individuals (Litz et al., 2002). Therefore, treating everyone exposed to a trauma fails to sufficiently consider the natural resiliency of some survivors and emergency personnel and their ability to find adaptive ways of managing reactions to the stressful demands of the event on their own (Gist and Devilly, 2002).

In terms of implementing CISD procedures within workplace environments, it is important to note that peers from affected organisations are often included as co-facilitators to enhance the team's credibility and personalize the experience for particular work cultures. Although this appears in line with the overarching goals of CISD, it can also create dual relationships and make some attendees feel unsafe, possibly making the intervention counter-therapeutic and potentially unethical (Litz and Gray, 2004). Moreover, employees are sometimes mandated or even coerced by their employers to attend a group debriefing session, which could create resentment and disengagement.

According to some, CISD should not be dismissed altogether (Richards, 2001), pointing to the putatively enhanced outcomes apparently associated with its integration into a more comprehensive series of interventions known as Critical Incident Stress Management (CISM; Everly and Mitchell, 2000). CISM adds additional components, such as stress management, but debriefing is still a core strategy. The CISM programme is designed to address the needs of emergency service organisations and personnel before and after engaging in dangerous work, using pre-trauma training and post-event debriefings. Also, in the CISM model, individual follow-up consists of future contact with victims, aiding in long-term management of trauma-related symptoms (Phipps and Byrne, 2003). However, more research is needed to further evaluate the effectiveness of follow-ups within the CISM model.

The most prominent criticism of CISD/CISM is the lack of sufficient evidence to support the use of these interventions as secondary prevention for PTSD or other types of significant stress reactions. Those who do CISD/CISM rely on uncontrolled studies that fail to employ treatment fidelity checks or the use of well-validated measures of post-traumatic stress (Everly et al., 2002). Although not specific to workplace settings, the Cochrane review of debriefing (Rose et al., 2001) reviewed six RCTs, using CISD/CISM among victims of various traumas (e.g. motor vehicle accidents, assault and acute burns). Of the six studies, two had positive outcomes, while the remaining four did not. Of these four, two of the studies showed debriefing to lead to small, albeit significantly worse, outcomes over time, which has led researchers to consider abandoning the use of these interventions entirely (Bisson et al., 1997; Hobbs et al., 1996). In addition, Adler et al. (2008) performed the only group randomized trial of CISD among US Army peacekeepers deployed in Kosovo, compared with a stress management class (SMC) and survey-only (SO) condition. Consistent with other findings, CISD was not found to reduce PTSD relative to no intervention. For only those soldiers reporting the highest degrees of exposure to mission stressors, CISD was barely and minimally associated with lower reports of PTSD and aggression (vs. SMC), higher perceived organisational support (vs. SO), yet more alcohol problems than SMC and SO. Thus, even well-designed and controlled studies using these interventions reveal them to be therapeutically inert, comparable to no intervention at all. Consequently, if CISD/CISM is to continue as a viable approach, future research must include independent, randomized, controlled trials to further verify its effectiveness, as well as examine its effectiveness within different types of settings.

Psychological first aid

Psychological first aid (PFA) was developed as an alternative to unproven and conceptually suspect crisis intervention and debriefing strategies. Designed by the National Centre for PTSD and the National Child Traumatic Stress Network, PFA is a systematic set of flexible conversational helping actions intended for use by disaster mental health responders, including mental health counsellors, who may be called upon to provide immediate support for trauma survivors (Brymer *et al.*, 2006). Although the core strategies are intuitive and typically applied in most contexts, PFA is groundbreaking because it is substantiated by evidence and valid conceptual frameworks, is manualized and potentially reliably applied, and it is systematic and replicable. When compared to potentially intrusive and inappropriately applied debriefing approaches, PFA is more flexible and formalizes human connection and support in the immediate aftermath of trauma (Litz and Bryant, 2009; Raphael, 1986).

PFA's approach does not assume that all survivors will develop severe mental health problems or long-term difficulties in recovery (Brymer *et al.*, 2006). Instead, PFA is administered with an understanding that disaster survivors will experience a broad range of early reactions, and each type of reaction may have an impact on physical, psychological, behavioural and spiritual capacities. For some, these reactions will cause enough distress to interfere with adaptive coping, and in those cases recovery may be facilitated by PFA.

Specifically, PFA is an evidence-informed modular approach for assisting victims, as well as disaster relief workers, in the immediate aftermath of disaster and terrorism (Brymer *et al.*, 2006). Its mission, to reduce the initial distress caused by traumatic events and to foster both short and long-term adaptive functioning, is accomplished by the use of eight conceptual models, described as *core actions*: (1) contact and engagement; (2) safety and comfort; (3) stabilization; (4) information gathering; (5) practical assistance; (6) connection with social supports; (7) information on coping support; and (8) linkage with collaborative services. Although detailed descriptions of these core actions are beyond the scope of this chapter, each core action was devised using theory and research on stress, coping and adaptation in the aftermath of extreme events (Hobfoll *et al.*, 2007). Additionally, for each action, specific recommendations for working with disaster survivors are offered while taking into account both the individual's needs and the context in which services are offered.

The PFA Guide outlines specific behaviours to avoid (e.g. refrain from making assumptions or debriefing) and stresses the importance of confidentiality in post-disaster settings. It is recommended that these behaviours are followed rigorously to ensure that the PFA's support services are developmentally appropriate, culturally sensitive and context-specific. Furthermore, PFA's guidelines are designed to be easily administered within the context of many different settings, including shelters, schools, hospitals, homes, rape crisis centres and warzones.

To date, PFA has yet to infiltrate work-systems and cultures (e.g. the military). We argue that PFA is well suited to work environments because it is practical, efficient, non-intrusive but formalized, and has a solid theoretical basis (Litz, 2008). However, PFA needs to be simplified and structured in a way that promotes acculturation to other organisational or occupational environments. Given that uniformed service personnel (fire rescue, police, emergency medicine and military) are united through a strong sense of group cohesion and often share similar trauma and loss, utilizing the PFA intervention in a group format may be useful (Everly *et al.*, 2006; Ulman, 2004).

PFA is also attractive because it emphasizes information gathering to help providers make timely assessments as well as provide recommendations about survivors' immediate concerns and needs (Brymer *et al.*, 2006; Litz, 2008). However, it is important to emphasize that, to date, there has been minimal research on the effects of PFA and the optimal time interval for its implementation (Litz, 2008). Research is needed to examine its efficacy. Dismantling which aspects particular to PFA prove most effective will ultimately increase its utility across work cultures and disciplines and reach a greater number of victims.

An alternative form of early intervention: cognitive-behavioural therapy

Cognitive-behavioural therapy (CBT) is a set of treatment strategies derived from experimental research to target a variety of different mental health problems. CBT is the prescriptive evidence-based treatment for chronic PTSD (e.g. Litz and Bryant, 2009). It is an individualized intervention that requires specialized training. CBT's framework uses techniques such as psycho-education, anxiety management training, stress inoculation training, cognitive restructuring, and imaginal and *in vivo* exposure therapy (Foa and Rothbaum, 1998).

The exposure component of CBT is a key therapeutic tool in the treatment of PTSD. The rationale for its use is that post-traumatic symptoms occur because the individual has not adequately processed the trauma, due to avoidance behaviours. The aim is to allow for sufficient and sustained activation of trauma memories so that the individual can learn that, while painful and anguishing, the memory is not harmful and the intensity of the emotional response rises but then falls, and is more tolerable than individuals expect (thus otherwise motivating their avoidance of the memory). One variant of exposure therapy, imaginal exposure, involves repeatedly revisiting feared events or memories of the trauma in their imagination. Alternatively, patients may be asked to write down a narrative account of the traumatic event, which is read aloud in-session and as homework.

Although few studies have been conducted on the efficacy of early intervention strategies for trauma, the inarguable success of CBT as an intervention for chronic PTSD suggests that some components might be useful to adopt in early interventions. Several controlled trials have found CBT to be significantly more effective than supportive counselling (SC) as a secondary prevention intervention for PTSD. For example, Bryant *et al.* (1998) compared five 90 minute weekly individual sessions of CBT to the same amount of SC in a randomized clinical trial within a month's time period of the trauma exposure. Significantly fewer participants receiving CBT (8%) than SC (83%) met criteria for PTSD at post-treatment. This pattern was maintained at 6 month follow-up, in addition to the

CBT participants experiencing greater clinically and statistically significant reductions in avoidance and intrusive and depressive symptomatology.

Comparably favourable results were found by Ehlers *et al.* (2003), who targeted motor vehicle accident survivors approximately 4 months after their accident, comparing 12 sessions and three monthly booster sessions of cognitive therapy with repeated assessment (no treatment), and a self-help booklet based on cognitive-behavioural principles. Symptoms of PTSD were assessed via self-report and independent evaluators at 3 and 9 month follow-up. Cognitive therapy was found to be significantly more effective in reducing symptoms than the self-help booklet or repeated assessments: 11% of CBT participants met criteria for PTSD at follow-up, compared to 61% of the self-help participants.

There are a number of considerations that must be resolved before adapting CBT as an acute, pre-clinical intervention. If this form of intervention is provided too early after a trauma, the net will be cast too widely, and many will be provided with treatment who do not need this labour-intensive form of expert care. In addition, there is a risk that, if provided too early, the traumatized individual may be bereft or consumed with other pressing needs, and may be unable to abide by the various demands of the treatment, such as homework (Litz *et al.*, 2002). Findings from the above-mentioned studies, however, suggest that CBT can be a feasible secondary intervention, having the potential to reduce, or even prevent, chronic or severe post-traumatic symptomatology. Indeed, practice guidelines from the UK's National Institute for Clinical Excellence, the International Society for Traumatic Stress Studies and the American Psychological and Psychiatric Associations all recommend CBT as the prescriptive secondary prevention intervention for trauma. Despite this, CBT is not yet regularly used within US organisations in the aftermath of workplace trauma. A variation of CBT, however, known as trauma-focused CBT (TF-CBT), is becoming more widely used among UK organisations in the attempt to increase employee resilience when faced with trauma. Its techniques, similar to CBT, target post-traumatic, depressive and anxiety symptoms and address cognitive distortions associated with trauma. These techniques may help educate employees on how to cope with common feelings and post-trauma behaviours (Chapter 16).

Summary and recommendations

To date, there are a limited number of published research trials of interventions initiated within the first few weeks following disasters, acts of terrorism and other traumas (Ruzek *et al.*, 2007) and no formal RCTs within the workplace (other than in the military). Consequently, a lack of empirical support has prevented the development of definitive recommendations on crisis management in the workplace. In addition, there are few published accounts of standard practices in the workplace in the aftermath of trauma, or in EAP programmes.

According to Galea *et al.* (2003), the current literature on the effects of disasters on mental health functioning suggests that people's reactions should not necessarily be regarded as pathological responses or even as precursors of subsequent disorder, as many will have transient stress reactions in the aftermath of mass violence, although such reactions may occur, occasionally, years later. Rather than traditional diagnosis and clinical treatment, most people are likely to need support and minimal provision of resources to ease the transition to normalty. As outlined above, simple PFA procedures appear to be the most promising in comparison to CISD/CISM and CBT, in the immediate aftermath of trauma in the workplace (hours and days after an event), and organisations should be cautious not to force disclosure, as set forth in the principles of CISD/CISM. Organisations have the responsibility to be aware of a minority who may develop PTSD, and to see that they receive the needed help, which should ideally be evidence-based. At present, CBT is the optimal form of secondary prevention, but CBT is not routinely used in work settings, nor are CBT principles necessarily used in primary prevention programmes in the workplace. We highly recommend that all disciplines germane to stakeholders in workplaces and organisations, and CBT experts bring their knowledge and experience to bear and create a version of CBT that fits various work cultures and is optimally useful and ecologically valid.

Responsibility for workplace trauma prevention and response does not fall neatly into any one segment of an employer's organisational domain. It is not exclusively a security issue, a human resources issue, an EAP issue or a management issue, but instead touches on each of these disciplines. Consequently, determining who within an organisation will be responsible for dealing with the many aspects of workplace trauma is not a simple matter. Developing the most effective trauma prevention and response procedures will require a multidisciplinary approach, drawing on various parts of the management structure, each bringing its own perspective, area of knowledge and skills. Finally, employers should focus on both pre-trauma prevention, with the goals of educating employees and management about the nature and types of risks they face and teaching them skills and behaviours that minimize risk, and trauma intervention, teaching employees how to respond if a traumatic event does occur.

References

Adler, A.B., Litz, B.T., Castro, C.A., Suvak, M., Thomas, J.L., Burrell, L. *et al.* (2008) A group randomized trial of critical incident stress debriefing provided to US peacekeepers. *Journal of Traumatic Stress* 21(3), 253–263.

Bender, E. (2006) When stress gets severe, police turn to POPPA. *Psychiatric News* 1 September, 21.

Benedek, D.M., Urasano, R.J., Fullerton, C.S., Vineburgh, N.T., Gifford, R.K. (2006) Responding to workplace terrorism: applying military models of behavioural health and public health response. *Journal of Workplace Disaster Preparedness, Response, and Management* 21(3/4), 21–33.

Bisson, J.I. (2008) Using evidence to inform clinical practice shortly after traumatic events. *Journal of Traumatic Stress* 21(6), 507–512.

Bisson, J.I., Jenkins, P.L., Alexander, J., Bannister, C. (1997) Randomized controlled trial of psychological debriefing for victims of acute burn trauma. *British Journal of Psychiatry* 171(July), 78–81.

Bryant, R.A., Harvey, A.G., Dang, S., Sackville, T., Basten, C. (1998) Treatment of acute stress disorder: a comparison of cognitive-behavioural therapy and supportive counseling. *Journal of Consulting and Clinical Psychology* 66(5), 862–866.

Brymer, M., Jacobs, A., Layne, C., Pynoos, R., Ruzek, J., Steinberg, A. *et al.* (2006) National Child Traumatic Stress Network and National Center for PTSD. *Psychological First Aid: Field Operations Guide*, 2nd edn: www.nctsn.org and www.ncptsd.va.gov [accessed 23 October 2009].

Center for the Study of Traumatic Stress (CSTS) (2006) Workplace preparedness for terrorism: report of findings to Alfred P. Sloan Foundation: www.usuhs.mil/csts and www.centerforthestudyoftraumaticstress.org [accessed 23 October 2009].

Edelman, S.E. (1978) Managing the violence patient in a community mental health center. *Hospital and Community Psychiatry* 29(7), 460–462.

Ehlers, A., Clark, D.M., Hackmann, A., McManus, F., Fennel, M., Herbert, C., Mayou, R. (2003) A randomized controlled trial of cognitive therapy, a self-help booklet, and repeated assessments as early interventions for posttraumatic stress disorder. *Archives of General Psychiatry* 60(10), 1024–1032.

Everly, G.S., Feldman, R.L. (1985) *Occupational Health Promotion: Health Behaviour at the Workplace*. New York: Wiley.

Everly, G.S., Flannery, R.B., Eyler, V.A. (2002) Critical incident stress management (CISM): a statistical review of the literature. *Psychiatric Quarterly* **73**, 171–182.

Everly, G.S., Mitchell, J.T. (2000) The debriefing controversy and crisis intervention: a review of the lexical and substantive issues. *International Journal of Emergency Mental Health* **2**(3), 211–225.

Everly, G.S., Sherman, M.F., Stapleton, A., Barnett, D.J., Hiremath, G.S., Links, J.M. (2006) Workplace crisis intervention: a systematic review of effect sizes. *Journal of Workplace Behavioural Health* **21**(3/4), 153–170.

Feldner, M.T., Monson, C.M., Friedman, M.J. (2007). A critical analysis of approaches to targeted PTSD prevention: current status and theoretically derived future directions. *Behaviour Modification* **31**(1), 80–116.

Foa, E.B., Rothbaum, B.O. (1998) *Treating the Trauma of Rape: Cognitive–Behavioural Therapy for PTSD*. New York: Guilford.

Galea, S., Vlahov, D., Resnick, H., Ahern, J., Sesser, E., Gold, J. *et al.* (2003) Threads of probably post-traumatic stress disorder in New York City after the September 11 terrorist attacks. *American Journal of Epidemiology* **158**(6), 514–524.

Gist, R., Devilly, G.J. (2002) Post-trauma debriefing: the road too frequently travelled. *Lancet* **360**(9335), 741–742.

Hobbs, M., Mayou, R., Harrison, B., Warlock, P. (1996) A randomized trial of psychological debriefing for victims of road traffic accidents. *British Medical Journal* **313**(7070), 1438–1439.

Hobfoll, S.E., Watson, P.E., Bell, C.C., Bryant, R.A., Brymer, M.J., Friedman, M.J. *et al.* (2007) Five essential elements of immediate and mid-term mass trauma intervention: empirical evidence. *Psychiatry: Interpersonal and Biological Processes* **70**(4), 283–315.

Litz, B.T. (2008) Early intervention for trauma: where are we and where do we need to go? A commentary. *Journal of Traumatic Stress* **21**(6), 503–506.

Litz, B.T., Bryant, R.A. (2009) Early cognitive–behavioural interventions for adults. In Foa, E.B., Keane, T.M., Friedman, M.J., Cohen, J.A. (eds), *Effective Treatments for PTSD: Practice Guidelines from the International Society for Traumatic Stress Studies*, 2nd edn. New York: Guilford; 117–135.

Litz, B.T., Gray, M.J. (2004) Early intervention for trauma in adults: a framework for first aid and secondary prevention. In Litz, B.T. (ed.), *Early Intervention for Trauma and Traumatic Loss*. New York: Guilford; 87–111.

Litz, B.T., Gray, M.J., Adler, A.B. (2002) Early Intervention for trauma: current status and future directions. *Clinical Psychology: Science and Practice* **9**(2), 112–134.

McLeod, J. (2008) *Counselling in the Workplace: A Comprehensive Review of the Research Evidence*, 2nd edn. Lutterworth: BACP.

Mitchell, J.T. (1983) When disaster strikes. *Journal of Emergency Medical Services* **8**(1), 36–39.

Mitchell, J.T., Everly, G.S. (1996) *Critical Incident Stress Debriefing: An Operations Manual for the Prevention of Traumatic Stress Among Emergency Services and Disaster Workers*, 2nd edn. Ellicott City, MD: Chevron.

Phipps, A.B., Byrne, M.K. (2003) Brief interventions for secondary trauma: review and recommendations. *Stress and Health* **19**(3), 139–147.

Raphael, B. (1986) *When Disaster Strikes: How Individuals and Communities Cope with Catastrophe*. New York: Basic Books.

Richards, D. (2001) A field study of critical incident stress debriefing versus critical incident stress management. *Journal of Mental Health* **10**(3), 351–362.

Rose, S., Bisson, J., Wessely, S. (2001) Psychological debriefing for preventing posttraumatic stress disorder (PTSD) (Cochrane Review). In *The Cochrane Library*. Oxford, UK: Update Software; 3.

Ruzek, J.I., Brymer, M.J., Jacobs, A.K., Layne, C.M., Vernberg, E.M., Watson, P.J. (2007) Psychological first aid. *Journal of Mental Health Counseling* **29**(1), 17–49.

Ulman, K.H. (2004) Group interventions for treatment of trauma in adults. In Buchele B.J., Spitz, H.I. (eds), *Group Interventions for Treatment of Psychological Trauma*. New York: AGPA.

WRAIR (2007) Battlemind psychological debriefing (Walter Reed Army Institute of Research, 20 February): https://www.battlemind.army.mil/ [accessed 27 July 2009].

Chapter 14

Supporting employees at risk of developing secondary trauma and burn-out

Noreen Tehrani

Introduction

Organisations engaged in activities that require their workers to come in direct contact with human misery, pain and destruction need to recognize their duty to safeguard the health, safety and welfare of their workforce (Tehrani, 2004). Whilst the legal duties that an employer has for employees may differ between nations (Bergman *et al.*, 2007), there are some common principles which apply in most developed countries. These include the need to undertake an assessment of the risks where the work has been shown to involve the possibility of employees developing mental health conditions such as stress, burn-out, anxiety or depression. Employers need to be working with employees and their representatives to provide information, training and support to enable the work to be carried out safely. Individual employees also have a personal responsibility to protect their own health and well-being and to ensure that their actions do not cause harm to others.

With workers in an increasing number of organisations having been found to suffer negative mental health conditions as a result of undertaking emotionally demanding work (see Part I), it is important to develop practical guidelines to help organisations adopt safe systems of work which will address the needs of the organisation and its vulnerable workers. This chapter describes a system of risk assessment–risk management designed to support workers involved in roles which are emotionally demanding, and where the workers are at high risk of developing secondary trauma, burn-out, anxiety and depression.

The control cycle and the management of secondary trauma

The UK Health and Safety Executive (HSE, 2006) has developed a five-stage model of risk assessment to help organisations deal with workplace hazards. The model, which deals with physical and psychological risks, recognizes that whilst it may not be possible to eliminate all hazards, organisations have a legal duty to take reasonable steps to protect workers from physical and psychological harm. An adapted version of the HSE model has been developed for the control and management of psychosocial risks (Cox, 1993) and it is this model which is used as the framework for the Trauma Support Model (TSM) in the assessment and management of the risk of developing secondary trauma. The six stages of the model are:

- Identification of the psychosocial risks and other hazards and the harm they cause.
- Selection of reliable measures to establish the association between the hazard and the harm caused.
- Design of reasonable and practicable interventions or control strategies.
- Implementation of the strategies.
- Monitoring and evaluating the strategies.
- Feeding back of information to facilitate a process of hazard reduction, resilience building and personal growth.

Whilst physical hazards are relatively easy to recognize and assess, psychological hazards tend to be more complex and hidden, and involve multiple interactions between: (a) the worker's capabilities, personality and personal history; (b) the level and nature of the demands or challenges; and (c) the availability of support and resources. In order to help organisations deal with the needs of their high-risk roles, some basic principles have been established on which a trauma support programme can be developed.

Principles of the secondary trauma support programme

- The roles of all workers with direct or indirect exposure to emotionally demanding material/activities will be risk assessed.

- All workers will undergo regular screening and be provided with ongoing training and support.
- Exposure to emotionally demanding material/activities will be controlled and minimized.
- Vulnerable workers[1] will be identified and protected from harm.
- Positive working relationships will be promoted to reduce the incidence of harm.
- Managers and workers will be trained to recognize symptoms of secondary trauma which may occur gradually (cumulative) or be delayed.
- The organisation and workers will be actively encouraged to work together to reduce the cause, incidence and impact of secondary trauma.

The trauma support model

Elements of the trauma support model (TSM) described in this chapter have been adopted by a number of organisations, including Fire and Rescue Services, Police Services, Ambulance Services, Health Trusts, Child Protection Agencies and NGOs. Critical to the success of the implementation of the model is the requirement for the organisation to consider how the model will fit, or can be adapted to match, its culture and practices and meet the precise needs of their high-risk workers. The model has nine elements: person specification; pre-employment screening; induction training; education; resilience building; demobilizing/defusing; trauma counselling; in-post screening and monitoring; and quality assurance. A brief description of each of the elements follows.

Person specification

A person specification is a description of the personal skills, experience, attributes and abilities that a person needs to possess when undertaking a particular role. Therefore, when organisations are developing a person specification, it is important to understand the nature of the work to be undertaken and what will be required of the job holder. The job description is a good starting point for developing a person specification, as it provides a description of the purpose

---

1 The HSE describes vulnerable workers as those workers who are at increased risk of suffering work-related disease and injury.

of the job, its main accountabilities and responsibilities and the key tasks to be performed. For emotionally demanding high-risk roles, the person specification should not only describe skills, qualifications and experience necessary to undertake the technical aspects of the role but also the personal attributes which enable the worker to deal with the personal demands of the role in terms of self-awareness, interpersonal sensitivity, coping skills, emotional hardiness and resilience (Paton *et al.*, 2003). However, organisations need to be careful, when developing the person specifications for their high-risk roles, to use well-supported and objective evidence when deciding which particular personal characteristics, skills or attributes are essential or desirable for the specific role. If organisations fail to demonstrate the reason for their selection criteria, they can be accused of unfairly discriminating against those employees who are not appointed on the basis of flawed criteria. The TSM uses a number of processes to help organisations develop well-supported person specifications; these include analysing the job description, gathering feedback from current job holders and their supervisors, and using the evidence provided by researchers into secondary trauma, particularly evidence which has been found to be associated with effective and resilient employees.

Pre-employment screening

Having established a valid personal specification, the next element of the TSM process is to ensure that, prior to appointment, all internal and external applicants for high-risk roles are screened against the criteria set out in the person specification. It is normal practice in many organisations to undertake a preliminary interview to assess the technical skills and experience of applicants, from which a short-list of candidates is formed. The short-listed candidates would then be offered an opportunity to undertake a pre-employment screening of their personal attributes and resilience. The aim of pre-employment screening is to provide an objective view on the candidate's physical and mental fitness to undertake a particular role and to identify whether there are any health problems which may require adjustments to be made to the way the work is undertaken or supported. The findings and recommendations that emerge from pre-employment screening will then be fed back to those responsible for recruitment, to help them in their final decision on whether or not a particular candidate is suitable for a particular vacancy.

One of the additional benefits of the pre-employment screening is the creation of a well-being base line for each employee prior to employment; these data can be used later in the monitoring of employee as part of the in-post screening programme. A range of psychometric screening tools have been used for pre-employment screening by the TSM (Chapter 7); their selection is determined by a number of factors, including their reliability, validity, fairness and relevance to the role being screened (a list of psychometric screening tools can be found at the end of this chapter). However, there are restrictions on who is allowed to administer and interpret the results of psychometric testing, therefore organisations wishing to undertake screening should ensure that the people they employ to undertake this work are professionally competent (BPS, 2006). When setting up pre-employment screening, it is important to provide the candidate with information in advance of the screening taking place. This information prepares the candidates for the screening and reduces the likelihood of any misunderstandings or ethical breaches occurring. The information should include a clear statement on the purpose of the screening, the relevance of particular tests being used, together with a description of the testing procedure, who will have access to the results and how these results will be used in the selection process (BPS, 2006). Organisations should also make sure that they have procedures for dealing with an interviewee's enquiries or any complaints from the pre-employment screening process.

Induction training

Induction training helps new recruits to settle into their roles more quickly. Induction programmes should be designed to support the recruits in forming positive working relationships with colleagues, gaining an understanding of the nature of the new working environment, their role and the organisation (CIPD, 2009). Whilst the induction programme is important to providing recruits with a good impression of the organisation during their first few days of employment, for those recruits about to be engaged in roles with a high risk of psychological harm, the induction programme has a greater importance, as it plays a part in preparing them for the work that they are about to undertake. Line managers drawing up induction programmes should begin by addressing any skills gaps or needs for adjustments that had been identified during the selection process. The induction training provides the first opportunity for line managers to tailor and adjust the training support to meet needs of a new team member. Another important function of the induction programme is the way in which it can assist a new recruit to create supportive cognitive frameworks or ways of thinking about the nature of work they are to undertake. The process of building protective cognitive frameworks (Pearlman, 1999) or dealing with negative thoughts (Lazarus and Folkman, 1984) takes time; therefore, wherever possible, line managers should introduce the emotionally demanding aspects of the work to new recruits gradually, allowing time for the team member to review and consolidate their experiences through personal reflection and discussion with colleagues. Whilst it is being increasingly recognized that throwing a new recruit in at the deep end without any preparation is likely to be psychologically damaging, it is also true that spending too much time preparing people for dealing with emotionally demanding work without offering any practical experience or exposure to psychologically demanding material or events can be equally damaging (Alexander and Wells, 1991). There is therefore a sensible balance between preparation and exposure to be achieved during the induction process. The responsibility for implementing, adapting and recording the induction training for team members and workers rests with their line manager; however, it is usually the role of a human resources practitioner to develop the induction policies, procedures and checklists, following consultation with senior management, line managers, health and safety and occupational health. A copy of the induction checklist should be held on every employee's personal file.

Education

Increasing the awareness of the nature and symptoms of secondary trauma and their impact on the organisation and its workers is an essential element of the TSM. Education programmes should be developed to meet the needs of front-line workers, line managers and senior managers, with the aim of reducing the incidence of secondary trauma and burn-out and enhancing opportunities for personal and organisational growth and development.

Worker education

Education sessions should be delivered to everyone working within the organisation, including workers with little or no direct exposure to traumatic events or materials. The aim of the education sessions is to provide simple information on the nature of secondary trauma and burn-out and a description of common symptoms with suggestions on ways to reduce the distress by simple lifestyle activities and building stress-reducing strategies. During the session, reference should be made to the individual and organisational responsibilities for protecting health and well-being. It is beneficial to have these education sessions delivered by line managers to all new recruits as part of their induction programme. However, the training material, process for recording and handouts should be developed in consultation with occupational health and human resources.

Line manager education

In addition to the core employee education which is provided for all workers, line managers require additional information and education to help them carry out their managerial role. During their management training, line managers and supervisors should be shown the importance of their role in maintaining a healthy workforce by promoting a supportive working environment. Line managers will also need to recognize when team members are showing signs of mental health problems and be able to use their communication skills to support troubled team members to look for ways to resolve their difficulties. Where a team member is experiencing more significant emotional or psychological problems, the line manager should know how to involve occupational health or refer the worker for specialist trauma counselling. Most line managers will have been trained to interview and carry out the induction and training of new team members in the technical skills required for working in a high-risk role. The education of line managers should show how the protection of emotional health and well-being of employees should be embedded within their technical training.

Senior manager education

The senior manager should be included in all aspects of the worker and line manager education programmes; however, they have the additional need to understand their roles in creating the organisational culture, policies and procedures which will promote healthy working relationships, methods of communication and organisational growth. The senior management team should also be regularly apprised of the results of the employee monitoring and any research which will help them deal with secondary trauma more effectively.

Resilience building

Resilience-building sessions provide workers who are engaged in emotionally demanding work with the opportunity to meet with colleagues and a facilitator, in order to share their experiences, coping skills and hints for the benefit of the whole team. This process is particularly helpful where there are teams of workers undertaking similar tasks, as it enables team members to discuss common issues or difficulties as they arise within their work and to encourage consultation on the way the difficulties can be resolved. The resilience-building approach adopted in the TSM is based on the principles of narrative therapy (White, 1995). The working team come together on a regular basis, usually every 4–6 weeks. The group is coordinated by a facilitator trained in the resilience-building model. The members of the group are offered the opportunity to talk about their concerns to the facilitator, who continually offers encouragement for persons to provide more details on the nature and extent of their experiences. Having achieved a detailed description of the concern, the focus is then changed from that of a personally owned problem to one in which the concern is externalized. This enables the nature of the concern to be challenged, reviewed and reframed. The concerned person is then invited to describe how he/she would prefer things be in the future and what else might be gained if the change occurred. The other members of the resilience team then have the opportunity to offer feedback to their colleague, during which time realistic solutions begin to emerge. Whilst this kind of conversation can occur naturally, organising time for people to get together provides opportunities for the team to learn from each other and to reduce the barriers to open discussions on the impact of the work.

Demobilizing/defusing

Where a team or individual team member has experienced an event or series of events that has caused them distress, it is useful for their line manager to offer an opportunity for the team to be demobilized or the distressed team member to talk about the event in a defusing session. Recovery from the impact of a traumatic exposure is improved when there is access to social support (Stephens, 1996) and where there is an opportunity to reflect on the experience with others (Pennebaker and Susman, 1988). Demobilizing and defusing sessions are normally undertaken by line managers or supervisors.

Demobilization

Where a team has been exposed to a distressing event, the line manager should use demobilization as a way of acknowledging what has happened and recognizing the efforts the team has made in dealing with the event. Whilst it is possible for members of the team to ask questions or make comments, the demobilization process is a relatively short session, designed to accept contributions of team members rather than to explore the event in great depth. Towards the end of the demobilization session, which would normally be around 10 minutes, the team is provided with information on the support that is available to them.

Defusing

Where a member of the team has been exposed to an event that has caused high levels of distress, the line manager may wish to undertake a defusing. This works best as a one-to-one session in which the line manager listens to the problems or concerns that are affecting the team member and then looks for any physical, social, emotional or psychological needs. The defusing process includes an incident risk assessment checklist, which can be used to help the line managers to identify whether it is appropriate to make a referral to Occupational Health for a medical or psychological intervention.

Trauma counselling

Where a worker is found to be suffering from secondary trauma related to his/her work, it may be necessary for him/her to be referred for trauma counselling. It has been shown that while trauma counselling and therapy is effective in treating traumatic stress, there is little evidence to show that any particular model is more effective than other models (Benish et al., 2007). However, for high-risk groups dealing with emotionally disturbing material, it is essential to find a counsellor familiar with dealing with secondary trauma and post-traumatic stress, in particular the kind of work undertaken by the distressed high-risk worker.

In-post screening and monitoring

All workers in organisations dealing with emotionally high-risk activities should have regular in-post screening. This should include a repeat administration of the clinical questionnaires used in the pre-employment screening: anxiety, depression, burn-out, secondary trauma, together with a survey of the worker's current lifestyle and experiences at work. However, there are likely to be other influences on mental health, including events outside the workplace. It is useful, therefore, to include screening tests which assess the impact of life events (Holmes and Rahe, 1967) and the worker's ability to establish meaning or coherence within his/her personal and workplace experiences (Antonovsky, 1993). The timing of the in-post screening will be determined by the nature of the role, the level of exposure to distressing material and the vulnerability of the worker. A common pattern of in-post screening would involve workers with a high risk being screened every 3 months, those at moderate risk every 6 months and workers with a low risk of secondary trauma once a year. However, supervisors and managers should be aware of their role in the screening process by monitoring the behaviours of all their workers, looking for any signs that suggest that a particular individual may need extra help or screening.

Quality assurance

Essential to the TSM is the need to assure the quality of the programme of support in maintaining the health and well-being of those working in an emotionally demanding work environment. In order to achieve a high quality and effective service, it is necessary to look at four aspects of quality assurance: (a) the guidelines and standards established for service delivery; (b) the supervision of the service provider; (c) the clinical audit of the service and its outcomes; and (d) the satisfaction levels achieved in consumer surveys (Cape, 1991).

Guidelines and standards

In order to audit the quality of a service, it is necessary to define the minimum acceptable level of performance as a good average service provision or as an ideal performance. Whilst guidelines are confined to general statements of the quality of service expected, standards provide a precise specification of the service required.

Professional supervision

Practitioners involved in delivering the TSM should attend professional supervision of their practice. Professional supervision for counselling and clinical psychologists is a professional requirement and must be undertaken at least once a month in face-to-face discussions between a clinical supervisor and the practitioner. During the supervision, a sample of cases may be examined, where the identity of the worker is kept confidential. The supervisor is also responsible for looking at the way the case has been handled and ensures that the practitioner is working competently. In addition, the supervisor is responsible for making sure that the psychologist is mentally fit and not suffering from a mental health condition and that the service being provided is fit for purpose.

Clinical audit

Clinical audit requires the service provider to collect data with the organisation to monitor particular aspects of the service. This may involve practical service elements, such as the availability of the services, speed of setting up appointments or preparing reports. The audit should also endeavour to undertake an assessment of the clinical effectiveness of the interventions.

Consumer surveys

Consumer opinion surveys provide an indication of the effectiveness of the service from the point of view of the users. They provide some indication of which aspects of the service might be changed to improve the user's response. These surveys could involve simple post-session feedback or could perhaps be part of a larger employee satisfaction survey.

Discussion

It has been recognized for some time that there are consequences to being directly involved in a traumatic event (Brewin, 2003); however, more recently it has been shown that traumatization is not confined to the direct victims of overwhelming events but can also affect those indirectly involved in investigating, supporting or reporting on traumatic events, such as fire fighters (Corneil et al., 1999), body handlers (Hyman, 2005), mental health workers (Buchanan *et al.*, 2006), therapists (Ennis and Home, 2009), insurance claims workers (Ludick *et al.*, 2007), solicitors (Vrklevski and Franklin, 2008), social workers (Adams *et al.*, 2007), online child abuse investigators (Burns *et al.*, 2008) and nurses (Mealer *et al.*, 2006).

Where occupational exposure to traumatic events is a normal part of a role, organisations nevertheless have a responsibility to put in place a system of support which is clinically and organisationally appropriate and effective. The Trauma Support Model provides a system of trauma care which, due to its flexibility, can be adapted to support workers in many different kinds of organisations. However, for the TSM to work, it is essential that it is supported by senior management, who agree to provide the necessary cultural climate, time and resources to carry out the programme. Fundamental to the process is the need for an organisational risk assessment involving the roles, the role holders and the development of the risk-control measures. The TSM provides a systematic approach to controlling the risk of secondary trauma and for identifying opportunities for creating positive learning and personal growth for workers.

References

Adams, R.E., Figley, C.R., Boscarino, J.A. (2007) The compassion fatigue scale: its use with social workers following urban disaster. *Research on Social Work Practice* **18**(3), 238–250.

Alexander, D.A., Wells, A. (1991) Reactions of police officers to body handling after a major disaster: a before and after comparision. *British Journal of Psychiatry* **159**, 574–555.

Antonovsky, A. (1993) The structure and properties of the sense of coherence scale. *Social Science Medicine* **36**, 725–733.

Benish, S.G., Imel, Z.E., Wampold, B.E. (2007) The relative efficacy of bona-fide psychotherapies for treating post-traumatic stress disorder: a meta-analysis of direct comparisons. *Clinical Psychology Review* **28**, 746–758.

Bergman, D., Davis, C., Rigby, B. (2007) *International Comparison of Health and Safety Responsibilities of Company Directors*. Norwich: HSE.

BPS (2006) *Psychological Testing: A User's Guide*. Leicester: British Psychological Society.

Brewin, C.R. (2003) *Post-traumatic Stress Disorder – Malady or Myth?* London: Yale University Press.

Buchanan, M., Anderson, J.O., Uhlemann, M.R., Horwitz, E. (2006) Secondary traumatic stress: an investigation of Canadian mental health workers. *Traumatology* **12**(4), 272–281.

Burns, C.M., Morley, J., Bradsaw, R., Domene, J. (2008) The emotional impact on coping strategies employed by police teams investigating internet child exploitation. *Traumatology* **14**(2), 20–31.

Cape, J.D. (1991) Quality assurance methods for clinical psychology services. *Psychologist* **4**(11), 499–503.

CIPD (2009) Induction: http//www.cipd.co.uk/subjects/recruitment/induction [accessed 25 May 2009].

Corneil, W., Beaton, R., Murphy, S., Johnson, C., Pike, K. (1999) Exposure to traumatic incidents and prevalence of posttraumatic stress symptomatology in urban fire fighters in two countries. *Journal of Occupational Health Psychology* **4**(2), 131–141.

Cox, T. (1993) *Stress Research and Stress Management: Putting Theory to Work*. Sudbury: HSE Books.

Ennis, L., Home, S. (2009) Predicting psychological distress in sex offender therapists. *Sexual Abuse: A Journal of Research and Treatment* **15**(2), 149–156.

Holmes, T.H., Rahe, R.H. (1967) The social readjustments rating scales. *Journal of Psychosomatic Research* **11**, 213–218.

HSE (2006) *Five Steps to Risk Assessment*. Sudbury: HSE Publications.

Hyman, O. (2005) Religiosity and secondary traumatic stress in Israeli–Jewish body handlers. *Journal of Traumatic Stress* **18**(5), 491–495.

Lazarus, R.S., Folkman, S. (1984) *Stress, Appraisal and Coping*. New York: Springer.

Ludick, M., Alexander, D., Carmichael, T. (2007) Vicarious traumatisation: secondary traumatic stress levels in claims workers in the short-term insurance industry in South Africa. *Problems and Perspectives in Management* **5**(3), 99–110.

Mealer, M.L., Shelton, A., Berg, B., Rothbaum, B., Moss, M. (2006) Increased prevalence of post-traumatic stress disorder symptoms in critical care nurses. *American Journal of Respiratory and Critical Care Medicine* **175**, 693–697.

Paton, D., Violanti, J.M., Smith, L.M. (2003) *Promoting Capabilities to Manage Posttraumatic Stress – Perspectives on Resilience*. Springfield, CT: Charles C. Thomas.

Pearlman, L.A. (1999). Notes from the field: What is vicarious traumatization? In Stamm, B.H. (ed.), *Secondary Traumatic Stress: Self-care Issues for Clinicians, Researchers and Educators*, 2nd edn. Lutherville, MD: Sidran Press.

Pennebaker, J.W., Susman, J.R. (1988) Disclosure of traumas and psychosomatic processes. *Social Science Medicine* **26**(3), 327–332.

Stephens, C. (1996) Debriefing, social support and PTSD in the New Zealand Police: testing a multidimensional model of organizational traumatic stress. *Australian Journal of Disaster and Trauma Studies*: www.massey.ac.nz/~trauma/issues/1997 [accessed 30 March 2009].

Tehrani, N. (2004) *Workplace Trauma – Concepts, Assessment and Interventions*. London: Brunner-Routledge.

Vrklevski, L.P., Franklin, J. (2008) Vicarious trauma: the impact on solicitors of exposure to traumatic material. *Traumatology* **14**(1), 106–118.

White, M. (1995) *Re-authoring Lives: Interviews and Essays*. Adelaide: Dulwich Centre Publications.

Useful psychometric tools

Carver, C.S., Scheier, M.F., Weintraub, J.K. (1989) Assessing coping strategies: a theoretically-based approach. *Journal of Personality and Social Psychology* **56**(2), 267–283 [a coping skills inventory].

Eysenck, H.J., Eysenck, S.B.G. (1975) *Manual of the Eysenck Personality Questionnaire (Junior and Adult)*. Sevenoaks, UK: Hodder and Stoughton [a useful personality test].

Felitti, V.J., Anda, R.F., Nordenberg, D. *et al.* (1998) Relationship of childhood abuse and household dysfunction to many of the leading causes of death in adults. The Adverse Childhood Experiences (ACE) study. *American Journal of Preventative Medicine* **14**(4), 245–258 [this study demonstrates the childhood experiences associated with physical and mental ill health].

Figley, C.R. (1995) *Compassion Fatigue*. New York: Brunner/Mazel [this book contains the Compassion Satisfaction, Fatigue and Burn-out Questionnaire].

Goldberg, D., Bridges, K., Duncan-Jones, P., Grayson, D. (1988) Detecting anxiety and depression in general medical settings. *British Medical Journal* **297**, 897–899 [a short anxiety/depression questionnaire].

Steiner, C. (1977) *Achieving Emotional Literacy*. London: Bloomsbury Publishing [this book includes the Emotional Awareness Questionnaire].

Support material

HSE Guidance on risk assessment/risk management: www.hse.gov.uk
DVD training package on crisis management demobilization and defusing: www.noreentehrani.com

Part IV

Building resilience and growth

Chapter 15

Sanctuary

An operating system for living organisations

Sandra L. Bloom

Background

The Sanctuary Model® represents a theory-based, trauma-informed, evidence-supported, whole-culture approach that has a clear and structured methodology for creating or changing an organisational culture. The objective of such a change is to more effectively provide a cohesive context within which healing from psychological and social traumatic experience can be addressed. As an organisational culture intervention, it is designed to facilitate the development of structures, processes and behaviours on the part of staff, clients and the community as a whole that can counteract the biological, affective, cognitive, social and existential wounds suffered by the victims of traumatic experience and extended exposure to adversity.

Although the roots of the Sanctuary Model go back to moral treatment and the Quaker philosophy of the eighteenth and nineteenth centuries, as well as the democratic therapeutic community movement and the human rights movements of the twentieth century, the Sanctuary Model was originally developed during 1980–2001 in a short-term, acute inpatient psychiatric setting for adults who were traumatized as children (Bloom, 1994, 1997; Bills and Bloom, 1998). The further development of the Sanctuary Model was facilitated by an NIMH research grant through the Jewish Board of Family and Children's Services in New York. The present training programme and implementation process has been a joint achievement of the author and the Andrus Children's Centre in Yonkers, New York. The model is currently being adopted by a number of human service delivery organisations in the USA, Scotland, Northern Ireland and Australia.

The impossibility of engineering human service delivery change

Embedded in the history of virtually all human service delivery systems are many debates about how services should be delivered, what constitutes help and how each institution should be structured and managed. It is clear from the initiation of the current projects in facilitating organisational change that these debates continue to surface in a number of ways today. Everywhere there is a lack of a clear, consistent, comprehensive and coherent theoretical model for delivering services that can be shared by staff, clients and families; lack of communication and feedback between and among component parts of the system; conflicts between various levels of staff as to what defines treatment; hierarchical management structures that encourage obedience to authority but do not encourage initiative, innovative problem-solving, or direct conflict resolution; a relative inability to sufficiently address the enormity of trauma-based problems in people's lives; only partially effective methods for dealing with aggressive acting-out; and unclear ideas about what constitutes success in these programmes.

From the staff's point of view, working in human services is often difficult, frustrating and stressful. People working in a care-giving environment are simultaneously leading their own lives and going through their own struggles, and these struggles often compound the stress of the workplace. Because of the exposure to adverse childhood conditions that so many people face, staff members are likely to have their own histories of experiences that consciously or unconsciously – for good or for ill – may collide and intersect with those of the clients in their care. Funding reductions for human services usually also result in decreases in training and supervision. To complicate this further, organisations are usually under a variety of pressures deriving from economic, performance and safety concerns, some of which spring directly from social and political forces that exist in the larger environment.

As a result, as described in Chapters 9 and 19 of this volume and elsewhere, complex, parallel process interactions occur between traumatized clients, stressed staff, pressured organisations and economic, political and social forces in the wider environment (Bloom, 2006, 2007, 2010, in press); Bloom and Farragher, 2011, in press. In this way, human service delivery systems become trauma-organised, inadvertently recapitulating the very experiences that have proved to be so toxic for the clients in their care (Bentovim, 1992). Not only does this have a detrimental effect on clients, but it also frustrates and demoralizes staff and administrators, a situation that can lead to worker burn-out, with all its attendant problems. Ultimately, the inefficient or inadequate delivery of service and the toll this takes on workers wastes money and resources. This vicious cycle also lends itself to a world view that the clients receiving the services are the cause of the problem, that their situations are hopeless and they cannot really be helped.

For such endemic problems there is no quick fix. Because systems of care are just that, interconnected systems, a piecemeal approach to change does not work. Every component of our human service delivery system must communicate with the others for proper service delivery, but presently they exist within silos, without a shared language or theoretical framework. This creates confusion that peaks at the interface between different kinds of service provisions. Sadly, it is usually those clients who are the most vulnerable and the least resourced who fall between the cracks. Many attempts have been and even are being made to alter this situation but, unfortunately, most organisational change methods are based on the idea of social engineering, which assumes cascading intention from the top to the bottom of a hierarchy, as leaders tell everyone else what to do and they do it.

Unfortunately, according to organisational change research, 70% of these change efforts in a wide variety of organisations fail. So dramatic is the failure of past methodology that organisational development investigators have declared that 'social engineering as a context is obsolete' (Pascale et al., 2000, p. 13). They reason that organisations are not machines but living systems and cannot be predictably engineered, and that 'Living Systems isn't a metaphor for how human institutions operate. It's the way it is' (Pascale et al., 2000, p. 7).

The explicit assumption of the Sanctuary Model is that most of the clients who present to human service delivery organisations have been exposed to significant adversity, chronic stress and frequently overwhelming trauma, and that they have the capacity to heal from these injuries and change the trajectories of their lives. But they frequently need help to do so and they cannot heal within the context of traumatizing – or traumatized – organisations that may actually create more, not less, pathology. The goal of the Sanctuary Model is to facilitate the development of an organisational culture that can contain, manage, and help transform the terrible life experiences that have moulded – and often deformed – the clients in care. But no one person can change an organisational culture – at least not for the better. Living systems are comprised of living people who tend to support what they help to create – and who fail to support change efforts that exclude them.

A new operating system for organisations

Confronted with the reality that our systems of care are both alive *and* trauma-organised, it is clear that three essential tasks need to be accomplished:

1 The development of a model of intervention that can be broadly applied across the population, can be shared between staff, clients and families, is consistent with established good practice, and allows for the uniqueness of each setting.
2 Practically integrate the system by developing more trust among organisational members, better communication networks, feedback loops, shared decision making, and conflict resolution practices.
3 Use the developed infrastructure to synthesize a variety of treatment approaches and techniques into a progressive map of recovery for each client.

What has emerged from our experience to date is the Sanctuary Model, an evidence-supported plan, process and method for creating trauma-sensitive, democratic, non-violent cultures that are far better equipped to engage in the innovative treatment planning and implementation that is necessary to adequately respond to the extremely complex and deeply embedded injuries that our clients have sustained.

A different model – a different metaphor

It has occasionally been difficult to explain to people who are training in the Sanctuary Model that it is *not* a specific treatment intervention, that it is structurally deeper than a specific intervention, although many interventions are compatible with it and are certainly necessary to obtain as complete a recovery as possible for the clients. Explanations required a new metaphor, since metaphors are especially useful in bridging knowledge gaps. Everyone who attends our Sanctuary Institutes has at least a rudimentary understanding of computers, so using a computer metaphor has become a useful way to explain how the Sanctuary Model works and how it integrates with other approaches.[1]

In brief, every computer has an operating system and every application – such as word processing and spreadsheet programmes – must be compatible with that operating system. Over the last few decades, research on the nature of attachment relationships has made clear that for human beings, healthy attachment is a fundamental requirement for physical, emotional, social and moral development. We can therefore understand attachment as the basic operating system for individuals. A useful way of understanding trauma and its impact on human beings is by recognizing that trauma fundamentally disrupts this human attachment system in a wide variety of ways, and that disruption wreaks havoc with a wide variety of the applications we use to adapt to the world, such as learning, emotional management, memory and many others. Trauma and sustained adversity do to the human operating system what a computer virus does to a computer. Social relationships are the basis of organisational functioning as well, so in a similar way, traumatic experience and adversity can profoundly disrupt the operating systems of organisations.

For people to heal from traumatic experience, that means not just changing their applications, the usual level of focus for treatment approaches, including trauma-specific approaches; it means changing things at a deeper level than that – changing their operating system – what we more commonly call their personality. This is why research that has extended over the last few decades, pertaining on the one hand to the impact of trauma, and on the other to the impact of disrupted attachment, offers a different paradigm for defining what we mean by 'treatment'. Particularly in the more complex cases that populate our mental health, substance abuse, child welfare and criminal justice systems, trauma-specific treatment approaches are necessary but not sufficient. In complex exposure to trauma and adversity, deeper, structural personality shifts have occurred – trauma-organised shifts in the individual's operating system – and shifting their personality on to a new trajectory of

---

1 Thanks to our colleague, Dr Joe Benamati, for the metaphor.

experience means changing that operating system. Likewise, in order to adequately address the needs of the traumatized clients who fill the ranks of our trauma-organised human service delivery system, we need a new operating system for organisations.

Compatibility with the Sanctuary Model

The Sanctuary Model is not a trauma-specific intervention but a way of reorganising whole organisational cultures. The Sanctuary Model is an operating system for a trauma-informed organisation. It is designed to get a number of people, from diverse backgrounds, with a wide variety of experience, on the same page, speaking the same language, living the same values, sharing a consistent, coherent and practical theoretical framework grounded in the science of cumulative, overwhelming, traumatic stress and disrupted attachment. It functions underneath all the other things that go on in a treatment programme – all the approaches, kinds of therapy, techniques and practices – as long as those practices are compatible with the Sanctuary operating system. It integrates long-established but often forgotten good organisational practice with the newer sciences of trauma and attachment studies.

The Sanctuary Model is designed to create the context within which groups of people within an organisation are encouraged and supported to make what are sometimes radical shifts in the very foundations of the way we think, what we feel, how we communicate and how we practise. This radical shift has become known as trauma-informed practice. The current challenge for everyone in human services is to consider how we unwittingly – and often in the name of science – erect barriers to recovery that prevent self-organising change in the individual lives of the clients in our care and in our organisational lives as well. We must wrestle with the fact that our diagnostic categories often shame clients from the moment they enter care. Our rigid hierarchies frequently prevent participation and innovation, when we need staff members to exercise almost constant creativity in order not to be drawn into traumatic replays of previous negative life experiences in the lives of the clients we serve. From chaos theory, we are learning that an organisation – even one as small as a child or individual family – will spontaneously know how to reorganise in the face of a challenge, *if* the obstacles hindering its capacity to self-organise are removed, and if the system can be drawn toward the edge of chaos and enabled to jump to a new and healthier set of attractors.

The Sanctuary safety spacesuit for exploring the edge of chaos

Organisational culture is 'the sum total of all the shared, taken-for-granted assumptions that a group has learned throughout its history' (Schein, 1999, p. 29), or how we do things around here. Organisational culture matters because cultural elements determine strategy, goals, and modes of operating (Schein, 1999). Danger and losses that attend the loss of safety are usually the wake-up calls that urge individual survivors and organisations to recognize that it is time for change. On the other hand, threat, dangers and loss arouse individual and organisational anxiety, and fear tends to drive us back to doing whatever is familiar. The familiar is our equilibrium state and, because it is familiar, that equilibrium state often feels safer than anything else. As a species we are fundamentally risk-aversive, at least in the short term. Deeply embedded in every organisational culture are the equilibrium attractors helping to guarantee that a system will return to its previous stable point, even after a radical divergence from that position.

Once we start facing organisational problems, they are generally bigger, more complex, than they appeared at first glance and it is difficult to know where to start. When faced with complexity, it is important to have some kind of cohesive framework that helps structure the formulation of an action plan for change, knowing that change is normally resisted because maintaining equilibrium is what all living systems achieve in order to stay viable. In a therapeutic situation, it is essential that the client and the helper get on the same page, so that their goals and strategies for achieving those goals are aligned. Similarly, in an organisational setting it is critical that staff members, administrators and, when relevant, board members agree on basic assumptions and beliefs about their shared mission, desired outcomes and methods for achieving their goals.

When an organisation has at least a vague outline of another set of attractors – something they want to do or be in the future – then and only then does it become possible to begin moving an organisation away from its stable equilibrium point. In organisations adopting the Sanctuary Model, those 'attractors' become things like eliminating seclusion and restraint, being more effective in treating traumatized children, adults and families, or having fewer staff injuries and sustaining less staff turnover. In chaos theory, the place of transformation, of true creative change, is out 'on the edge of chaos', and for individuals and organisations that can be a very scary place to be. The Sanctuary Model is designed as a kind of organisational spacesuit that allows an organisation to venture out into and explore unknown territory while remaining tethered to its own vehicle for sufficient safety to make the trip. Once the members of the community have found a place they want to go to, and the attraction of that place is sufficiently strong, they can let go of the tether and, with some degree of reliability, go to the new place. The Seven Commitments, SELF, and the Sanctuary Toolkit are all vital elements of the organisational spacesuit.

The Seven Commitments

Creating Sanctuary refers to the shared experience of creating and maintaining physical, psychological, social and moral safety within a social environment – any social environment – and thus reducing systemic violence. For a complex organisation to function, you need just the right number of principles that guide short-term, everyday conduct as well as long-term strategy. Too many rules and a system becomes rigid, inflexible and even paralysed; too few and it becomes purely individualistic and chaotic. The Seven Commitments structure the organisational norms that determine the organisational culture. The Seven Sanctuary Commitments represent the guiding principles for implementation of the Sanctuary Model – the basic structural elements of the Sanctuary 'operating system' – and each commitment supports trauma recovery goals for clients, staff and the organisation as a whole:

1 *Commitment to non-violence* – to build safety skills, trust and inspire a commitment to wider socio-political change.
2 *Commitment to emotional intelligence* – to teach emotional management skills and expand awareness of problematic cognitive-behavioural patterns and how to change them.
3 *Commitment to social learning* – to build cognitive skills, improve learning and decisions and create/sustain a learning organisation.
4 *Commitment to open communication* – to overcome barriers to healthy communication, discuss the undiscussables, increase transparency, develop conflict management skills and reinforce healthy boundaries.
5 *Commitment to democracy* – to develop civic skills of

self-control and self-discipline, to learn to exercise healthy authority and leadership, to develop participatory skills, overcome helplessness and honour the voices of self and others.

6   *Commitment to social responsibility* – to harness the energy of revenge by rebuilding social connection skills, establishing healthy attachment relationships and transforming vengeance into social justice.

7   *Commitment to growth and change* – to work through loss in the recognition that all change involves loss, and to envision, skilfully plan and prepare for and be guided by a different and better future.

Leadership commitment

The Seven Commitments apply to everyone. Organisational leaders must be fully committed to the process of the Sanctuary Model for it to be effective – that means the board of directors, managers at all levels and staff. If the organisational leaders do not get on board, it will not work. If the middle managers do not get on board, it will not work. If the staff do not get on board, it will not work. At first glance, many organisational leaders hear a review of the Seven Commitments and believe that those commitments already constitute their organisational culture. In many cases this is at least partially true. It is only when leaders engage in a different kind of dialogue with other members of their organisational community that they find out how divergent people's views are on what these commitments mean and how to make them real in everyday interactions. Experience has taught that courageous leadership is critical to system change, and without such leadership substantial change is unlikely to occur.

This change process, however, can be frightening for people in leadership positions and they rightfully perceive significant risk in opening themselves up to criticism, in levelling hierarchies and sharing legitimate power. The gains are substantial, but a leader only finds that out after learning how to tolerate the anxiety and uncertainty that inevitably accompanies real change. It should also be noted that change does not occur just because a leader wants it to occur. Leaders may be willing to share power with others, but this does not necessarily mean that others are always willing to assume power and the responsibility that comes with it. Although staff and clients may indicate that they want a greater voice, creating the conditions in which others have a greater voice is not always welcomed. It is easy to stay in or slide back to a familiar and comfortable arrangement.

Learning how to be an effective democratic leader necessitates a sharp, often steep and sometimes painful learning curve. It is through participation in work groups, teams and meetings that routine emotional management occurs within organisational settings. Crisis-driven organisations sacrifice communication networks, feedback loops, participatory decision making and complex problem-solving under the pressures of chronic stress and, in doing so, lose healthy democratic processes and shift to an increasingly hierarchical, top-down control structure that discourages creativity, innovation and risk-taking, resulting in an inability to manage complexity. The cure for this situation is more democracy. This requires leadership buy-in and immersion in the change process, an increase in transparency and deliberate restructuring to ensure greater participation and involvement.

SELF: a non-linear organising framework

SELF is an acronym that represents the four interactive key aspects of recovery from bad experiences. SELF provides a non-linear, cognitive-behavioural therapeutic approach for facilitating movement – regardless of whether we are talking about individual clients, families, staff problems or whole organisational dilemmas. SELF is a compass that allows us to explore all four key domains of healing:

- *Safety* – attaining safety in self, relationships and environment.
- *Emotional management* – identifying levels of various emotions and modulating emotion in response to memories, persons and events.
- *Loss* – feeling grief and dealing with personal losses and recognizing that all change involves loss.
- *Future* – trying out new roles, ways of relating and behaving as a survivor to ensure personal safety and help others.

Using SELF, clients, their families and staff are able to embrace a shared, non-technical and non-pejorative language that allows them all to see the larger recovery process in perspective. The accessible language demystifies what sometimes is seen as confusing and even insulting clinical or psychological terminology that can confound clients and line-staff, while still focusing on the aspects of pathological adjustment that pose the greatest problems for any treatment environment.

The further utility of SELF is that it can simultaneously be employed in a parallel process manner to deal with problems that arise within the treatment setting between staff and clients, among members of staff and between staff and administration. Applied to such issues of staff splitting, poor morale, rule infraction, administrative withdrawal and helplessness and misguided leadership, SELF can also assist a stressed organisation to conceptualize its own present dilemma and move into a better future through a course of complex decision making and conflict resolution.

The Sanctuary Institute

Our belief in the power of community led us to develop the Sanctuary Institute. Creating and sustaining a normative culture requires a large up-front investment of time, energy and resources, but in the long term produces compound interest in the investment. For individuals and for systems, this requires a rigorous process of self-examination and the development of a core system of meaning that will guide behaviour, decision-making, problem-solving and conflict resolution. Such a process involves the willingness to temporarily reflect on the past, create a culture of inquiry to examine the present, and commitment of sufficient time to engage in honest dialogue. Productive discourse, however, depends on good communication, and recovering individuals need to learn how to listen and how to talk. Likewise, chronic systemic problems lead to communication breakdowns and the loss of feedback loops within organisations. As a result, an organisation must learn how to reconnect and integrate with the various parts of itself.

The Sanctuary Institute is a 5 day intensive training experience.[2] Teams of five to eight people, from various levels of the organisation, come together to learn from our faculty, colleagues from other organisations and one another, and begin to create a shared vision of the kind of organisation they want to create. These teams will eventually become the Sanctuary Steering Committee for their organisation. The training experience usually involves several organisations

---

2 The Sanctuary Institute is a part of the Andrus Center for Learning and Innovation, at Andrus Children's Center in Yonkers, NY: www.andruschildren.org

and generally these organisations are very different in terms of size, scope, region and mission. This diversity helps to provide a rich learning experience for the participants.

Participation in the Sanctuary Institute is the gateway to the Sanctuary Network, a community of organisations committed to the development of trauma-informed services. We are all committed to the belief that we can do better for our clients and our colleagues, as well as our society, if we can accept that the people we serve are not sick or bad but injured, and that the services we provide must provide hope, promote growth and inspire change. We believe that clients can change if they find themselves in a community that tolerates risk, values creativity, inspires hope and believes that the future can be different from the past. We believe organisations require the same kind of community if they are going to improve, heal from their own stresses and injuries, and realize their full potential. It is hard to change your old patterns without help and support. What we know about trauma theory tells us that our old patterns are difficult to break and that it is easy to slide back into established habits without even thinking about it.

Sanctuary Steering Committee and the Sanctuary Toolkit

During the training, the Steering Committee engages in prolonged facilitated dialogue that serves to surface the major strengths, vulnerabilities and conflicts within the organisation. By looking at shared assumptions, goals and existing practice, staff members from various levels of the organisation are required to share in an analysis of their own structure and functioning, often asking themselves and each other provocative questions that have never overtly surfaced before. Many of these questions have not been raised before because participants have never felt safe enough to say what has been on their minds or in their hearts, even after many years of working together. Although the continual focus is on the fundamental question of 'Are we safe?', participants quickly learn that in the Sanctuary Model being safe means being willing to take risks, by being willing to say what needs to be said and hear what needs to be heard.

Participants look at the change process itself and are asked to anticipate the inevitable resistance to change that is a fact of life in every organisation. They look at management styles, the way decisions are made and conflicts resolved. In the process of these discussions, they learn about what it means to engage in more democratic processes on the part of leaders, staff and clients in terms of the simultaneous increase in rights and responsibilities. They evaluate the existing policies and procedures that apply to staff, clients and families and ask whether or not they are effective in achieving their shared goals. They are asked to learn about, and become thoroughly familiar with, the psychobiology of trauma, the way PTSD, complex PTSD and other trauma-related disorders present in the children, adults and families they work with, and begin to think about the implications of that knowledge for treatment. They also learn how high levels of stress in the organisation can impact relationships, emotions and decision making at every level of the organisation. They develop an understanding of the conceptual tool for organising treatment – SELF. They learn about vicarious trauma, traumatic re-enactment and the importance of understanding themselves and providing support for each other. And they are introduced to the various components of the Sanctuary Toolkit, including community meetings, safety plans, Red Flag reviews, SELF Psycho-education, SELF treatment planning, and Sanctuary team meetings.

Developing a Core Team and guided implementation manuals

The Sanctuary Steering Committee are instructed to go back to their organisation and create a Core Team – a larger, multidisciplinary team that expands its reach into the entire organisation. It is this Core Team that will be the activators of the entire system. The Core Team are armed with a *Sanctuary Staff Training Manual*, a *Sanctuary Implementation Manual* and ongoing consultation and technical assistance from Sanctuary faculty members to guide them through the process of Sanctuary implementation. This process takes several years to really get traction and then continues – hopefully – forever. The objective of the implementation and technical assistance is to edge an organisation closer and closer to the edge of chaos, where creative, self-organising change occurs, without destabilizing it to such a point that it becomes chaotic and dangerous. As the CEO of Andrus Children's Center, Nancy Ment, has noted:

> The Sanctuary Model doesn't keep bad things from happening but it allows an organisation to deal with those bad things

without losing its way so it can bounce back and continue to function.[3]

The Core Team should have representatives from every level of the organisation to ensure that every voice is heard. It is vital that all key organisational leaders become actively involved in the process of change and participate in this Core Team.

The responsibility of Core Team members is to actively represent and communicate with their constituents and to become trainers and cheerleaders for the entire organisation. The Core Team works out team guidelines and expectations of involvement for individual team members, as well as a meeting schedule, and decides on safety rules for the constructive operation of the team itself. The Core Team is ultimately responsible for the development of an implementation process, aimed at including the entire organisation in the change process, that involves teaching everyone about the Seven Commitments, trauma theory, SELF and the Sanctuary Toolkit. The Core Team facilitates the development of changed human resource, supervision, orientation, and training programmes and policies. They oversee a plan for significantly greater client participation in planning and implementation of their service plan. The ultimate goal is to take meaningful steps to change the organisation's culture and engage as many community members as possible in that process.

As discussions begin in the Core Team, participating staff begin to make small but significant changes. Members take risks with each other and try new methods of engagement and conflict resolution. They feed these innovations and their results back into the process discussions. The Core Team must always maintain a balance between process and product. It is not enough to talk about how we will change things. We must also make actual changes in the way we do business. The Core Team therefore not only plans together how best to share what they are learning with the larger organisation, but also plans how to train all agency personnel and clients in the Sanctuary principles, how to integrate the Sanctuary Toolkit into the day-to-day operation of the organisation and how to evaluate how these initiatives are taking hold in the organisation.

Through the implementation steps of the Sanctuary Model, staff members engage in prolonged dialogue that serves to surface the major strengths, vulnerabilities and conflicts within the organisation.

3 Personal communication.

By looking at shared assumptions, goals and existing practice, staff members from various levels of the organisation are required to share in an analysis of their own structure and functioning, often asking themselves and each other provocative questions that have never overtly surfaced before. As this happens, the development of more democratic, participatory processes begins to emerge. These processes are critical because they are most likely to lend themselves to the solution of very complex problems while improving staff morale, providing checks and balances to abuses of power and opening up the community to new sources of information.

Evaluation and expected outcomes

Finally, the Core Team must decide on indicators they want to use to evaluate their Sanctuary programme in an ongoing way – their Sanctuary Programme Evaluation Plan. The indicators should be observable, measurable and consistent with standards established by Sanctuary leaders. There should be a regular process of evaluation and review that involves all core team members. It is vital that there be a thorough method for reviewing problems and failures and establishing remedial courses of action; but likewise there must be methods for reviewing and capturing successes.

The impact of creating a trauma-informed Sanctuary Model culture should be observable and measurable. The outcomes we expect to see include, and are applicable to, all community members:

- Less violence, including physical, verbal and emotional forms of violence, including but not limited to reduced/eliminated seclusion and restraint.
- System-wide understanding of complex biopsychosocial and developmental impact of trauma and abuse and what that means for the service environment.
- Less victim-blaming; fewer punitive and judgemental responses.
- Clearer, more consistent boundaries, higher expectations, linked rights and responsibilities.
- Earlier identification of, and confrontation of, abusive use of power in all of its forms.
- Better ability to articulate goals, create strategies for change and justify the need for a holistic approach.
- Understanding and awareness of re-enactment behaviour, resistance to change and how to achieve a different outcome.

- More democratic environment at all levels.
- Better outcomes for children, staff and organisation.

Sanctuary certification and research

Sanctuary is a registered trademark and the right to use the Sanctuary name is contingent on engagement in the Sanctuary Institute training and certification programme and an agreement to participate in an ongoing, peer-review certification process. Programmes usually seek Sanctuary Certification in the 2–3 year period after participation in the Sanctuary Institute.

The Sanctuary Model is considered an evidence-supported practice by the National Child Traumatic Stress Network in the USA and it is accumulating a growing research base of support (Rivard *et al.*, 2004; McSparren, 2007; Bloom and Farragher, 2009; Banks and Vargas, 2008, 2009).

References

Banks, J., Vargas, L.A. (2008) *Preliminary Outcomes: Sanctuary in Childcare Settings*. Yonkers, NY: Andrus Center for Learning and Innovation: www.andruschildren.org

Banks, J., Vargas, A.L. (2009) *Sanctuary in Schools: Preliminary Child and Organizational Outcomes*. Yonkers, NY: Andrus Center for Learning and Innovation: www.andruschildren.org

Bentovim, A. (1992) *Trauma-organized Systems: Physical and Sexual Abuse in Families*. London: Karnac Books.

Bills, L.J., Bloom, S.L. (1998) From chaos to sanctuary: trauma-based treatment for women in a state hospital system. In Levin, B.L., Blanch, A.K., Jennings, A. (eds), *Women's Health Services: A Public Health Perspective*. Thousand Oaks, CA: Sage.

Bloom, S.L. (1994) The Sanctuary Model: developing generic inpatient programs for the treatment of psychological trauma. In Williams, M.B., Sommer, J.F. (eds), *Handbook of Post-traumatic Therapy: A Practical Guide to Intervention, Treatment, and Research*. New York: Greenwood Publishing.

Bloom, S.L. (1997) *Creating Sanctuary: Toward the Evolution of Sane Societies*. New York: Routledge.

Bloom, S.L. (2006) Organizational Stress as a Barrier to Trauma-sensitive Change and System Transformation. White paper for the National Technical Assistance Center for State Mental Health Planning (NTAC), National Association of State Mental Health Program Directors: http://www.nasmhpd.org/publications.cfm [accessed 20 October 2009].

Bloom, S.L. (2007) Loss in human service organizations. In Vargas, A.L., Bloom, S.L. (eds), *Loss, Hurt and Hope: the Complex Issues of Bereavement and Trauma in Children*. Newcastle, UK: Cambridge Scholars Publishing.

Bloom, S.L. (2010, in press) Trauma-organized systems and parallel process. In Tehrani, N. (ed.), *Managing Trauma in the Workplace*. London: Routledge.

Bloom, S.L., Farragher, B. (2009) Expected outcomes and research: developing an evidence base. Yonkers, NY: Andrus Center for Learning Innovation: www.andruschildren.org

Bloom, S.L., Farragher, B. (2011, in press) *Destroying Sanctuary: The Crisis in Human Service Delivery*. New York: Oxford University Press.

McSparren, W. (2007) Models of Change and the Impact on Organizational Culture: The Sanctuary Model Explored. Unpublished manuscript.

Pascale, R.T., Millemann, M., Gioja, L. (2000) *Surfing the Edge of Chaos: The Laws of Nature and the New Laws of Business*. New York: Crown Business.

Rivard, J.C., McCorkel, D., Duncan, M.E., Pasquale, L.E., Bloom, S.L., Abramovitz, R. (2004) Implementing a trauma recovery framework for youths in residential treatment. *Child and Adolescent Social Work Journal* **21**, 529–550.

Schein, E.H. (1999) *The Corporate Culture: A Survival Guide. Sense and Nonsense About Culture Change*. San Francisco, CA: Jossey Bass.

Chapter 16

A resilience-building toolbox

Noreen Tehrani

Introduction

In organisations where workers are known to be exposed to traumatizing material, incidents or environments, it is helpful to provide training to support the workers in recognizing and dealing with their trauma responses. Having chosen to work in careers which involve traumatic exposure, workers will find that the work brings about changes in their responses, attitudes and beliefs, which can be both positive and negative. Post-trauma growth occurs when a worker is able to transform the negative emotional and physiological reactions to his/her work into positive learning and personal development. This chapter has been written for workers engaged in careers that expose them to experiences where their lives are put in danger, where they are involved in rescuing others, need to support traumatized people or are exposed to material which depicts or describes potential or actual traumatic events. The tools described in this chapter are therefore useful for a wide range of workers, including counsellors, nurses, social workers, police officers, foster parents, emergency services workers, psychologists, teachers, human resources workers and others. The tools are easy to learn and can be employed safely whenever a worker begins to notice the indicative signs of a trauma response to his/her work. However, the tools are not intended to replace professional supervision or therapy, but rather to build workers' self-awareness and knowledge and empower them to use skills to protect their health and well-being by increasing their personal resilience.

Background to the toolbox

The tools in the toolbox have been selected from a wide range of interventions that are commonly in use by trauma therapists to help in dealing with troubling post-trauma responses. Many of these interventions, however, can be learnt and used by anyone, provided that they have a basic knowledge of the biology and psychology of traumatic stress. Training workers to use these skills prior to the onset of traumatic stress serves a number of purposes by: (a) increasing the understanding of the role of post-trauma responses in the recovery process; (b) demystifying the trauma recovery; (c) enabling workers to take an active role in enhancing their own well-being and resilience; and (d) making the tools available to the workers who need them at a time when they are needed.

Traumatic stress involves three main symptoms: re-experience, hyperarousal and avoidance. It is accepted that, in the immediate aftermath of a traumatic event, these acute responses are adaptive and have the ability to protect rather than be injurious to well-being (Shalev and Yehuda, 1998). The ability to understand the adaptive purpose of post-trauma responses in increasing personal security and reducing the incidence of physical or psychological injury is an essential part of the psycho-educational training for workers engaged in emotionally demanding work. All living creatures have evolved biological processes, drives and instincts that maximize their survival. These primeval processes are largely outside conscious awareness and control; nevertheless, they are extremely powerful and adaptive. Normal living is challenging, with 60% of the general population being exposed to at least one traumatic event in their lives (Kessler *et al.*, 1995). However the majority of people exhibit only transient symptoms, which tend to resolve within a few weeks or months, and only a small proportion of people going on to develop PTSD (Yehuda *et al.*, 2005). Nevertheless, in organisations where traumatic exposure is a regular feature of working life, it is important to help workers to return to pre-traumatic exposure levels of functioning and performance as soon as reasonably possible, and for this reason it is beneficial for the organisation and the worker to be proactive in addressing post-trauma reactions and symptoms, however mild and transitory.

Underpinning principles

All living creatures are born with devices designed to solve the basic problems of life and to maintain homeostasis. At the most fundamental level, this involves the autonomic nervous system and basic reflexes which are nested within the body's other systems and processes. These systems involve automatic and instinctive behaviours, including those concerned with: (a) the avoidance of pain and maximization of pleasure; (b) basic drives and motivations for satisfying appetites for food, drink, sex and safety; (c) emotions such as disgust, fear, happiness and shame; and (d) feelings, thoughts and perceptions which draw attention to the state of all the body's systems. However, the goal of this complex nest of systems is not merely to survive, but rather to provide opportunities for achieving an enhanced state of well-being (Damasio, 2006). Unfortunately, in their zealousness to protect, the innate systems occasionally create trauma responses which, whilst adaptive in the short term, become fixed or conditioned and detrimental to the flexibility essential to healthy living. The goal of the resilience-building toolset is to identify the output of this faulty conditioned learning and to offer the troubled body and mind alternative solutions in a form which encourages adaptive systemic learning. As much of the trauma learning takes place at a pre-conscious sensory level, the tools require the worker to actively engage with his/her trauma memories and reactivate his/her sensory responses. The tools help to address the three groups of trauma symptoms: re-experience; arousal; and avoidance. Ideally, the skill training should be undertaken by an experienced traumatologist or trauma counsellor with an understanding of the underlying therapeutic theories. The sequence of skills is best delivered in a series of six 90 minute sessions.

Preparation

Before attempting to use any of the resilience-building tools, it is important to help the workers to build some general skills which will assist them to learn how to become relaxed, and to find a safe place which becomes a refuge or safe haven that they can enter whenever they feel distressed or overwhelmed by their symptoms. Spending time practising relaxation is essential preparation, as there is a tendency for employees and trainers to underestimate the importance of the preparation phase, particularly when a worker is currently

experiencing distressing trauma symptoms. The worker should practise the relaxation and safe place exercises for at least a week before
attempting any of the other exercises. Deep breathing is a very
simple and useful technique for increasing relaxation; the following
exercise is particularly helpful and involves simply taking in a slow
deep breath for the count of 7 seconds, then holding the breath
for 7 seconds, and finally breathing out slowly and smoothly for
7 seconds. The whole process is then repeated 10 or more times. The
slow breathing is physically relaxing, whilst the rhythmic counting
calms the mind and reduces the incidence of intrusive thoughts. The
second relaxation exercise (Exercise 1) involves guided imagery; in
this exercise, a script is read which takes the worker to a safe place
where he/she feels comfortable and relaxed. During the exercise, all
the senses are used to add sensory depth to the experience of safety.
Initially it helps to have someone read the script, but after a short
while the worker will find quicker ways to enter his/her place of
safety without having to use the script. In order to learn these skills,
it is necessary to practise this exercise at least twice a day for 2 weeks.

Re-experience

The re-experience symptoms of flashbacks, nightmares and other
recurrent responses to the trauma are perhaps the most distressing
feature of traumatic stress. Following traumatic events, workers may
find that one or more of their senses is involved in triggering some
aspect of the incident. It is helpful to train the workers in ways to
deal with their trauma responses to triggers involving each of their
senses. Many people, faced with a distressing image or feeling, will
try to avoid them; unfortunately, this makes matters worse and the
distress returns. In the re-experience exercises the objective is to call-
up the feared sensory experience in a safe and controlled way, then to
demonstrate that the sensory experience is not real but rather an
illusion that the mind and body is creating. The following exercises
deal with visual images, sounds, smells, physical sensations and
tastes. It is helpful to use the safe place exercise (Exercise 1) at the
beginning and the end of each of these trauma memory exercises.

Exercise 1. Establishing a safe place
In this exercise, we are not going to think about bad memories,
but we will practise using our imagination to create positive

images and feelings. I am going to ask you to imagine a place or scene where you feel calm, secure and happy. This could be somewhere real that you remember, maybe a holiday, or it could be somewhere you have heard about or perhaps a place that you create in your imagination.

Make yourself comfortable, by sitting on a chair which fully supports your back or by lying flat on the floor or bed. Relax and close your eyes. Concentrate on your breathing – as you breathe out, concentrate on the tip of your nose – feel how it slightly tingles as the air flows out through your nostrils. Breathe out – feeling the air pass out of your nostrils – your nostrils slightly tingle. Breathe out once more – the air flowing out of your nostrils.

Let the relaxation radiate over your body – already you are at a deeper level of relaxation – deeper than before. In order to increase your level of relaxation, imagine that you are standing at the top of a staircase – this may be a wide and winding staircase or perhaps a staircase you know well at home – soon you will take hold of the rail and take the first step down the stairs. As you take the first step down, you can feel the carpet soft and thick beneath your feet. There are 10 more steps to the bottom of the stairs; as I count, you will take steps down the stairs – every step you take will make you more and more mentally and physically relaxed. You are standing on the staircase, you are now ready to take another step down – ten – nine – take some more steps down – eight – seven – six – you are halfway down the staircase – you are deeply relaxed – five – four – three – two – one – you have reached the bottom of the staircase – feeling deeply mentally and physically relaxed.

In front of you is a door. Walk over to the door – turn the handle – open the door. On the other side of the door is the most beautiful place you have ever seen. It is totally perfect – you stand looking at this perfect place; as I count to three, you will walk through the door into your perfect place. One – two – three. You step through the door into the place where you feel at home and at ease. I want you to notice your surroundings, notice the colours all around you – the blue of the sky – the green of the grass and trees – look at all the shapes around you – the shapes of the land – change anything which is not perfect – make it as beautiful a place as you ever could wish for.

Examine all your surroundings, become familiar with all the

colours and shapes – touch your surroundings – feel the warmth of the ground – the hardness of a pebble – the softness of a leaf. Listen to the sounds in your special place – can you hear the sounds of birds singing – the sounds of the breeze in the trees – can you hear any water sounds – the rush of water in a stream or the gentle lapping of the sea? Smell the fragrance in this place – can you smell the scent of flowers – the smell of damp earth – or the salty smell of the sea – wood smoke – pine needles and other pleasant fragrances. Spend some time relaxing in this place – absorb the atmosphere of calm and peace. Every time you come to this place it will become more familiar and vivid than before – each time you come here you will feel calm and at peace.

Look around in your imagination once more. Remember that this is your special place. It will always be there. You can always imagine being here when you want to feel calm and secure and happy. Now get ready to open your eyes and leave your special place for now. You can come back when you want. As you open your eyes, you will feel calm and happy.

Visual flashbacks and nightmares

This exercise deals with visual images and requires workers to identify a particular flashback or recurrent nightmare which is troubling to them. The workers do not need to talk about their trauma images, but rather are asked to project them as a film onto a wall or other surface. For some workers this may be very difficult, as they are afraid of the trauma film that their minds are creating. It is important that workers are reassured that they are in complete control of the projection and that they can turn the film off or freeze it as they wish. Having created the trauma film, the workers are then encouraged to begin to change it by, for example, making it appear in black and white, or running it backwards, speeding it up or slowing it down, taking it out of focus or make the film frame narrow or wide. Any change, even a small change, is important to notice and reward. The workers are then able to introduce new elements into the film; like a director, they can bring in a supporting hero or friend to help them deal with the situation, or they can run the film forward to a place where they feel safe. At the end of the exercise it is important to switch the film off; in some people this may involve creating a switch to turn off or a plug to pull out.

Auditory flashbacks and triggers

Auditory flashbacks and triggers can be reduced by bringing to mind the feared sound. The sound is heard as if it is on a radio or CD. The worker begins to change the sound by altering the volume, pitch or tempo of the sound; if the feared sound is a voice then the voice can be altered to sound like a humorous cartoon character. When the worker has gained control over the sounds then the radio or CD is switched off.

Trauma-related smells and tastes

For some people, trauma memories are strongly attached to a smell or taste. The smell of burning flesh many cause flashbacks for a firefighter or the taste or smell of semen for a rape victim. Here it is important to pair a pleasant smell or taste with the safe place exercise, for example, the smell of lavender or pine needles and the taste of cool fresh water. In the smell exercise, the bad smell in the trauma memory is made visible by colouring it black, so that it appears like a black cloud; the worker is then asked to visualize him/herself holding an empty balloon, which gradually sucks in the smelly black cloud. The worker is then asked to look around the scene in his imagination and check that there are no pieces of the black cloud hiding under stones or behind objects. Only when he is satisfied that all the smells are in the balloon is he asked to tie the neck of the balloon and let it float away. He then returns to his safe place and becomes aware of his favourite smell.

The taste exercise is similar to that used to deal with bad smells, but this time the worker becomes aware of the taste and identifies where she experiences the taste – is it in her mouth, her throat, her stomach? When she knows exactly where the taste has gone, she visualizes a glass of cool, fresh water, which she can drink. As she watches herself drink, she notices that the water is washing away the bad taste; it cleanses her mouth, her throat and stomach, washing away all traces of the bad taste until all she can taste is the cool, fresh water.

Body sensations

In this exercise the worker is encouraged to become more aware of his/her physical reactions to his/her trauma experience. He needs to think of a time when he has felt distress or discomfort and then to check out his body to identify the changes in his body. The responses to distress are often in the body's central core: the stomach, chest, throat or head; however, the sensation may be in other parts of the body, particularly limbs. The worker is then asked to talk about the sensation, its size, temperature, texture, colour and weight. Having established the position and nature of the sensation the worker, is then asked to see if the sensation is connected to anything else in the body – or it is a single sensation? When the worker becomes certain of the sensation, he is asked to take one of the features of the sensation and begin to change it slightly. If it is hot, can it become cooler? If black, can it become grey? If big, can it become smaller? It is not necessary to make large changes; a small change is enough. The final stage is to move the sensation out of the body; a slight movement is sufficient. The worker is then asked how he feels, having been able to change the sensation, and what it means to have this ability to bring about the change.

Dual attention

This exercise brings all the senses together and helps the brain to process the information and to begin to create a greater sense of calm. The process is based on the principles found in eye movement desensitisation and reprocessing EMDR (Shapiro, 2001). The worker is asked to tap her knees to a slow rhythm. As she taps, she calls up a memory that has been upsetting her. With her eyes open, she creates pictures, sounds, smells and other sensations. Then she begins tapping her knees while she observes the images and sensations. Then she stops and describes what happened during the tapping. The worker is asked to repeat the process a number of times until her trauma pictures and other sensations become less distinct and distressing. Finally the worker is asked to think of a pleasant image and sensation; as she looks at this image, she begins tapping her knees, making the image sharper and brighter.

Dreams

Many people have bad dreams or nightmares after a traumatic event. The next exercise will help workers deal with bad dreams and nightmares. Whilst nightmares seem real when one is asleep, they are created in the mind and are not real. The best way to fight nightmares is to get them into the open during the daytime, when it is clear that they cannot cause harm. Dealing with dreams during the day means that they come back less often at night. Any of the re-experience tools can be used to call up and change the dream; however, it is also possible to stop nightmares by drawing them and then finding a supportive friend or colleague to talk to about the drawing and the dream and what it means. Some workers may find it helpful to make their drawings into a cartoon strip, where the last drawing represents how they would like the dream to end.

Arousal

Workers who have been exposed to a traumatic event will have an immediate arousal response, in which their autonomic nervous system primes their bodies to deal with the physical and psychological demands of the situation. During the first few days and weeks following the traumatic exposure, hyperarousal is regarded as a feature of acute stress disorder and includes physical and psychological restlessness, insomnia, hypervigilance, concentration difficulties and irritability (Bryant and Harvey, 2000). There are three tools which can be learnt to deal with hyperarousal, in addition to the deep breathing exercise already described. These tools are progressive relaxation, graded relaxation and creating a healthy lifestyle.

Progressive relaxation (PR)

There are two steps to the progressive relaxation procedure: (a) deliberately tensing muscle groups; and (b) releasing the induced tension. PR should be practised twice a day for a week and then used regularly until the arousal symptoms disappear. During the PR, all the major muscle groups are tensed and then relaxed in sequence. In order to prepare for the exercise, the worker should be sitting on a chair or lying down with his eyes closed. It helps to establish a regular sequence for this exercise. It is important that when the worker is tensing his muscles, he tries to make them as tight and hard as possible; he should then hold the tension for a few seconds, recognizing how it feels, and then let the tension go, concentrating on the feeling of relaxation.

Exercise 2. Progressive relaxation

Progressive relaxation requires the worker to be seated or lying down. It is important that time is given to allow for the experience of tension and relaxation to be recognized in each part of the exercise. After experience using this exercise, the body will begin to identify when tension is creeping into the body and will automatically introduce relaxation.

Legs and lower body

Taking one leg at a time tense your foot by curling your toes up, then allow your foot to become relaxed. Tense your ankle and calf by pulling your toes up, hold it for a few seconds, then relax them, then tense your thigh and buttock – and relax. Finally notice the relaxation in the whole of your leg.

Hands, arms and shoulders

Taking one arm at a time tense your hand by forming a fist, then relax. Bend your elbows to tense your biceps and relax, pull your shoulders up towards your ears and then let fall down and relax. Notice the relaxation in the whole of your arms and shoulders.

Face, neck and upper back

Wrinkle forehead, hold it and then let it relax, clench teeth hard notice the tension in your mouth and throat then relax, roll your head to the side, back and then to the other side, watch as the tension moves then allow it come back to a relaxed place. Notice the relaxation in your head and upper body.

Chest, stomach and lower back

Breathe in slowly, feeling the tension in your chest, hold your breath and then let the breath flow out of your mouth slowly.

Tighten your stomach muscles, hold it and then relax. Arch your lower back, notice any tension, then relax. Finally check the whole of your body, make sure that no tension has crept in, if you notice any tension try to increase the tension then relax and let the tension melt away.

Distress reduction

The distress-reducing tool is helpful in enabling workers to identify how they have been feeling over a period of a week. The worker is given a chart with four boxes (Example 16.1) and is asked to estimate the percentage of time during the week she has spent in each of the boxes. She is then asked to give details of what kinds of things were put into each box. The goal then is to take one of the boxes and to identify what is preventing them moving some of the experiences into the next box.

Example 16.1. Distress reduction

Very relaxed	Quite relaxed	Rather tense	Very tense
0%	5%	30%	65%
I have not felt very relaxed at all	For a short time when I was listening to music I forgot about things	When I walk into my work Meeting new people	When I think about what happened When I have flashbacks

In Example 16.1 the discussion could be around how you can make yourself quite relaxed whilst walking to work; this could include walking with a friend, listening to music or taking a different route. The next week the worker looks at what she has achieved and reallocates the time spent in each of the boxes. Breaking down time into smaller chunks, it is possible to identify small areas where improvement is possible, leading to an overall reduction of distress.

Creating a healthy lifestyle

Everyone involved in a role that exposes them to traumatic stress should be aware of the need to adopt a healthy lifestyle. Taking regular exercise, getting enough sleep, eating healthy food, drinking enough water, meeting and talking with friends are all helpful in reducing arousal. In the following Well-being checklist, the aim is to have all the ticks in the left-hand column. During the training, the trainer helps the worker to identify areas for improving his/her lifestyle and explains why a healthy lifestyle is important in reducing hyperarousal.

Well-being checklist

How many healthy meals do you eat a day?	3	2	1
How many cups of coffee/tea/cola do you drink a day?	1–3	4–5	7+
How many units of alcohol do you drink a week?			
Men	0–10	11–20	21+
Women	0–7	8–14	15+
(1 unit = 1/2 pint, small glass wine, small sherry, small spirits)			
How often do you take exercise outside of work each week?	4+	1–3	0
How many interests/activities do you have outside work?	3+	1–3	0
How many hours do you sleep each night?	7+	5–6	1–4
How often do you meet friends socially each week?	3+	1–2	0
How many cigarettes do you smoke a day?	0–10	11–25	26+

Avoidance

Avoidance may be cognitive, in that the worker will try to stop thinking about a distressing event, or behavioural, in that the worker may avoid places, people or things associated with a traumatic event. The effect of avoidance is the restriction of normal functioning, impacting on the worker's ability to undertake his/her role effectively. Although avoidance may provide temporary relief, in the longer-term it serves to maintain the trauma symptoms. In many ways, teaching skills for dealing with re-experience and arousal prior to dealing with avoidance lessens the hold of avoidance, as the worker now has the skills to deal with the possible triggering re-experience and arousal symptoms that may arise when he/she removes avoidance. The avoidance-reducing tools include: graded exposure; and imaginal exposure, including drawing, writing and talking and learning from the experience.

Graded exposure

To use this tool, the worker has to identify all the things which are causing him/her distress or discomfort; these should then be allocated to one of six boxes, which are labelled 'places', 'things', 'people', 'situations', 'thoughts' and 'sensations'. After the worker has filled in the boxes, it is important to notice that some boxes may be fuller than others. The worker should then grade the level of discomfort felt by each of the things identified on a scale of 1–10. The worker should then identify the things he/she is avoiding because he/she believes that any exposure will cause him/her distress. One of the least distressing avoided activities, people, places or things should then be selected and a ladder created, which defines the five steps leading from 'where I am now' to 'where I want to be in the future'. The aim then is to work out how to move from the first to the second step, identifying the support that may be available and the rewards that will be present when the goal is reached.

Imaginal exposure

Using one's imagination to deal with avoidance can be very helpful. This can be as simple as imagining coming in contact with the trauma trigger whilst maintaining a state of relaxation until such time that recalling the trigger no longer causes arousal, or some more specific techniques for dealing with avoided memories in a safe way. These tools involve drawing, writing and talking.

Drawing

Drawing is useful in dealing with thoughts and fears as it allows them to be made more tangible and real. Drawing fears helps workers to process their experiences and begins to create a way of understanding what has happened. Talking about the drawings with a colleague or friend is even more helpful.

Writing

There is a lot of evidence to show that writing about distressing events has a wide range of psychological and physical benefits (Graybeal et al., 2002). It is not known how this process works, but it is likely that writing helps to make sense of chaotic emotional experience. The writing tool involves spending 5–10 minutes each day for a week, writing about the things which have been causing distress. After the set period of time, the paper is then folded and put in an envelope. At the end of the week the worker should reflect on what has changed during the week. The worker then needs to decide what to do with the written sheets. Some people decide to burn them, others to bury them or to lock them in a box where they will be safe.

Talking and explaining

For many people, talking about their experiences is helpful; however, the listener has to be appropriate and prepared to listen. Workers will also find that if they are able to talk about the toolbox to others they will find that they begin to understand it better, learn when to use the various skills and identify which tools they find most helpful.

Learning from the experience

Although avoidance may be maladaptive, this is not always the case. It is helpful for workers to identify, from the things that they are avoiding, those avoidance behaviours that are more likely to protect than harm them. For example, crime analysts investigating rape will learn about the dangers of taking lifts in unregistered minicabs and may well avoid them. This exercise involves looking at all the things that are being avoided and working out whether these avoidances are rational and based on real dangers, or irrational, based on unfounded fears.

Discussion

The pervasiveness of traumatic events and the increasing awareness of the persistent and often devastating effects on those whose work involves them in dealing directly or indirectly with the outcome of disasters, crisis and traumatic events make the provision of a resilience-building toolbox valuable. The toolbox is designed to guide workers through a number of self-directed techniques to enable them to build and grow their resilience in the face of danger and human suffering, thus reducing the incidence of secondary trauma and post-traumatic stress. The tools are based on tools that are currently being employed in trauma-focused cognitive-behavioural therapy, and therefore well-established as effective tools.

The programme is versatile and can be carried out either alone or with groups. It is important to recognize that these are first aid tools, and that where employees have experienced a major incident they may find that their emotions are too overwhelming to use these tools, in which case they should seek the support of a trained trauma therapist to help them resolve their difficulties.

References

Bryant, R.A., Harvey, A.G. (2000) *Acute Stress Disorder – A Handbook of Theory, Assessment and Treatment.* Washington, DC: American Psychiatric Association.

Damasio, A. (2006) *Descartes' Error.* London: Vintage Books.

Graybeal, A., Sexton, J.D., Pennebaker, J.W. (2002) The role of story-making in disclosure writing: the psychometrics of narrative. *Psychology and Health* **17**(5), 571–581.

Kessler, R.C., Sonnega, A., Bromet, E., Hughes, M., Nelson, C.B. (1995) Posttraumatic stress disorder in the National Comorbidity Survey. *Archives of General Psychiatry* **52**, 1048–1060.

Shalev, A.Y., Yehuda, R. (1998) Longitudinal development of traumatic stress disorders. In Yehuda, R. (ed.), *Psychological Trauma.* Washington, DC: American Psychiatric Press.

Shapiro, F. (2001). *Eye Movement Desensitization and Reprocessing: Basic Principles, Protocols and Procedures*, 2nd edn. New York: Guilford .

Yehuda, R., Bryant, R., Marmer, C., Zohar, J. (2005) Pathological responses to terrorism. *Neuropsychopharmacology* **30**, 1793–1805.

Chapter 17

Growth in relationship

A post-medicalized vision for positive transformation

David Murphy, John Durkin and Stephen Joseph

Introduction

In this chapter we set out a vision for the future with regard to the understanding of trauma and helping survivors of potentially devastating events. There is little doubt that when unexpected events happen we will be faced with challenges we had previously not considered. We need to deal with what had hitherto been the unthinkable. In this chapter we begin by outlining some of the unthinkable yet common things that happen to people, and review the evidence that suggests that the way people respond to traumatic events is often transformational in nature. Whilst we recognize the deleterious effects of trauma and the legitimate suffering many incur as a result, the struggle with trauma is also known to provide a springboard to greater psychological well-being.

For some time, the trauma literature has been dominated by a medicalized way of thinking that supports the view that people who experience severe psychological distress following traumatic events can be considered as ill and in need of specific treatment interventions. Such trauma-related illness is known to most as post-traumatic stress disorder (PTSD). The specific treatments aimed at eliminating and minimizing the various reactions that people have to traumatic events can involve either medication or manual-based therapeutic treatments, which leave little room for the uniqueness of idiosyncrasies and individual reactions to trauma. The view taken in this chapter is that, while much of this knowledge of how to help people is useful, it is also true that the experience caused by upsetting thoughts, attempts at avoidance and increased arousal are natural and normal reactions to extreme situations. We question the conceptual conversion of these experiences into symptoms of an illness in need of treatment.

One of the consequences of the medicalization of traumatic distress has been the development of a research agenda into the causes of PTSD and the effectiveness of specific interventions for the treatment of PTSD. While this has led to much valuable knowledge, it may inadvertently have distracted researchers from understanding that positive effects can emerge from the distress that people experience. In this chapter we will suggest that an alternative aim to the treatment of PTSD is the facilitation of growth.

Post-traumatic growth: a background of theory and context

There are two broad categories of well-being, psychological well-being and subjective well-being, which refer to the eudaimonic and hedonic philosophical traditions, respectively (Ryan and Deci, 2001). Eudamonia, the philosophical perspective promoted by Aristotle, emphasizes such qualities as virtue, meaning and authenticity. Hedonism is the historical counter to the eudaimonic view, and is one that emphasizes positive emotional states and the pursuit of pleasure. The experience of distress, in the eudaimonic view, is part of the human experience, whereas in the hedonic view it negates positive emotional experience and is therefore seen as an obstacle. Post-traumatic growth is a concept that derives from the eudaimonic rather than the hedonistic tradition.

Positive changes are often reported by people who have experienced psychological trauma (Tedeschi and Calhoun, 2004). Three broad dimensions of change have been described. First, people may report that their relationships are enhanced in some way, for example, that they now value their friends and family more and feel an increased compassion and altruism toward others. Second, survivors may develop improved views of themselves in some way. For example, they may report having a greater sense of personal resiliency and strength, which may be coupled with a greater acceptance of their vulnerabilities and limitations. Third, survivors may report positive changes in life philosophy, such as finding a fresh appreciation for each new day, or renegotiating what really matters to them in the full realization that their life is finite. Although these three dimensions seem well supported in the literature, further factor analytic studies are needed in order to establish the most parsimonious structure and to clarify the boundaries of enquiry (Joseph and Linley, 2008).

Post-traumatic growth is the most widely used term in the literature at present for describing such changes following psychological trauma, but other recent terms include stress-related growth, adversarial growth, benefit finding, perceived benefits, thriving, flourishing, and growth following adversity. Although this is a new field of enquiry for empirical psychology, it has roots dating back to the existential work of Viktor Frankl and his observations of survivors of the Nazi holocaust, and of course is a theme echoed in the world's major religions. In contrast to PTSD, the idea that trauma can provide a springboard to positive changes offers a different way to think about how trauma affects people.

Positive changes have been assessed using one or other of several retrospective self-report measures, the most widely used being the Posttraumatic Growth Inventory and the Changes in Outlook Questionnaire. Other measures of positive changes following trauma and adversity include the Stress-Related Growth Scale, the Perceived Benefits Scales and the Thriving Scale, as well as a number of other measures developed for use with specific trauma populations. A number of methodological issues are, however, raised with regard to retrospective measures of positive change, and it is not certain that asking people to recall what positive changes have occurred as a result of their experiences is a valid measure of the changes that actually occurred.

While psychological trauma is the trigger, positive changes have been reported following a wide range of life stressors (Linley and Joseph, 2004): transportation accidents (shipping disasters, plane crashes, car accidents); natural disasters (hurricanes, earthquakes); interpersonal experiences (combat, rape, sexual assault, child abuse); medical problems occurring to oneself or significant others (cancer, heart attack, brain injury, spinal cord injury, HIV/AIDS, leukemia, rheumatoid arthritis, multiple sclerosis, illness); and loss (marital separation, bereavement, loss of parents, immigration). Further, vicarious experiences of post-traumatic growth have been shown in those not suffering themselves but exposed to the suffering of others, including counsellors, therapists, clinical psychologists, funeral directors, disaster workers and spouses and parents of people with cancer (Linley and Joseph, 2004). Theoretical models of post-traumatic growth include the Functional-Descriptive Model (Tedeschi and Calhoun, 2004), the Organismic Valuing Theory (Joseph and Linley,

2005), and the Janus-face Two-component Model (Zoellner and Maercker, 2006).

It is thought that distress may be a necessary condition for the development of growth following adversity (Calhoun and Tedeschi, 2006; Tedeschi and Calhoun, 1995). Distress can force people to confront the unpleasant realities of life. The tension between how we thought the world worked and the painful realization that we were wrong may be reconciled by emotional processing in ways that accommodate the new information (Joseph and Linley, 2005). Several variables have been found to correlate with positive changes. Positive change has been found to be associated with the extent that the person believes that there was a high degree of threat and harm, and at the same time that he/she was able to exert some influence over the events or their outcomes (i.e. controllability) (Linley and Joseph, 2004). There may, however, be a curvilinear relationship between post-traumatic growth and perceptions of threat and harm, resulting in growth being less likely when events are perceived as either very low or high in the degree of threat or harm. People's reported approaches to coping have also been found to be correlated with positive change, with a greater use of acceptance, positive reinterpretation, optimism, religion and cognitive processing being associated with greater positive change (Linley and Joseph, 2004).

Growth and social support

It is clear from the studies that effective social support assists recovery from distressing life-events (Joseph and Williams, 2005), even in cases of psychiatric disorder (Brugha, 2009). Empirical literature that has tested the relation between social support and growth following adversity has generally found greater social support to be related to higher levels of growth. Statistically significant associations have been reported in studies of emergency services and civic volunteers (Prati and Pietrantoni, 2006), earthquake survivors (Sattler et al., 2006), former prisoners of war (Erbes et al., 2005), mixed adult samples following various life events (Park et al., 1996), women following sexual assault (Borja et al., 2006; Frazier et al., 2004), churchgoers following various traumatic experiences (Harris et al., 2008) and Gulf War veterans (Maguen et al., 2006). Although a few other studies of disaster workers (Linley and Joseph, 2006), women with chronic arthritic illness (Abraido-Lanza et al., 1998) and survivors of a ship-sinking (Joseph *et al.*, 1993) have not reported association, overall it seems appropriate to conclude that social support appears to be related to growth.

Facilitating post-traumatic growth

Research into the clinical facilitation of positive change among survivors of a variety of events is beginning to flourish, with reports of interventions with war veterans, cancer patients, survivors of sexual abuse and terrorism, for example, reporting positive results (Calhoun and Tedeschi, 2006; Joseph and Linley, 2008). Research indicates that reports of growth are related to longer-term adaptation, such as lower levels of depression and post-traumatic stress as well as higher levels of well-being. Frazier *et al.* (2001), for example, found that self-reported positive changes in the initial weeks following a sexual assault predicted lower subsequent levels of distress when the initial positive changes were maintained, but not when the initial positive changes were lost.

Common factors or specific ingredients?

It is a long-established and generally accepted fact within the field that psychotherapy is effective. However, *how* psychotherapy works has been the focus of much debate, seeing proponents taking either the view that psychotherapy's effectiveness is attributable to specific elements of a particular treatment approach (e.g. systematic desensitization) or that effects are due to non-specific factors believed to be common to all approaches (e.g. therapeutic relationship). The overall combined effects of these two elements on successful outcome is thought to account for approximately 45% of the total variance in outcomes (Asay and Lambert, 2002). Of these, specific techniques only contribute about 15%, a fraction of the overall variance in outcome of successful psychotherapy treatments, with the therapeutic relationship accounting for approximately 30% (Lambert and Ogles, 2004). The remainder of the variance in outcomes is thought to be due to placebo/expectations (15%) and extra therapeutic factors (40%), such as a client's situation changing regardless of therapeutic intervention. However, despite being equipped with this knowledge, and contrary to the equivalence in findings from thousands of randomized clinical trials together with countless process-outcome studies, practitioners and policy makers continue to promote and invest in technique-orientated therapies. Perhaps even more remarkably, all this is in spite of the overwhelming evidence presented to us by our *clients* that they respond best to the authenticity and genuine human relatedness of the therapist, and not to the constraints of proscribed personal involvement (Eugster and Wampold, 1996).

In the UK, most health service providers try where possible to adhere to the clinical guidelines set out by the National Institute for Clinical Excellence (NICE), with Guideline 26 specifically relating to PTSD. The guidelines recommend trauma-focused cognitive-behavioural theory (CBT) or eye movement desensitization and reprocessing (EMDR) for PTSD sufferers, yet there is little or no place for approaches that focus on relationship-based therapy. This is perhaps a rather narrow and blinkered method for helping people and will certainly do little to foster the potential for post-traumatic growth. This is because, within this medical model, the reactions to trauma are seen as pathological symptoms in need of amelioration, and gives the message that one should not feel this way after a traumatically stressful event. However, relationship-based approaches do not aim to ameliorate the reactions, as they are viewed as neither positive nor negative but, rather, are accepted at face value, and understanding and meaning is sought. In this model, greater potential for facilitating growth will exist.

There is a vast number of different contexts in which people are exposed to traumas which create opportunities for growth, and the evidence suggests that, when people experience growth, this is more likely to be as a result of enhancing psychological well-being, in addition to, or more probably in place of, the enhancement of subjective well-being. As an example, consider the following. Subjective well-being as a goal for therapy becomes the reduction of symptoms, e.g. minimizing intrusive thoughts via distraction techniques. In this scheme, the view is that the client will feel less distressed by the removal of the 'unwanted symptom/thought'. However, psychological well-being is more concerned with the acceptance of the intrusive thought, the possible meaning it may carry for future living and the lessons learned about the self as a consequence of both the event and the intrusive thought. However, the theoretical literature from the field of psychotherapy continues to focus on therapeutic interventions that are primarily concerned with enhancing subjective well-being. Whilst this may be satisfactory for the medicalized approach to therapeutic intervention specifically designed for PTSD, such therapeutic strategies may not generalize to the facilitation of post-traumatic growth (Durkin and Joseph, 2009). If clients are to experience post-traumatic growth, and if therapy is to play a role, it is incumbent upon both individual therapists and the organisations which employ them to consider which therapeutic interventions will best serve their clients. Such decisions are likely to be driven by the underlying philosophical principles of eudaimonism and hedonism and the view of what really matters within the life of the particular organisation, that is, whether a higher value is placed on subjective or psychological well-being.

There is evidence to suggest that some therapeutic factors may be more helpful than others in facilitating post-traumatic growth. For instance, therapist variables that contribute to outcome tend to fall into four categories: observable traits; observable states; inferred traits; and inferred states. Beutler *et al.* (2004) provide a comprehensive review of the literature in this area. It has been suggested above that relational factors, or observable traits of the therapist, are key in order for the client to activate his/her potential for post-traumatic growth. However, it would appear that the association between the presence of a therapeutic relationship and positive change in psychotherapy is not as straightforward as it may first seem, as some studies within the psychotherapy literature appear to show a greater effect of the relationship on outcome than others (Waddington, 2002). After all, it could be argued that all therapy is relational, as it takes place between and involves at least two people (Barrett-Lennard, 2005), yet we can see that not all clients respond in the same way on experiencing the relational environment. There are two points that need to be clarified here: first, for post-traumatic growth to occur, it is the *nature* of the therapeutic relationship that exists between the client and therapist that is important; second, the therapeutic relationship is a *bi*directional phenomenon.

The nature of the therapeutic relationship

There are a number of facilitative elements of the therapeutic relationship, first proposed by Rogers (1951, 1957), which have been shown to be helpful in promoting positive therapeutic change and are generally accepted by all therapeutic traditions as a necessary requirement. These include therapist empathy (Bohart *et al.*, 2002), positive regard (Farber and Lane, 2002) and congruence (Klein *et al.*, 2002). In addition to this, a specific component of the therapeutic alliance, known as the therapeutic bond, which is made up of therapist relational qualities, has been associated with positive outcome across a range of approaches (Horvath and Bedi, 2002). In addition to the therapist qualities, a key element in psycho-therapeutic work, which is also likely to facilitate post-traumatic growth, is the therapist adopting a non-directive stance. This has been proposed as the ethical stance of the therapist (Grant, 1990), where the therapist adopts a position of either instrumental or prin-cipled non-directivity. These two stances have different aims, with the former being goal-directed towards facilitating growth or empower-ment in the client; the latter, principled non-directivity, is grounded in a fundamental respect for the other where the therapist does not try to make anything happen. In the principled non-directive form, post-traumatic growth becomes a welcome but unintended con-sequence of the therapeutic endeavour. The therapist is required to provide the core conditions, with the intention of creating an environment in which the client can make best use of them.

It is important to note here that this position directly challenges the current political rhetoric surrounding psychotherapy, which calls for the implementation of a narrow set of specific treatments chan-nelled through restrictive clinical guidelines, such as those promoted by NICE. A significant amount of politics currently surrounds psy-chotherapy, with a whole industry based on the identification and categorization of distinct psychological illnesses. The notion of post-traumatic growth lies beyond this and requires a paradigm shift to a non-medicalized view of trauma. Whilst this creates increased opportunities for enhanced well-being, it also requires practitioners to relinquish power over their clients and an acknowledgement that treatment approaches based on specificity are inappropriate for facilitating post-traumatic growth. It is difficult to ask those who have highly invested in the specificity model people to envision, let alone engage with, a therapeutic approach which advocates this pos-ition. We recognize the challenge, even 50 years on since the notion of the client as a self-healer and of the therapeutic relationship creat-ing the climate for activating growth was first proposed, in accepting that it is relationship-based principles which are the most potent agents within the psychotherapy encounter. However, to fully appre-ciate and grasp the concept of post-traumatic growth, this is pre-cisely what is required. Here you are called to let go of the notion that what works in psychotherapy is *what you do to* your client, and to openly consider the contrary, that with regards to post-traumatic growth, you may be better served by doing nothing *to* your client.

It's important to acknowledge that this view may be challenging and to consider there is nothing or little to gain from adopting such a position if the interests being served are such to be seen as 'expert practitioner'. However, if you are genuinely concerned with facilitating growth, then this is the position best adopted. Finally, it is important to state the paradox of this position: rather than suggesting that therapy consists of nothing, principled non-directivity calls upon the therapist, to the contrary, to be prepared to do everything required to facilitate growth. This means that, in contrast to the caricature of non-directive therapy involving a passive nodding therapist who does little but reflects back the utterances of the client, non-directive therapy is dynamic, creative, challenging and growthful for both client and therapist. The therapist is client-centred and responsive to the call of the client's needs and movement towards growth, as they are stated and identified by the client. A non-directive approach can and often does include all those elements of more directive manual-based therapies; however, it is in their application that they differ. Non-directive approaches respond to individual client need and have the flexibility to incorporate techniques such as homework tasks or the use of psychometric measures. However, each would be provided by the therapist in his/her attempt to understand and communicate acceptance of the client, and not in an attempt to reduce or treat symptoms or force the client towards change and growth. Growth comes from the client's response and making meaning of their traumatic experience.

Relationship, bidirectional process and post-traumatic growth

Recently, research focusing on the therapeutic relationship has turned towards considering bidirectional process, as opposed to the view of the relationship conditions as unilateral phenomena (Orlinsky et al., 2004). This has in part been a result of alliance research focusing on the therapeutic bond itself, concerned with reciprocal processes between client and therapist. For example, under the generic model of psychotherapy (Orlinsky and Howard, 1986), therapeutic bond research has covered the concepts of mutual affirmation, the affective environment and self-relatedness as interrelated areas of psychotherapy process contributing to outcome. This notion suggests that when therapist and client engage as a dyadic interaction set, characterized by reciprocal patterns and exchange of understanding, acceptance and genuineness, post-traumatic growth is most likely to occur.

Mutual therapist and client openness (Ablon and Jones, 1999; Eugster and Wampold, 1996; Kolden, 1996), acceptance (Muran *et al.*, 1997; Saunders, 1999, 2000) and understanding (Hill *et al.*, 1993) have all been shown to be related to positive change. All this suggests that when the therapeutic relationship is defined by a mutual experiencing of the other as distinct and worthy of respect, positive growth will likely follow. For this to be a valid and reliable notion, it is necessary for the theory to withstand the test of application in practice. So far, evidence in support of this has been found in the field of eating disorders (Tantillo and Sanftner, 2003) and for adults following sexual abuse (Murphy, 2009). Here it is perhaps helpful to also return to the social support literature, where recent empirical research has shown that failures in support can be attributed to inequities or a lack of mutuality. This has been shown to be the case for sufferers of serious illnesses and their closest partners (Gleason *et al.*, 2003; Kleiboer *et al.*, 2006) and between managers and employees (Dabos and Rousseau, 2004). Mutuality in relationship is helpful in both professional and non-professional helping relationships. What is required is for the field of post-traumatic growth to take these notions forward through the development of a research programme focused on this agenda.

Applications to organisations

Growth and individual support

People employed in occupations at high risk for psychological distress, such as the medical and emergency services, may find their emotional balance upset in ways that temporarily threaten their competence. In order to keep working effectively, they may seek ways to find relief from the stressful consequences as quickly as possible. In such cases, they would be seeking to enhance their subjective well-being, a target that could be met by little more than the companionship, sympathy and assistance of familiar colleagues. However, if the goal were to enhance psychological well-being, a different way of relating to others may be needed. Theoretically, growth is more likely to result from a direct engagement in emotional reactions than from the consolation of having others help us feel better. If an emotional upset is quickly rebalanced without engaging in its painful expression, little processing will have taken place. While recovery seeks a restoration of prior assumptions, growth demands a revision of those assumptions. Growth has been reported as 'feeling sadder but wiser', so a distinction between growth and recovery can be made by whether the experience appears to have fundamentally changed their view of the world. The distress experienced in the aftermath of a traumatic event is known to alternate through cycles of intrusion and avoidance that abate when the event has been successfully processed (Horowitz, 1986).

Organisations, growth and support

The two forms of well-being offer a distinction that may serve organisations seeking to encourage psychological growth amongst their people. When a job goes as expected and nobody in the team appears to be badly affected afterwards, the interactions between the members of the team will most likely run in comfortable and familiar ways that allow rest, recuperation and preparation for the next job. However, when the job does not go as expected and something goes badly wrong, such as a life being lost unnecessarily or an error that causes a loss of confidence within the team, the old ways of interacting may not work. What does the organisation do in these circumstances? Does it encourage its people to consider new viewpoints? To rework habitual ways of thinking and modify actions in similar situations in the future? Or merely to encourage its people to get on with it, look on the bright side, forgive mistakes and find consolation in humour and companionship? The latter approach might reduce uncomfortable social emotions, such as blame and guilt, bring early consolation to those involved. However, if individual or collective incompetence contributed to what went wrong and efforts to simply feel better are prioritized, important lessons may be missed. The team may not acknowledge its limitations and so fail to prepare for similar encounters in the future. Those motivated to improve the team's future performance may see their concerns being trivialized and settle for behavioural and mental disengagement, both markers of maladaptive coping (Carver, 1989). However, several personal and relational qualities can be enhanced by purposeful engagement with life's difficulties (Ryff and Keyes, 1995). This suggests that developmental gains, including personal growth, more likely await those who endure the unpleasant emotional consequences of failure than those who avoid them.

Direct confrontation of the emotional elements of traumatic experience has been justified in established therapeutic practices, including crisis-intervention (Caplan, 1964), client-centred therapy (Rogers, 1957) and exposure therapy. It is important, therefore, to seek the company of a colleague, friend or counsellor who will not dismiss, explain, ignore or otherwise invalidate the worker's emotional reactions, but rather attune him/herself to the dilemma, listen with interest and put him/herself at the emotional disposal of his/her colleague. Students of Rogers' (1957) core conditions will doubtless recognize the theoretical climate for personal growth in such a relationship. If this type of supported confrontation leads to growth and the survivor enjoys improved affect as a result, both eudaimonic and hedonic forms of well-being will have been served, in which case the optimal outcome may not be one type of well-being over another, but the emergence of both.

A list of the principles for facilitating post-traumatic growth is shown in Table 17.1.

Conclusion

In this chapter the goal has been to provide an introduction to the literature on growth following adversity. Post-traumatic growth is an important yet understudied topic. While traditional therapies for trauma have largely been concerned with increasing subjective

Table 17.1 Principles to help facilitate growth

1. To let the idea of growth and its directions emerge from the client
2. To recognize that growth emerges from the struggle to make sense of the experience, not from the experience itself
3. To adopt a principled, non-directive stance, based on a fundamental respect of the client
4. To show the client unconditional respect as a person of worth
5. To aim towards an understanding of the client's experience as it is for him/her
6. To be open and communicate understanding and acceptance of the client's experience
7. To be always prepared to work with the traumatic material
8. To acknowledge, respect and respond to the whole of the client's experience
9. Not to place an expectation for growth on the client
10. To acknowledge and work towards a therapeutic relationship based on mutuality

well-being, the notion of growth following adversity focuses attention on increasing psychological well-being.

These are alternative conceptualizations of the ways in which people can change following trauma. How we construe the role of therapy at any given time must inevitably relate to how society values hedonic versus eudaimonic principles. Society changes as the pendulum between hedonism and eudaimonism swings. Our expectations of therapy follow suit.

References

Ablon, S.J., Jones, E.E. (1999) Psychotherapy process in the National Institutes of Health Treatment of Depression collaborative research program. *Journal of Consulting and Clinical Psychology* **67**, 64–75.

Abraido-Lanza, A.F., Guier, C., Colon, R.M. (1998) Psychological thriving among Latinas with chronic illness. *Journal of Social Issues* **54**, 405–424.

Alloy, L.B., Abramson, L.Y. (1979) Judgment of contingency in depressed and nondepressed students: sadder but wizer? *Journal of Experimental Psychology: General* **108**, 441–485.

Asay, T.P., Lambert, M.J. (2002) Therapist relational variables. In Cain, D.J., Seeman, J. (eds), *Humanistic Psychotherapies: Handbook of Theory and Practice*. Washington, DC: American Psychological Association; 531–557.

Barrett-Lennard, G.T. (2005) *Relationship at the Centre: Healing in a Troubled World*. London and Philadelphia: Whurr.

Beutler, L.E., Malik, M., Alimohamed, S., Harwood, T.M., Talebi, H., Noble, S., Wong, E. (2004) Therapist variables. In M.J. Lambert (ed.), *Bergin and Garfield's Handbook of Psychotherapy and Behaviour Change*, 5th edn. New York: Wiley; 227–306.

Bohart, A.C., Elliott, R., Greenberg, L.S., Watson, J.C. (2002) Empathy. In Norcross, J.C. (ed.), *Psychotherapy Relationships that Work: Therapist Contributions and Responsiveness to Patients*. New York: Oxford University Press; 89–108.

Borja, S.E., Callahan, J.L., Long, P.J. (2006) Positive and negative adjustment and social support of sexual assault survivors. *Journal of Traumatic Stress* **19**, 905–914.

Brugha, T.S. (2009) *Social Support and Psychiatric Disorder*. New York: Cambridge University Press.

Calhoun, L.G., Tedeschi, R.G. (eds) (2006) *Handbook of Posttraumatic Growth: Research and Practice*. Mahwah, NJ: Erlbaum.

Caplan, G. (1964) *Principles of Preventive Psychiatry*. London: Tavistock Publications.

Carver, C.S. (1989) Assessing coping strategies: a theoretically based approach. *Journal of Personality and Social Psychology* **56**, 267–283.

Dabos, G.E., Rousseau, D.M. (2004) Mutuality and reciprocity in the psychological contracts of employees and employers. *Journal of Applied Psychology* **89**, 52–72.

Durkin, J., Joseph, S. (2009) Growth following adversity and its relation with subjective well-being and psychological well-being. *Journal of Loss and Trauma* **14**, 228–234.

Erbes, C., Eberly, R., Dikel, T., Johnsen, E., Harris, I., Engdahl, B. (2005) Posttraumatic growth among American former prisoners of war. *Traumatology* **11**, 285–295.

Eugster, S.L., Wampold, B.E. (1996) Systematic effects of participant role on evaluation of the psychotherapy session. *Journal of Consulting and Clinical Psychology* **64**, 1020–1028.

Farber, B.A., Lane, J.S. (2002) Positive regard. In Norcross, J.C. (ed.), *Psychotherapy Relationships that Work: Therapist Contributions and Responsiveness to Patients*. New York: Oxford University Press; 175–194.

Frazier, P., Conlon, A., Glaser, T. (2001) Positive and negative life changes following sexual assault. *Journal of Consulting and Clinical Psychology* **69**, 1048–1055.

Frazier, P., Tashiro, T., Berman, M., Steger, M., Long, J. (2004) Correlates of levels and patterns of positive life changes following sexual assault. *Journal of Consulting and Clinical Psychology* **72**, 19–30.

Gleason, M.E.J., Iida, M., Bolger, N., Shrout, P.E. (2003) Daily supportive equity in close relationships. *Personality and Social Psychology Bulletin* **29**, 1036–1045.

Grant, B. (1990) Principled and instrumental nondirectiveness in person-centred and client-centred. In Cain, D.J. (ed.), *Classics in the Person-Centred Approach*. Ross-on Wye: PCCS Books; 371–377.

Harris, J.I., Erbes, C.R., Engdahl, B.E., Olson, R.H.A., Winskowski, A.M., McMahill, J. (2008) Christian religious functioning and trauma outcomes. *Journal of Clinical Psychology* **64**, 17–29.

Hill, C., Thompson, B.J., Cogar, M.C., Denman, D.W. III (1993) Beneath the surface of long-term therapy: therapist and client reports of their own and each other's covert processes. *Journal of Counseling Psychology* **40**, 278–287.

Horowitz, M.J. (1986) *Stress Response Syndromes*. Northville, NJ: Jason Aronson.

Horvath, A.O., Bedi, R.P. (2002) The alliance. In Norcross, J.C. (ed.), *Psychotherapy Relationships that Work: Therapist Contributions and Responsiveness to Patients*. New York: Oxford University Press; 37–70.

Joseph, S., Linley, P.A. (2005) Positive adjustment to threatening events: an organismic valuing theory of growth through adversity. *Review of General Psychology* **9**, 262–280.

Joseph, S., Linley, P.A. (2008) Psychological assessment of growth following adversity: a review. In Joseph, S., Linley, P.A. (eds), *Trauma, Recovery and*

Growth: Positive Psychological Perspectives on Posttraumatic Stress.
Hoboken, NJ: Wiley.

Joseph, S., Williams, R. (2005) Understanding posttraumatic stress: theory,
reflections, context, and future. *Behavioural and Cognitive Psychotherapy*
33, 423–441.

Joseph, S., Williams, R., Yule, W. (1993) Changes in outlook following disaster: the preliminary development of a measure to assess positive and
negative responses. *Journal of Traumatic Stress* **6**, 271–279.

Joseph, S., Worsley, R. (2005) *Person-centred Psychopathology: A Positive
Psychology of Mental Health.* Bath, UK: PCCS Books.

Kleiboer, A.M., Kuijer R.G., Hox, J.J., Schreurs, K.M.G., Bensing, J.M.
(2006) Receiving and providing support in couples dealing with multiple
sclerosis: a diary study using an equity perspective. *Personal Relationships*
13, 485–501.

Klein, M.H., Kolden, G.G., Michels, J.L., Chisholm-Stockard, S. (2002)
Congruence. In Norcross, J.C. (ed.), *Psychotherapy Relationships that
Work: Therapist Contributions and Responsiveness to Patients.* New York:
Oxford University Press; 195–215.

Kolden, G.G. (1996) Change in early sessions of dynamic therapy: universal
processes and the generic model of psychotherapy. *Journal of Consulting
and Clinical Psychology* **64**, 489–496.

Lambert, M.J., Ogles, B.M. (2004) The efficacy and effectiveness of psychotherapy. In Lambert, M.J. (ed.), *Bergin and Garfield's Handbook of
Psychotherapy and Behavior Change*, 5th edn. New York: Wiley.

Linley, P.A., Joseph, S. (2004) Positive change following trauma and adversity: a review. *Journal of Traumatic Stress* **17**, 11–21.

Linley, P.A., Joseph, S. (2006) The positive and negative effects of disaster work: a preliminary investigation. *Journal of Loss and Trauma* **11**,
229–245.

Maguen, S., Vogt, D.S., King, L.A., King, D.W., Litz, B.T. (2006) Post-
traumatic growth among Gulf War I veterans: the predictive role of
deployment-related experiences and background characteristics. *Journal
of Loss and Trauma* **11**, 373–388.

Muran, J.C., Samstag, L.W., Jilton, R., Batchelder, S., Winston, A. (1997)
Development of a suboutcome strategy to measure interpersonal pro-
cess in psychotherapy from an observer perspective. *Journal of Clinical
Psychology* **53**, 405–420.

Murphy, D. (2009) Client-centred therapy of severe childhood abuse: a case
study. *Counselling and Psychotherapy Research* **9**, 3–10.

Orlinsky, D.E., Howard, K.L. (1986) Process and outcome in psychotherapy.
In Garfield, S.L., Bergin, A.E. (eds), *Handbook of Psychotherapy and
Behaviour Change*, 3rd edn. New York: Wiley; 311–384.

Orlinsky, D.E., Ronnestad, M.H., Willutzki, U. (2004) Fifty years of psychotherapy process–outcome research: continuity and change. In Lambert,

M.J. (ed.), *Bergin and Garfield's Handbook of Psychotherapy and Behaviour Change*, 5th edn. New York: Wiley; 307–389.

Park, C.L., Cohen, L.H., Murch, R. (1996) Assessment and prediction of stress-related growth. *Journal of Personality* 64, 71–105.

Prati, G., Pietrantoni, L. (2006) Crescità post-traumatica: un'opportunita' dopo il trauma? *Psicoterapia Cognitive e Comportmentale* 12, 133–144.

Rogers, C.R. (1951) *Client-centered Therapy: Its Current Practice, Implications and Theory*. Boston, MA: Houghton Mifflin.

Rogers, C.R. (1957) The necessary and sufficient conditions of therapeutic personality change. *Journal of Consulting Psychology* 21, 95–103.

Ryan, R.M., Deci, E.L. (2001) On happiness and human potentials: a review of research on hedonic and eudaimonic well-being. *Annual Review of Psychology* 52, 141–166.

Ryff, C.D., Keyes, C.L.M. (1995) The structure of psychological well-being revisited. *Journal of Personality and Social Psychology* 69, 719–727.

Sattler, D.N., de Alvarado, A.M.G., de Castro, N.B., Van Male, R., Zetino, A.M., Vega, R. (2006) El Salvador earthquakes: relationships among acute stress disorder symptoms, depression, traumatic event exposure and resource loss. *Journal of Traumatic Stress* 19, 879–893.

Saunders, S.M. (1999) Clients' assessment of the affective environment of the psychotherapy session: relationship to session quality and treatment effectiveness. *Journal of Clinical Psychology* 55, 597–605.

Saunders, S.M. (2000) Examining the relationship between the therapeutic bond and the phases of treatment outcome. *Psychotherapy* 37, 206–218.

Sherman, A.R. (1972) Real life exposure as a primary therapeutic factor in desensitization treatment of fear. *Journal of Abnormal Psychology* 79, 19–28.

Tantillo, M., Sanftner, J. (2003) The relationship between perceived mutuality and bulimic symptoms, depression, and therapeutic change in group. *Eating Behaviors* 3, 349–364.

Tedeschi, R.G., Calhoun, L.G. (1995) *Trauma and Transformation: Growing in the Aftermath of Suffering*. Thousand Oaks, CA: Sage.

Tedeschi, R.G., Calhoun, L.G. (2004) Posttraumatic growth: conceptual foundations and empirical evidence. *Psychological Inquiry* 15, 1–18.

Waddington, L. (2002) The therapy relationship in cognitive therapy: a review. *Behavioural and Cognitive Psychotherapy* 30(2), 179–191.

Zoellner, T., Maercker, A. (2006) Posttraumatic growth in clinical psychology – a critical review and introduction of a two-component model. *Clinical Psychology Review* 26, 626–653.

Chapter 18

One disaster after another

Building resilience in the trauma therapist and the role of supervision

Stuart McNab

> Ring a-ring o' roses,
> A pocket full of posies,
> A-tishoo! A-tishoo!
> We all fall down

Introduction

This chapter is concerned with the impact of repeatedly working with psychological trauma in a therapeutic relationship, and specifically with the role of supervision in facilitating effective and safe trauma work. It concludes by offering a model of how the supervisory relationship may be used and the necessary activities for supervisor and supervisee.

Trauma is contagious; when anyone comes into contact with it they risk a piercing impact leaving them infected and vulnerable. This contagion may be more subtle, absorbed through any of the five senses – the sound of a collision, the smell of a fire, the touch of a corpse. Working with trauma means recognizing not that this contagion is possible but that repeated exposure to trauma in any capacity will have consequences. These consequences may be negative and range widely across a continuum from a half-full outlook on the world to full-blown PTSD or burn-out. The consequences may also be positive and involve post-traumatic growth, or indeed an increase in personal resilience from exposure to others' resilient narratives (Hermandez *et al.*, 2007).

This chapter is concerned with the nature of the contagion and how supervision can play a key role in mitigating the negative impact of trauma work, enhancing the positive and building resilience in trauma therapists. There is a danger, however, in engaging in dualistic thinking, where the impact of trauma is regarded as either negative or positive when a non-duality approach offers the opportunity of both negative and positive.

Trauma attracts and repels. The rubber-necker in me strains to see the crash on the other carriageway, whilst the ostrich in me (a term apparently inappropriately allocated to this bird) pulls me away in repulsion and keeps my eyes fixed on my side of the motorway. So, too, in my trauma work; I seek to know but then wish I didn't. This, too, may be echoed in the supervisory relationship; I seek to know my supervisee's experience but wish he/she would protect me from the distressing detail. To not react to the description of the pain of the incident is to adopt a non-empathic, cold and potentially inhuman position which fails to witness the suffering of another. However, to feel too intensely and to be overwhelmed is also to fail the other by drowning alongside him/her. The task is thus one of balance, to hear, to feel and to respond, but from a safe, contained and, most importantly, aware position.

Witnessing another's survival and adaptation can be inspiring and developmental. Human capacity is at times breathtaking and the meanings people make of their trauma infinitely surprising. As trauma therapists and supervisors, our lives may be enriched by our work and this may indeed be a motivation for choosing this work or continuing to expose ourselves to others' traumatic pain. The motivation of the trauma therapist is crucial and understanding the wounds of the therapist provides a lens upon the therapeutic dynamics and those reflected within the supervisory relationship.

Five areas may be identified as key in negotiating the safe passage in trauma therapy and supervision:

- Personal characteristics.
- Personal awareness.
- Understanding the relational dynamics.
- Using support mechanisms.
- Building resilience.

Personal characteristics

Empathy may be seen as a necessary characteristic of an effective therapist, and although it may be seen as central in some theoretical orientations, it is more peripheral in others. Witnessing suffering requires some ability to enter the frame of reference of another, and this journey brings dangers. Rogers (1959) saw empathy as the ability to:

> ... perceive the internal frame of reference of another with accuracy and with emotional components and meanings which pertain thereto as if one were the person, but without ever losing the as if condition (pp. 210–211).

Being wounded by the deep experience of empathy comes from losing this 'as-if' experience. The greater the ability of an individual to establish an empathic connection, the more dangerous the therapeutic journey will be. Whilst the concept of identification is used to label this dangerous development of empathy, the distinction seems very difficult to recognize. This is a continuum along which effective therapists walk on a daily basis. The risks may be seen as heightened where trauma is the focus of exploration, as the existential dilemmas it raises are at the heart of human life. The skill for the effective trauma therapist or supervisor is recognizing the degree and quality of one's empathic connection with another.

Trauma involves being out of control, and consequently for the individual whose life exists firmly rooted in the reliability of certainty, the sense of being in control, trauma can be particularly devastating. An individual's assumptions about the world have become shattered (Janoff-Bulman, 1992). For the therapist or supervisor whose personal characteristics include some needs for being in control may find they are struggling at various points in the journey through trauma, and may unconsciously or consciously attempt to impose structure, and hence control, on the therapeutic or supervisory relationship. Some therapeutic models may be seen as more rooted in control and structure than others, and thus the personal characteristics of therapists and supervisors will draw them to those that support their motivations. The skill is to gain an understanding of these motivations and characteristics.

Personal characteristics most importantly include the trauma history of the therapist or supervisor. Through the experience of running an MSc in Psychological Trauma, it is apparent that those who choose this work are often trauma survivors. At times the trauma will be very well known to the individual and at other times it will be hidden in the darker recesses. Sometimes the trauma has been approached through therapy and may be seen as fully accommodated, or indeed fully overcome and assimilated. Whatever individuals believe about their location on their trauma journeys, it is important for them to recognize that their sensitivity to trauma will remain. Indeed, this sensitivity may be the very thing that aids therapists' or supervisors' ability to empathize, and at the same time be the thing that renders them unavailable or liable to responding without awareness. The skill is for therapists or supervisors to identify their own experiences of trauma, to understand the meaning they have attached to them and to recognize the triggers that will activate the feelings, thoughts and conditioned responses related to them.

Personal awareness

For therapists and supervisors, personal awareness is usually regarded as a key requirement if they are not to be meeting their own psychological difficulties rather than meeting the needs of their clients or supervisees. Communication may be blocked if painful memories or vulnerabilities fail to be understood, leading to unconscious or out-of-awareness processes coming into play. Sensitivity to another person may be seen as beginning with sensitivity towards self. Some therapeutic models see this awareness as central, and require the would-be therapists to engage in personal development groups and personal therapy. Others place less emphasis on the use of self in the therapeutic process but increasingly recognize the importance of the relationship. This, by definition, requires an awareness of self and an awareness of self in interaction with others.

In the trauma arena, awareness of how witnessing another's trauma is likely to affect the therapist and counsellor is crucial. This may involve direct reporting to the therapist or indirect reporting of case work from a supervisee to a supervisor. In the indirect reporting, the personal reactions and filters of the supervisee are likely to shape the nature of the communication of the trauma to the supervisor. Understanding the nature of one's own wounds, and most importantly how these may be triggered, is vital. This involves a willingness to describe and examine one's trauma history within the supervisory relationship, so that potential triggers can be identified and the learned response styles understood. If, for instance, the therapist has a history that involves suffering the abuse of power, his/her response to witnessing another's abuse may involve some unconscious closing-down behaviours, making it hard for the client to feel safe enough to talk about his/her experiences. Thus, a therapist may fail to respond to a comment made by a client that relates to abuse, or fail to show empathy for fear (unconscious) of a deeper exploration by the client that would be too hard for the therapist to hear. Alternatively, the response may be a triggering of anger in the therapist, which may be directed at the client, the supervisor and/or the therapist's family and friends. This level of self-awareness is not only required for trauma therapists but the potential for activating the out-of-awareness behaviour is even greater when dealing with traumatic exposure.

Appropriate coping mechanisms need to be identified and discussed, so they may be mobilized when needed or reinforced when necessary. These might include such things as engaging in activities outside of therapy that are nurturing, such as walking, reading or enjoying music, as well as identifying appropriate breaks between clients and having personal therapy. Equally important is the discussion that should take place in the supervision relating to the personal growth that trauma can bring, and the ultimate resilience that humankind can show. The active seeking of potential outcomes is a fundamental position which, when embedded in positive psychology, can facilitate the growth within the client, the therapist and the supervisor. What people learn about life through the facing of death can be profound, and witnessing the changes that people make following trauma in their relationships, their ability to live in this moment and in their enhanced congruence, can be inspiring. The skill is to be able to hear and see this opportunity and recognize the possible point of metanoia. Crisis brings a challenge; in loss can be gain, from death can come rebirth.

Understanding the relational dynamics

There may be a complex web of relational dynamics surrounding trauma counselling, with the trauma therapist relating to the client, the client relating to the trauma therapist, the trauma therapist relating to the supervisor, and the supervisor relating to the trauma therapist as supervisee, the supervisor relating to a consultant supervisor, and the consultant supervisor relating to the supervisor. A key issue in understanding the relational dynamics is that of transference and counter-transference. Freud (1953) saw the need for analysts to be blank screens upon which patients could project or transfer aspects of previous relationships, which could then give clues to the origins of their difficulties. Thus, anger towards the analyst might be interpreted as to do with a significant relationship in the patient's past, and on further investigation this might be identified as the patient's relationship with his/her father. At first Freud saw negative transference, e.g. anger, as an obstacle to the therapeutic process, but later saw all transference as valuable in understanding the patient. Countertransference has been defined in many ways, particularly as the analyst's response to the transference which came from the analyst's previous significant relationship. For the purposes of this chapter, I am using 'countertransference' to mean all reactions of the therapist which have their origin in the therapist's past relationships. Thus, each relationship may be seen to offer the opportunity for transference, for the nature of relating to contain historic relationships. It also offers the opportunity for countertransference where the relating is based on historic aspects of the trauma therapist or supervisor, or where the trauma therapist relates to the transference of the client, the supervisor relates to the transference of the supervisee or the consultant supervisor relates to the transference of their supervisee. The client–therapist relationship may also be mirrored or paralleled in the relationship of the supervisor/supervisee or indeed supervisor and consultant supervisor. The matrix of possibilities of relationships is complex and daunting.

Transference and countertransference are, by definition, unconscious processes and not easily identified and accessed. The supervisory relationship provides an ideal environment for the archaeological dig to be undertaken and the parallel process offers a live recreation of the therapist–client relationship. A skilful and open supervisor equipped with an appropriate 'trowel' can unearth the matrix and enable learning and change to occur, whilst ensuring that the client receives a therapy which is as 'clean' as possible. These supervisory skills are not easily acquired, and trauma supervisors need experience and well-developed self-awareness. Supervisors need to be open to examining their own processes and to be honestly open to receiving feedback from their supervisees. Whilst supervisors are inevitably the primary holders of power within the supervisory relationship, and hence often the subject of transference reactions, they must work in collaboration with their supervisees in order to unveil the two-way processes at work. This openness of approach requires supervisors to recognize their own trauma histories, their impact in the past and the present, and to become fearless warriors in their willingness to confront their own pain and despair in order to be able to join others in their trauma history. They need also the knowledge that undertaking trauma work, whether as a therapist or as a supervisor, has a shelf-life. Confronting, in the raw, the existential questions of meaning and unfairness on a daily basis is exhausting and, whatever the self-care mechanisms, potentially a net loss activity. The skill is to continue to recognize the presence of a process beyond the visible and in relationship with another to bring that process into view and understand its impact. The skill is also to know when enough is enough, that is, to know when it is time to take a sabbatical from the work or when it may be time to consider alternative work.

Using support mechanisms

Research tells us that social support is a key factor in predicting the impact of a traumatic event (Brewin et al., 2000). If one has a well-developed and supportive social network, long-term damage is much less likely to occur than when one is isolated and alone. Therapists and supervisors working with trauma need to connect with others; however, the quality of the connection is paramount. There is a need to feel able to disclose, to show vulnerability and to be accepted without being judged. They need a witness strong enough to bear the unbearable and weak enough to feel the pain, someone with resilience, which is sometimes seen as strength. However, resilience in this context may more usefully be viewed as elasticity, flexibility and an ability to go with the flow. In Taoist philosophy, the strongest material is water; it finds its way but 'goes with' on its journey. The nature of resilience is examined in more detail in the next section.

Social support is a crucial factor for trauma therapists and trauma therapists' supervisors. It is not enough, however, to have a widely developed social and professional network if it is not used effectively. One burden of the therapist and supervisor in any therapeutic work is to carry the thoughts, images, feelings and physical sensations of their clients and supervisees but only being able to express these in a limited professional context. Confidentiality is a vital requirement of therapeutic and supervisory work but there can be costs to both therapist and supervisor. Debriefing has become a controversial mechanism, although it appears that the evidence which suggests its potential harm is limited and, indeed, very specific in terms of the potentially harmed client group. Some form of debriefing for trauma therapists and trauma supervisors is necessary if retained experiences are not to corrode and disable. Listening to a client vividly describe a sustained and protracted assault can cause a replaying of the assault by the counsellor in profoundly disturbing nightmares that could only be resolved by supervision or debriefing (Chapter 14). Making meaning of the random thunderbolt of trauma is often a complex activity and may not provide a clear outcome; the struggle, however, is a necessary undertaking, even though the results may not be apparent at the time. Supervision should provide the arena, the safe, holding environment within which the struggle can be acknowledged, witnessed and held. To be safe, however, the special nature and impact of trauma has to be recognized. Trauma therapists need trauma-experienced supervisors in terms of practical experience and up-to-date theoretical knowledge. At the beginning of the supervisory relationship, both the supervisor and supervisee need to acknowledge the impact of this work; there needs to be openness from both parties about their trauma histories and the potential triggers for activation of these histories. From the beginning there needs to be recognition of the potential shelf-life of such work. The supervisory contract needs to pay special attention in the recognition of the significance of repeated trauma exposure found in trauma therapists. Building the supervisory relationship is crucial from the first meeting. This requires both trauma therapist and trauma supervisor to be prepared to be vulnerable and share this vulnerability in session. A prerequisite of this is psychological safety, formed in a relationship of trust and mutual confidence; this is necessary in any therapeutic supervisory relationship but its importance is heightened in the sometimes precarious domain of trauma. The skill here is one of relationship building and facilitating an environment within which congruence and mutuality can be enabled and a meeting at relational depth (Means and Cooper, 2005) can be developed. Fearless relating in the trauma arena requires a depth of shared vulnerability and the facilitation of this may be seen as primarily in the hands of the supervisor, at least in the initial stages of the supervisory relationship.

Building resilience

In order to build resilience, it is necessary to define it within the context of working with trauma and supervising trauma therapists. Life involves suffering, but resisting and fighting the suffering fosters further suffering and can eventually lead to becoming overwhelmed and eventually to breakdown. Given the suggested need for shared vulnerability, it would seem inappropriate for both the relationship between the therapist and the client and between the supervisor and the therapist to be based on a form of resilience stemming from stoical unyielding strength. In other words, failing to feel the impact of the trauma one is hearing, that is lacking insight into its effect or denying the impact, may appear like strength but is in fact the very opposite. Going with (as indicated above) and experiencing the pain and horror of the trauma and the personal reactions to it feels more like the resilience needed. 'Going with' requires awareness, a reflexive ability, elasticity and creativity of approach. Most definitions of resilience involve returning to the original position, shape or state, after being exposed to stress of some form. Concepts of post-traumatic growth and vicarious resilience imply change and assimilation, rather than a return to the original (Hernandez *et al.*, 2007; Calhoun and Tedeschi, 2006; see also Chapters 17 and 19). Key factors identified in the research into personal resilience focus around an ability to be positive in one's perspective on life, to be able to rethink a situation and to reframe it in a positive way, to have a range of coping strategies, to have an effective social support system which is also perceived as supportive, and to have a sense of mastery, that is, to feel one can solve the problems life throws up.

Therapists and supervisors may be seen as needing to explore these concepts in terms of their personal characteristics and ways of being; however, an ability to have a positive outlook and to positively reframe traumatic life events may need further consideration in the trauma therapy relationship and in the trauma therapist supervisory relationship. Trauma work means regular exposure to existential issues which may not readily lend themselves to a positive perspective or reframing; however, this depends on one's definition of positive. If 'positive' means an acceptance of the vicissitudes of life and a relatively coherent sense of meaning, then positive reframing is appropriate. If, on the other hand, 'positive' means always looking on the bright side, then the reframing will be fraught with danger. Misinterpreted positive psychological principles can lead to an overemphasis on looking at the positive, with insufficient focus on acknowledging the underlying pain and suffering (Chapter 17).

Resilience may also be seen as requiring an ability to self-protect. A blurring of experiences between therapist and client and therapist and supervisor creates a greater danger of contagion. Boundaries need to be clear and acknowledged if vulnerability is being experienced in the safety of a contained space. Sometimes these boundaries need to be worked on, as they are a key feature of building resilience. Therapists or supervisors may experience empathy with the impact of the trauma, and the 'as-if' experience can be powerful and piercing. What is needed is a permeable suit of armour, but that the permeability is controllable. When trauma triggers a trauma history or is in danger of becoming overwhelming, action needs to be taken. During my training as a psychotherapist I was introduced to the concept of the psychic cloak, which could be used to wrap myself in for self-protection. Trauma therapists and supervisors of trauma therapists need well-developed cloaks and the wisdom to recognize when to use them and the thickness of the cloth required.

The skill for the counsellor or therapist is a moment-to-moment self-knowledge; knowledge of what makes resilience, knowledge of how to meter and alter levels of resilience, and knowledge of what will increase resilience.

In summary, the skills identified in the previous five sections refer to therapy and supervision and will be applied in the next section with regard to the supervisory relationship. These skills are:

- Focusing on the crucial role and dangers of empathy when working with trauma.
- Exploring why I as therapist or supervisor have chosen to work in the trauma field.
- Openly acknowledging trauma histories and actively seeking to understand how these will be triggered (therapists and supervisors).
- Seeking to hear, see and promote growth that may come from traumatic experiences.
- Actively seeking to uncover unconscious or out-of-awareness processes at play in therapy and supervision.
- Relationship building in supervision.
- Resilience building.

A model of mindful trauma supervision

The term 'mindfulness' is defined by Kabat-Zinn (1994) as: '. . . paying attention in a particular way: on purpose, in the present moment, and non-judgementally' (p. 4). Germer *et al.* (2005) describe mindful moments as being non-conceptual, present-centred, non-judgemental, intentional, involving participant observation, non-verbal, exploratory and liberating. Ryan (2007) uses the term 'mindful supervision' and defines it 'as a form of compassionate enquiry, a consciousness-raising activity' (p. 70). In this chapter, mindful trauma supervision is based on this premise and involves a curiosity as to the experience of the moment and activities that supervisors and supervisees can engage in to facilitate awareness, self-care and, most importantly, effective therapeutic contact, in order to work with those who have been traumatized. It should also involve work at relational depth, as defined by Mearns and Cooper (2005) as 'a feeling of profound contact and engagement' (p. 36). This process requires, in particular, presence, which is a two-part process involving emotional availability and congruence. In this place there is an opportunity for sharing vulnerability in a way which is both possible and meaningful.

Pre-engagement

One of the first considerations for the would-be supervisor of trauma therapists is suitability. Walker (2004) researched supervisors of counsellors working with survivors of sexual abuse and identified the 10 qualities needed. These included being: emotionally robust; non-defensive; able to model good interpersonal interaction; and able to create a safe enough supervisory space. Walker also highlighted the need for supervisors to have a sound knowledge of the nature of psychological trauma as an essential prerequisite. This work should not be undertaken without careful consideration and preparation; a developed understanding of current knowledge about the impact of traumatic events on survivors is crucial if supervisors are to offer the most appropriate supervisory environment. Potential supervisors also need to have a developed sense of what brings them to this work. Recognition and knowledge of one's personal wounds and specific understanding of personal experiences of trauma is vital, together with a knowledge of how trauma history will be activated in the supervisory relationship and the ability to openly explore this with their supervisees at the early stages of forming the supervisory relationship.

Potential supervisors also need to identify a consultant supervisor who also has current knowledge of trauma theory and who demonstrates the qualities already mentioned. Locating suitable individuals is difficult and there is a real need for a centralized resource where therapists and supervisors can find suitable consultant practitioners. Finally in this pre-engagement stage, potential supervisors need to give careful consideration to how they will care for themselves and continue to be psychologically available to their supervisees. They need to consider how they can positively influence their resilience given the repeated distressing and painful exposure that supervisors of trauma therapists experience.

Supervision training courses will contribute to all of these areas and are clearly an essential part of preparation; however, there may need to be a move towards more specialist preparation for this role. Establishing core competencies for both trauma therapists and supervisors of trauma therapists may be a part of the way forward. There may also be a need to examine the curriculum for supervision courses to ensure that appropriate areas are covered.

Engagement and contract

At the point of first contact between supervisor and supervisee, there is a need to establish the nature of the process. The relationship requires a safe space within which the supervisor and therapist can meet at relational depth and engage in activity which is consciousness raising. The need for openness and fearlessness within the relationship should be present from the beginning, which requires the supervisor to acknowledge that trauma work is demanding and will impact on the therapist and on the therapist's wider life, and will have a shelf-life. The supervisor has an ethical responsibility to ensure that the therapist is fit for practice, and if he/she considers the shelf-life has been exceeded, he/she must take every step to ensure that the therapist discontinues his/her practice. Supervisor and supervisee need to engage in a discussion on their trauma histories and to examine what trauma triggers exist. In this place of mutuality the encounter can begin and, as long as boundaries are carefully defined and made visible, there is a contained space for experiential learning with a focus in the moment. Supervisor and supervisee can begin the journey of mindful trauma supervision.

In-session

Once the ground work has been undertaken, each supervision session needs to be based on the recognition that not only will the impact of trauma work be present within the session, affecting the therapist and the supervisor, but it may be difficult to access. Developed self-awareness and a seeking mind are not sufficient, therefore appropriate tools or practices are needed to unearth the processes at work. One significant route of access is through increased body awareness, as highlighted by Rothschild (2006), who identified the need in trauma work to regularly focus on the body and capture current physiological states and possible changes. Engagement in this activity within supervision can help to access areas of tension, sensations of discomfort or pain, differences in temperature and metaphoric experiences of trauma, such as feeling the wind has been knocked out of you, or you have been knocked off your feet. Accessing these body states can give a powerful experiential quality to the response to another's trauma. These physical reactions can enhance empathy but may also enhance the potential for contagion and vicarious traumatization, particularly when the body's responses remain out of cognitive awareness. Recognition of changes in body state when discussing a particular client increases the spectrum of awareness for therapist or supervisor and can enable physical responses to the experience, rather than continued cognitive appraisal. Rothschild (2006) suggests exercises to strengthen parts of the body that are particularly impacted by a specific client, and this activity may be seen as building resilience.

Another tool of focusing in-session can be the use of the 3 minute breathing space (Segal *et al.*, 2002), which involves three processes: first, a deliberate connection with current experience in terms of thoughts, feelings and body sensation (awareness); second, focusing on the breath to create a sense of stillness and presence (gathering); and third, expanding the focus to the whole body (expanding). This process can be used to aid presence and as a route to clarifying the experience in the moment. Sommer and Cox (2006) suggest a way of capturing one's experience of client work by asking therapists to imagine the name they would give to a book about themselves. The title may enable a less conscious process which accesses more of the lived experience of a client. 'The Tightrope Walker', 'Just Hanging On', 'No Way Out' and 'Hope Springs Eternal' may each be worthy of investigation to try to expand the experience and access the impact of client work. Sommer and Cox (2006) also suggest the use of titles of fairy tales as another way of accessing less manifest processes. Thus, 'Little Red Riding Hood' may be the fairy tale a therapist connects with in supervision when recounting his/her experience of a particular client. This again can be worked with to uncover the possible processes at play. Any tool may be a good tool in developing creativity and collaboration in the supervisory relationship in trying out new ways of exploring an experience and of connecting with the processes at the edge of awareness of both the therapist and supervisor.

The ultimate objective of trauma supervision is the protection of, and effective establishment of, the mental well-being of the client. This process needs a resilient therapist with high levels of self-awareness, who can use supervision effectively; this requires a knowledgeable, skilled and aware supervisor. Trauma therapists and supervisors need the ability to demonstrate self-compassion. Neff (2003) sees self-compassion as involving three elements: (a) demonstrating kindness towards oneself and avoiding self-criticism; (b) recognizing that one is part of the whole of personkind, not a separated individual; and (c) having the ability to be mindful. This latter skill is defined by Neff (2003) as 'holding one's painful thoughts and feelings in balanced awareness, rather than over-identifying with them' (p. 89). There is no better way to define that which therapists and supervisors should seek to be.

References

Brewin, C.R., Andrews, B., Valentine, J.D. (2000) Meta-analysis of risk factors for post-traumatic stress disorder in trauma-exposed adults. *Journal of Consulting and Clinical Psychology* **68**(5), 748–766.

Calhoun, L.G., Tedeschi, R.G. (eds) (2006) *Handbook of Posttraumatic Growth*. Mahwah, NJ: Lawrence Erlbaum.

Freud, S. (1953) *The Standard Edition of the Complete Psychological Works of Sigmund Freud*. London: Hogarth Press (original work published 1915).

Germer, C.K., Siegal, R.D., Fulton, P.R. (eds) (2005) *Mindfulness and Psychotherapy*. New York: Guilford.

Hermandez, P., Gangsei, D., Engstrom, D. (2007) Vicarious resilience: a new concept in work with those who survive trauma. *Family Process* **46**(2), 229–241.

Janoff-Bulman, R. (1992) *Shattered Assumptions: Towards a New Psychology of Trauma*. New York: Free Press.

Kabat-Zinn, J. (1994) *Wherever You Go, There You Are: Mindfulness Meditation in Everyday Life*. New York: Hyperion.

Mearns, D., Cooper, M. (2005) *Working at Relational Depth in Counseling and Psychotherapy*. London: Sage.

Neff, K. (2003) Self-compassion: an alternative conceptualization of a healthy attitude towards oneself. *Self and Identity* **2**, 85–101.

Rogers, C.R. (1959) A theory of therapy, personality and interpersonal relationships as developed in the client-centred framework. In Kosh, S. (ed.), *Psychology: A Study of Science., vol 111. Formulations of the Person and the Social Context*. New York: McGraw Hill; 184–256.

Rothschild, B. (2006) *Help for the Helper*. London: W.W. Norton.
Ryan, S. (2007) Mindful supervision. In Shohet, R. (ed.), *Passionate Supervision*. London: Jessica Kingsley.
Segal, Z.V., Williams, J.M.G., Teasdale, J.D. (2002) *Mindfulness-based Cognitive Therapy for Depression*. London: Guilford.
Sommer, C.A., Cox, J.A. (2006) Sexual violence counsellors' reflections on supervision: using stories to mitigate vicarious traumatisation. *Journal of Poetry Therapy* **19**(1), 3–16.
Walker, M. (2004) Supervising practitioners working with survivors of childhood abuse: counter transference; secondary traumatisation and terror. *Psychodynamic Practice* **10**(2), 173–193.

Chapter 19

Building resilient organisations in a complex world

Noreen Tehrani

Introduction

This chapter looks at resilience from an organisational perspective, dealing with organisations with the same level of care and understanding that would be expected when supporting and treating a traumatized individual. Workers expect their organisation to behave in ways that are compassionate, supportive and responsive to their needs; however, what happens if the organisation itself is traumatized and in need of help? Is it helpful to berate the organisation for its failings? Or time to look for ways to support organisations so that they are more able to provide an environment in which workers, leaders and the organisation can work together to recognize and deal with the symptoms of extreme stress? During period of crisis, high levels of perceived organisational support, particularly support from supervisors and leaders, are important in helping workers feel appreciated and valued (Chen *et al.*, 2009). Where organisations are unable to handle their own traumas, the likelihood of them being able to provide adequate support for their workers is reduced.

The nature of resilience

Resilience is a capacity inherent in individuals, groups and organisations to maintain the ability to function, relate and grow in the presence of significant disturbances and challenges. Resilient organisations and individuals are able to manage the demands, challenges and changes brought about by a crisis or disaster and to emerge with at least an ability to function at their previous level, but at best to have used the experience to achieve an increased level of understanding, self-knowledge and growth (Paton *et al.*, 2003). Richardson

(2002) identified three ways of looking at resilience: (a) as a set of unique characteristics; (b) as a set of processes and skills; and (c) as ways of thinking and adapting to danger or other forms of extreme demand. Agaibi and Wilson (2005) describe resilience as a complex set of behavioural tendencies, a cluster of personality traits (extraversion, high self-esteem, assertiveness, hardiness and internal locus of control) and ego resilience factors (flexibility, energy, humour, detachment and affect regulation). Whilst much of the emphasis in resilience research has focused on the individual, it is important to recognize that resilience is also affected by organisational and cultural factors (Paton and Burke, 2007), including the nature and availability of training (Harrison *et al.*, 2008; Arnetz *et al.*, 2009) and the provision of employee support (Gray and Litz, 2005). However, to be resilient it is not sufficient for employees and organisations to merely cope with a crisis or disaster; true resilience requires the demonstration of an ability to transform the traumatic experiences into individual and organisational learning and growth. The focus in this chapter is the organisation, and includes a review of some of the sources of organisational trauma and recognition of how an organisation's character, culture and behaviours can be affected by trauma. Ways of describing an organisation's personality or character are examined, together with how the organisational character can be transformed by extreme pressure or trauma to create the organisation's shadow side. The evidence on building resilient organisations is reviewed, including the role of emotional intelligence and decision making, which balances emotional and rational awareness. Finally, the chapter looks at the need to develop skills and knowledge and the means by which organisations can create an environment in which workers are able to build trust in each other.

The creation of traumatized organisations

Organisations, like individuals, experience traumatic stress. The source of trauma can result from a number of events or incidents; however, the four most common sources of organisational trauma are:

1   *Organisations born out of a trauma.* These organisations are typically created by an individual or group of individuals who have experienced, or been touched by, a traumatic event. Victim organisations are created by an individual or group who experience a

lack of recognition, support or action at a time when it was expected. These organisations tend to view the world through the lens of distress and vulnerability resulting in the absorption of the founder's perceptions of the external world as unsupportive, uncaring and sometimes malevolent (Hormann and Vivian, 2005). Organisations born out of the distress of their founder(s) tend to embed that experience within the fabric of the organisation's culture, influencing the organisation's perceptions and behaviours. If not recognized, the victimized culture can create an organisation which projects defensive attitudes, authoritarian dictates and punitive actions towards potential partners, stakeholders and workers. In such organisations, a minor criticism may be viewed as an attack and a creative suggestion as a criticism, with the result that the organisation is vulnerable to splintering, with new organisations being set up in competition with the parent organisation in such a way that much of the organisation's energy is diverted from their primary aim to one which is focused on destroying the heretic group.

2   *Internally damaged organisations.* The second source of trauma is internal to the organisation, and results from the activities of one or more employees. In recent years many organisations have become traumatized through the activities of rogue traders, transport organisations failing to adhere to safety standards or practices and other corporate scandals (Skeel, 2006). In addition, other internal organisational traumas, such as the untimely death of a CEO, the outbreak of workplace bullying or a decision to outsource work, cause large numbers of employees to become redundant. An action which causes shock to the workforce can result in a rapid negative shift in the perception of workers towards their organisation, causing feelings of anger, disbelief and shock similar to those found in a traumatic bereavement. The response of the workers can lead the organisation to overreact, overcompensate or engage in distracting activities, rather than acknowledge and deal with the real problems of organisational distress.

3   *Externally attacked organisations.* Organisations may also be affected by events which have their origin outside the organisation. These events might include a terrorist bomb, a fire or flood, a hostile take-over or even the overly excessive external monitoring or regulation of the organisation. Similar to the way individual survivors of disaster react, organisations often

respond to external threats by fighting, fleeing or freezing. For some organisations, being faced with an obvious threat or danger appears to bring out the best in them, particularly when they are led by a warrior hero able to mobilize the workers to fight the perceived traumatic agent (Thompson and Hickman, 2008). Other organisations bury their heads in the sand, denying the presence of the dangers that surround them, and continue to operate as if nothing was happening, while other organisations become so shocked that they stop functioning, becoming frozen and unable to make any decisions for fear of making the wrong decision (Flin, 1996).

4   *Secondary traumatized organisations.* Finally, there are a number of organisations which are serially affected by traumatic exposures that are indirect, insidious, gradual or hidden. This is the case in emergency services and other organisations interfacing with distressed clients or customers, such as social services or insurance claims handlers. The development of secondarily traumatized workplaces can be potentiated when the workers have their own unresolved traumas, passionate personal beliefs or a strong empathetic attachment to the people they support. If the secondarily traumatized or victimized organisational culture is not recognized and treated, the organisation can become a major source of trauma to the workers and customers (Chapter 9).

Some organisations have the misfortune to experience more than one form of traumatic exposure, with, for example, a victim-led charity being affected by the embezzlement of funds by a trustee, or a financial organisation emerging from a trading scandal being exposed to an arson attack on its head office.

Traumatized organisations: character and cultural shadow sides

Traumatized organisations behave in ways which make them appear irrational, aggressive and out of touch with their workers. Whilst the individual's responses to traumatic stress are well understood, there is less understanding or recognition of the nature or impact of organisational trauma. The response of the public to traumatized individuals has changed over the past 100 years from one in which people who develop trauma symptoms are viewed as weak cowards (Jones and Wesseley, 2005) to one in which trauma symptoms are the accepted and predictable outcome of being exposed to a traumatic event. However, organisations are not generally given this level of understanding. When organisations go through internal, external or secondary traumatic exposures, their workers and the public expect them to cope, with any organisational failure being viewed by the workforce as poor management and by external stakeholders and public as a sign that the organisation is failing or deficient. It is rare for anyone to recognize that the traumatization of the organisational system is as challenging to the life of the organisation as is the trauma which affects the individual. Without some recognition that an organisation has suffered an injury, it is difficult for organisations to use their traumatic experience to help them learn, develop and become more resilient in their functioning.

Understanding organisational character and culture is complex. As the Gestalt psychologist Kurt Koffka remarked:

> It has been said that the whole is more than the sum of its parts. It is more correct to say that the whole is something other than the sum of its parts, because summing up is a meaningless procedure, whereas the whole–part relationship is meaningful (Koffka, 1935, p. 176).

To be able to understand organisations, it is necessary to take time to understand the drives, motivations, feelings and character of the organisation and how these are affected by relationships with workers and other stakeholders. In order to help to understand organisational functioning, one could view the organisational character and culture as analogous to an individual's personality, attitudes and behaviours. Therefore anything which attacks the organisation's existence, integrity or functioning would be experienced by the organisation in a similar way to how an individual might respond to a threat of death or serious injury. It should not be surprising, therefore, that the organisation's response to a traumatic event is similar to those experienced by the individual. Whilst there have been many researchers looking at the impact of trauma on individuals, there is little research into the traumatized organisation. This failure has resulted in an over-emphasis on maladaptive organisational behaviours, such as reactive management, authoritarian attitudes and poor communication (e.g. Brown and Campbell, 1990; Hart et al., 1995; Regehr et al., 2003), rather than regarding these behaviours as organisational symptoms of traumatic stress.

Organisational character and cultures

There is a lack of definition around the concepts of organisational character and culture. It could be argued that, like personality, an organisation's character is made up of a number of reasonably stable dimensions or attributes which are largely determined by the influence of the organisation's founder or leader and the nature of the work it undertakes. Whilst some of the characteristics are open and clearly visible, others may be less easy to recognize and may only emerge in times of difficulty (Bligh, 2006). The expression of organisational characteristics can and will be modified over time and, as a result of interactions with workers and other stakeholders, lead to the establishment of the organisation's culture. There is some debate over the extent to which the organisational character influences organisational culture and vice versa (Oishi, 2004); however, it is clear that both are important in determining how organisations cope with organisational challenges.

Organisational character or personality

Organisational characters are unique and varied in the same way that people are different from each other. However, despite these differences, personality theorists (e.g. Costa and McCrae, 1995; Jackson *et al.*, 2000) have found that a small number of characteristics account for most of the individual variations. Surveys of workers exposed to traumatic events indicate that the personality characteristics of extroversion and emotional stability are most strongly associated with high levels of resilience (e.g. Moran and Shakespeare-Finch, 2003). These personality resilience indicators taken from personality tests can be translated into organisational characteristics, with 'extroverted organisations' taking proactive actions and being independent, hard working, competitive and willing to stand up for their rights, whilst 'introverted organisations' would be more likely to try to avoid taking sudden actions, preferring to absorb and interpret information, examining all options with great care before coming to a decision. The personality of emotional stability would find 'emotionally stable organisations' having an awareness of their strengths and optimism for the future; they would be flexible, calm and difficult to upset. In contrast, the emotionally neurotic organisation would be concerned about failing, with a desire to meet the needs of authority and a high level of self-discipline and conscientiousness. Whilst most personality tests are only designed for the use of individuals, the Organizational Character Indicator questionnaire (OCI), based on the MBTI (Myers and Myers, 1995), can be used to identify the character of organisations (Bridges, 1992). The MBTI has four dimensions: extrovert–introvert; sensing–intuitive; thinking–feeling; and judging –perceiving. Although the MBTI does not include the stability–neuroticism dimension, it gives an insight into how organisations respond to the demands of dealing with a traumatic event. Studies using the MBTI have shown that when an individual or organisation is faced with danger, there is a tendency to over-use a preferred behavioural style, rather than identifying a more effective or appropriate way of responding (Quenk, 1996; Edwards, 1994). When the preferred coping method fails to produce the anticipated outcome, the organisation may experience a level of frustration and exhaustion which causes it to flip into what appears, on the surface, to be out-of-character behaviours. The flipping reveals the presence of the normally hidden part of the organisation, which has been named 'the shadow side' (Egan, 1994; Karpiak, 2003), 'wicked problems' (Stoppelenburg and Vermaak, 2009) or 'the toxic trench' (Gallos, 2008). The psychological process which has been used to explain this behaviour is known as projection (Jung, 1977), involving the organisation attributing to workers and others the organisation's own negative qualities and behaviours, which it is has been unable to recognize, accept or deal with appropriately. The impact of the shadow side can be observed in the traumatized organisation as a parallel process in which the negative behaviours or challenges which impact the organisation and its workers can be found in the distressed organisation's own behaviours (Chapter 9).

Whilst it is not possible in this chapter to look at the eight shadow sides identified in the OCI, the following organisational case study is illustrative of the usefulness of this tool.

Case study

A newly formed organisation has been identified as extroverted, intuitive (E/I), it has a passion for new ideas, tends to take on risks and seek new challenges and opportunities, with little thought of the strain this may cause to its people and resources. Given its drive to bring about change, the organisation often takes on too much work and as a result is often over-extended. A crisis occurs when the organisation is faced with an increased pressure to comply with some ineffective and prescriptive procedures, which blocks it from achieving its goals. The organisation responds by pointing out the importance of its work but does not get a sensitive hearing and finds that its values are being questioned and challenged. Under pressure of limited resources, a pressure to conform and feelings of being undervalued, the organisation's culture flips into its shadow side. The once-confident E/I organisation becomes withdrawn and depressed, reducing its internal and external communication to a minimum; instead of holding onto its global vision, it begins to concentrate on minor issues or problems, becoming punitive and seeing things in black and white without any objective justification.

The shadow side is uncomfortable and unproductive and can continue for some time unless there are insightful leaders able to handle the distress (Marshak, 2009). To break out of the shadow, the leaders of the E/I organisation will need to allow time for the organisation to recharge its batteries and to find ways to say 'No' to unnecessary or fanciful projects or activities. This is not easy for an E/I organisation, where the normal behaviour is to welcome challenge. The organisation will also need to re-engage with its creative side, by using its inherent creativity to find ways to develop new approaches and strategies which will avoid similar situations arising in the future. By creating systems for giving meaning to its experience, the E/I organisation is able to move back into its more familiar, energized, creative and communicative self.

Building resilient organisations

Whilst organisations are unable to eliminate all the threats and dangers they may have to face, they can find ways to respond to traumatic events and to build resilience. Even organisations that are regularly exposed to traumatic incidents can find opportunities to create post-trauma growth and resilience (Paton, 2005). Organisations are well placed to build organisational resilience capacity, as they have the power, resources and opportunity to introduce systems which encourage organisational resilience, as well as directly influencing the selection, training and support of their workers. Studies of resilient teams (Cannon-Bowers *et al.*, 1995) have shown adaptability, shared awareness, feedback, leadership, interpersonal relationships, coordination, communications and decision making to be essential skills. Emotional intelligence is an essential element to each of these skills, as the ability to identify, empathize and respond to the mood of an individual, team or organisation leads to greater flexibility and a broader perspective (George, 2000).

Emotional intelligence

The construct of emotional intelligence was originally developed by Salovey and Mayer (1990) and has been described as the ability to:

> ... perceive, access and generate emotions so as to assist thought, to understand emotions and emotional knowledge, and to reflectively regulate emotions so as to promote emotional and intellectual growth (Mayer and Salovey, 1997, p. 5).

People differ in terms of their awareness of the emotions they experience and in their ability to express these emotions appropriately to others; for some the identification and expression of emotions is almost impossible, whilst for others the experience of strong emotions can rule their behaviour and their lives. Exhibiting emotional intelligence entails not only being able to recognize and manage one's own feelings but also the ability to recognize and manage emotions in others. Leaders and organisations need to be able to excite and motivate workers to take action or to instil within them the need to exhibit extreme care or caution. The ability to show emotional intelligence is an important interpersonal skill which can help organisations recognize and deal with extreme pressure, crisis or disaster. James and Arroba (2005) identified two dimensions to emotional intelligence: first, the need to turn attention outside and to read the wider organisational context; second, the ability to tune into the inner world and be aware of all the thoughts and feelings that are stimulated. This process requires workers and leaders to be aware of aspects of the organisation which are often missed or not attended to, and perhaps even avoided, as they are perceived as having a negative effect on the organisation. Without emotional awareness of the difficulties that exist within organisations, too much energy may be focused on individual organisational failures, rather than on building resilience.

Decision making in resilient organisations

Resilient organisations can function and make decisions in situations based on incomplete, ambiguous or competing information. Researchers working in the army and emergency services have studied decision making in crisis situations for over 20 years (Flin, 1996). The research has found that resilient organisations need leaders and teams able to make decisions quickly, without the need to spend valuable time comparing and contrasting a wide array of options (Shattuck and Miller, 2006). Real-life studies found that resilient leaders faced with a decision initially assessed their gut feel or hunch on what would be the best solution. The leaders would then test out their feelings and hunches by creating an imaginary scenario, in which the selected solution was played out. The leader would then assess whether the solution was good enough to be acted upon or to run the scenario again with a modified or alternative solution (Klein, 2008). As leaders gain experience in dealing with difficult and demanding situations, they become quicker at accessing solutions; these instinctive solutions are assisted by somatic markers (Damasio, 2003). Damasio's somatic marker hypothesis is based on the finding that when individuals undertake an action that creates a pleasurable or unpleasant outcome, when the opportunity to undertake the same or a similar action arises again, there is an automatic restimulation of the emotional response (somatic marker), leading to the decision being repeated or rejected. The recognition-primed decision (RPD) model describes how leaders skilled in dealing with critical situations use their prior experience to form a repertoire of emotional markers which can be instantly accessed (Klein *et al*, 1986). These hidden emotional biases, related to prior experiences of similar situations, are able to rapidly highlight the most relevant cues, goals and the actions necessary to achieve those goals. Effective leaders are skilled at recognizing their intuitive gut feeling and can assess which of the options is most likely to be successful. The role of the somatic markers is not to replace the reasoning process; their role increases the efficiency and speed of decision making (Damasio, 2003). An example of this process is graphically illustrated in the decision-making capacity and processes of Captain Sullenberger when landing a disabled aircraft in the Hudson River (Sullenberger and Zaslow, 2009).

Developing knowledge

Developing skills in reading situations and understanding what needs to be done to address the demands which face organisations needs takes time, training and practice. There is also a need for a 'professional' attitude of mind, which spurs workers on to engage in a process of continual improvement where they are found to be constantly refining their practice by reflection. Every day workers spend actively engaged in a role, they automatically extract information and decision rules that underlie the roles, processes and procedures (Goleman, 2002). However, to merely understand one's own role is insufficient; if workers are to become organisationally resilient, they also need to understand the overt and hidden drivers, connections and processes involved in organisational life (James and Arroba, 2005). Organisations faced with the task of building organisational resilience might need to consider the characteristics of their workforce, including their cognitive abilities, self-efficacy and motivation (Salas and Cannon-Bowers, 2001). Whilst there is a commonly held view that practice makes perfect, the simple repetition of actions with the intention of bringing about an increased level of proficiency has not been shown to be particularly successful. It is possible, however, to increase the effectiveness of training practice by providing pre-practice advice, frameworks, strategies, goals and information, together with an opportunity to reflect on the practice outcomes (Cannon-Bowers et al., 1998). In this way, workers will be able to create cognitive maps or mental models within which they can place their new and existing experience and learning. This training opportunity is particularly important when considering business continuity management (Chapter 11); here the members of the crisis management team are unlikely to have real-life experience of the events for which they are preparing in their incident simulations. Developing effective training programmes requires that the trainers understand the nature of the demands faced by organisations dealing with a crisis, and how this expertise can be used to develop and evaluate training simulations and exercises. Specially designed simulations provide opportunities to practise dealing with high-pressure situations in a safe and supportive environment, to review processes and procedures and to assess the skills of workers in realistic circumstances (Pollock et al. 2003).

Building trust

Trust is essential to effective interpersonal relationships, group processes and organisational resilience (Payne and Clark, 2003). Kee and Knox (1970) describe trust as a willingness to become vulnerable to the actions of another in the belief that the other person will perform an action which will be of benefit or value, without the need to be managed or controlled. Therefore, an important aspect of a trusting relationship is the presence of a risk. In situations where there is no risk, workers may choose to cooperate because they cannot perceive any risks to themselves of working with another person; however, if the situation involves a real danger involving a risk to health or well-being, cooperation becomes dependent upon where the parties trust each other. The factors that lead to trust have been described as confidence in the ability, benevolence and integrity of the trustee (Mayer *et al.*, 1995). The level of trust within a team or organisation evolves over time as the parties interact with each other. When workers, teams and organisations work together to improve their technical and interpersonal skills, they treat each other with respect and uphold shared values and principles and the organisation becomes stronger and increasingly resilient.

Discussion

The role of the organisation is critical to the protection of the health and well-being of the workforce. If an organisation is to undertake its role effectively, it needs to be resilient when faced with challenges and disasters. Organisational resilience needs to be created and is dependent upon the characteristics of the organisation, the development of a supportive and responsive culture and the building of individual skills and competencies in the workforce. Where workers become emotionally aware and are able to trust their colleagues, supervisors and organisation, it is possible to create an environment in which decision making becomes more responsive and effective in the face of extreme pressure or crisis. Workers who become emotionally attached to their organisation regard their actions as an expression of their feelings of loyalty and commitment to the organisation and their desire to help the organisation to grow and flourish in the future.

References

Agaibi, C.E., Wilson, J.P. (2005) Trauma, PTSD and Resilience: a review of the literature. *Trauma, Violence and Abuse* **6**(3), 195–213.

Arnetz, B.B., Nevedal, D.C., Lumley, M.A., Backman, L., Lublin, A. (2009) Trauma resilience training for the police: psychophysiological and performance effects. *Journal of Police Criminal Psychology* **24**, 1–9.

Bligh, M.C. (2006) Surviving post-merger 'culture clash': can cultural leadership lessen the casualties? *Leadership* **2**(4), 395–426.

Bridges, W. (1992) *The Character of Organisations: Using Jungian Type in Organisations*. Palo Alto, CA: Davies Black Publishing.

Brown, J., Campbell, E. (1990) Sources of occupational stress in the police. *Work and Stress* **4**(4), 305–318.

Cannon-Bowers, J.A., Tannenbaum, S.I., Salas, E., Volpe, C.E. (1995) Defining team competencies and establishing team training requirements. In Gusso, R., Salas, E. (eds), *Teams: Their Training and Performance*. Norwood, NJ: Ablex.

Cannon-Bowers, J.A., Rhodenizer, L., Salas, E., Bowers, C.A. (1998) A framework for understanding pre-practice conditions and their impact on learning. *Personnel Psychology* **51**, 291–320.

Chen, Z., Eisenberger, R., Johnson, K.M., Sucharski, I.L., Aselage, J. (2009) Perceived organisational support and extra-role performance: which leads to which? *Journal of Social Psychology* **149**(1), 119–124.

Costa, P., McCrae, R. (1995) Primary traits of Eysenck's P–E–N system: three and five factor solutions. *Journal of Personality and Social Psychology* **69**, 308–317.

Damasio, A. (2003) *Looking for Spinoza: Joy, Sorrow and the Feeling Brain*. London: Heinemann.

Edwards, J.R. (1994) The determinants and consequences of coping with stress, In Cooper, C.L., Payne, R. (eds), *Causes, Coping and Consequences of Stress at Work*. Chichester, UK: Wiley.

Egan, G. (1994) *Working with the Shadow Side: A Guide to Positive Behind the Scenes Management*. San Francisco, CA: Jossey-Bass.

Flin, R. (1996) *Sitting in the Hot Seat – Leaders and Teams for Critical Incident Management*. Chichester, UK: Wiley.

Gallos, J.V. (2008) Learning from toxic trenches: the winding road to healthier organisations and to healthy everyday leaders. *Journal of Management Inquiry* **17**(4), 354–367.

George, J.M. (2000) Emotions and leadership: the role of emotional intelligence. *Human Relations* **53**(8), 1027–1055.

Goleman, D. (2002) *The New Leaders: Transforming the Art of Leadership into the Science of Results*. London: Time Warner.

Gray, M.J., Litz, B.T. (2005) Behavioural interventions for recent traumas: empirically informed practice guidelines. *Behavior Modification* **29**(1), 189–215.

Harrison, J., Sharpley, J., Greenberg, N. (2008) The management of post-traumatic stress reactions in the military. *Journal of the Royal Army Medical Corps* **154**(2), 110–114.

Hart P., Wearing, A., Headley, B. (1995) Police stress and wellbeing: integrating personality, coping and daily work experiences. *Journal of Occupational and Organisational Psychology* **68**, 133–136.

Hormann, S., Vivian, P. (2005) Towards an understanding of traumatized organisations and how to intervene in them. *Traumatology* **11**(3), 159–169.

Jackson, C.J., Furnham, A., Forde, L., Cotter, T. (2000) The structure of the Eysenck Personality Profiler. *British Journal of Psychology* **91**, 223–239.

James, K.T., Arroba, T. (2005) Reading and carrying: a framework for learning about emotion and emotionality in organisational systems as a core aspect of leadership. *Management Learning* **36**(3), 299–316.

Jones, E., Wesseley, S. (2005) *Shell Shock to PTSD: From 1900 to the Gulf War*. Hove, UK: Psychology Press.

Jung, C.G. (1977) Relations between the ego and the unconscious. In *Collected Works of C.G. Jung: Two Essays on Analytical Psychology*; 123–169.

Karpiak, I.E. (2003) The shadow: mining its dark treasury for teaching and adult development. *Canadian Journal of University Continuing Education* **29**(2), 13–27.

Kee, H.W., Knox, R.E. (1970) Conceptual and methodological considerations in the study of trust and suspicion. *Journal of Conflict Resolution* **14**(3), 357–366.

Klein, G.A. (2008) Naturalistic decision making. *Human Factors* **50**(3), 456–460.

Klein, G.A., Calderwood, R., Clinton-Cirocco, A. (1986) Rapid decision making on the fireground. *Proceedings of the Human Factors and Ergonomics Society* (30th Annual Meeting) **1**, 576–580.

Koffka, K. (1935). *Principles of Gestalt Psychology*. New York: Harcourt, Brace, and World.

Marshak, R.J. (2009) Reflections on wicked problems in organisations. *Journal of Management Inquiry* **18**(1), 58–59.

Mayer, R.C., Davies, J.H., Schoorman, F.D. (1995) An integrated model of organisational trust. *Academy of Management Review* **20**(3), 709–734.

Mayer, J.D., Salovey, P. (1997) What is emotional intelligence? Implications for educators. In Salovey, P., Sluyter, D. (eds), *Emotional Development, Emotional Literacy and Emotional Intelligence*. New York: Basic Books.

Mohan, M.L. (1993) *Organisational Communication and Cultural Vision*. Albany, NY: SUNY Press.

Moran, C., Shakespeare-Finch, J. (2003) A trait approach to posttrauma vulnerability and growth. In Paton, D., Violanti, J.M., Smith, L.M. (eds), *Promoting Capabilities to Manage Posttraumatic Stress: Perspectives on Resilience*. Springfield, IL: Charles C. Thomas.

Myers, I.B., Myers, P.B. (1995) *Gifts Differing: Understanding Personality Type*. Palo Alto, CA: Davies Black Publishing.

Oishi, S. (2004) Personality in culture: a neo-Allportian view. *Journal of Research in Personality* **38**, 68–74.

Paton, D. (2005) Posttraumatic growth in protective services professionals: individual, cognitive and organisational influences. *Traumatology* **11**(4), 335–346.

Paton, D., Burke, K.J. (2007) Personal and organisational predictors of posttraumatic adaptation and growth in police officers. *Australian Journal of Disaster and Trauma Studies* **1**, 1–12.

Paton, D., Violanti, J.M., Smith, L.M. (2003) Posttraumatic psychological stress: individual, group and organisational perspectives on resilience and growth. In Paton, D., Violanti, J.M., Smith, L.M. (eds), *Promoting Capabilities to Manage Posttraumatic Stress: Perspectives on Resilience*. Springfield, IL: Charles C. Thomas.

Payne, R.L., Clark, M. (2003) The process of trusting: its relevance to vulnerability and resilience in traumatic situations. In Paton, D., Violanti, J.M., Smith, L.M. (eds), *Promoting Capabilities to Manage Posttraumatic Stress: Perspectives on Resilience*. Springfield, IL: Charles C. Thomas.

Pollock, C., Paton, D., Smith, L., Violanti, J. (2003) Training for resilience. In Paton, D., Violanti, J.M., Smith, L.M. (eds), *Promoting Capabilities to Manage Posttraumatic Stress: Perspectives on Resilience*. Springfield, IL: Charles C. Thomas.

Quenk, N.L. (1996) *In the Grip: Our Hidden Personality*. Palo Alto, CA: Consulting Psychologist Press.

Regehr, C., Hill, J., Goldberg, G., Hughes, J. (2003) Postmortem inquiries and trauma responses in paramedics and firefighters. *Journal of Interpersonal Violence* **18**(6), 607–622.

Richardson, G.E. (2002) The meta-theory of resilience and resiliency. *Journal of Clinical Psychology* **56**(3), 307–321.

Salas, E., Cannon-Bowers, J.A. (2001) The science of training: a decade of progress. *Annual Review of Psychology* **52**, 471–499.

Salovey, P., Mayer, J.D. (1990) Emotional intelligence. *Imagination, Cognition and Personality* **9**, 185–211.

Shattuck, L.G., Miller, N.L. (2006) Extending naturalistic decision making to complex organisations: a dynamic model of situational cognition. *Organisation Studies* **27**(7), 989–1009.

Skeel, D. (2006) *Icarus in the Boardroom: the Fundamental Flaws in Corporate America and Where They Came From*. Oxford: Oxford University Press.

Stoppelenburg, A., Vermaak, H. (2009) Defixation as an intervention perspective. Understanding wicked problems at the Dutch Ministry of Foreign Affairs. *Journal of Management Inquiry* **18**(1), 60–62.

Sullenberger, C.B., Zaslow, J. (2009) *Higher Duty – My Search for What Really Matters*. New York: Harper Collins.

Thompson, J., Hickman, M. (2008) More retailers fighting for survival. *The Independent*, 23 December 2008: http://www.independent.co.uk/news/business/news/more-retailers-fighting-for-survival-1208549.html [accessed 16 October 2009].

Index

Note: Tables and figures are denoted by *t* and *f*.